Ethics, Politics and Justice in Dante

Ethics, Politics and Justice in Dante

Edited by Giulia Gaimari and Catherine Keen

First published in 2019 by
UCL Press
University College London
Gower Street
London WC1E 6BT

Available to download free: www.uclpress.co.uk

ISBN: 978-1-78735-229-2 (Hbk.)
ISBN: 978-1-78735-228-5 (Pbk.)
ISBN: 978-1-78735-227-8 (PDF)
ISBN: 978-1-78735-230-8 (epub)
ISBN: 978-1-78735-231-5 (mobi)
ISBN: 978-1-78735-232-2 (html)
DOI: https://doi.org/10.14324/111.9781787352278

Contents

List of figures

List of contributors

Nicolò Crisafi is stipendiary fellow at Berlin ICI (Institute of Cultural Inquiry) in Germany, working on a new project on 'Possibility and the Utopian Imagination in Dante, Petrarch, and Boccaccio'. At Oxford his DPhil thesis 'Dante's Masterplot and the Alternative Narrative Models in the *Commedia*', argued for narrative pluralism in Dante's poem by focusing on paradoxes, detours and the future as alternatives to the teleological 'masterplot'.

Sabrina Ferrara is Associate Professor in Italian (Département Langues Étrangères Appliquées) at the University of Tours. She is also a member of the Centre d'Études Supérieures de la Renaissance (Tours), and of the research groups 'Recherches en Humanités – Humanités numériques' and 'Savoirs: théories, pratiques, circulations'. She sits on the editorial boards of several book series and journals, including *Revue des études dantesques, Arzanà: Cahiers de civilisation médiévale* and *Dante e l'arte*. Her research interests extend from Dante Studies to medieval and humanistic Latin and vernacular epistolography, and to medieval and humanist receptions of classical texts. She has published extensively on Dante and Boccaccio, especially on political themes (e.g. exile, the idea of justice), on readership and on the concept of time. She has recently published a monograph, *La parola dell'esilio. Autore e lettori nelle opere di Dante in esilio* (2016) and co-edited the volume *Boccace. Les tensions d'un écrivain entre Moyen Âge et Renaissance* (2015).

Giulia Gaimari recently completed her PhD as a Wolfson Postgraduate Scholar at University College London. Her doctoral thesis, entitled '"Tutto suo amor là giù pose a drittura". The Concept of Justice in Dante's Works', assesses Dante's idea of justice by taking into account both the historical circumstances and the philosophical, rhetorical culture that contributed to shaping his texts, as well as the diverse scope of his works. Her research interests focus on Dante's knowledge and employment of classical philosophy, including Aristotle's *Nicomachean Ethics* and *Politics* and Cicero's *De officiis* and *De amicitia*; on medieval encyclopaedic and didactic culture, including Brunetto Latini's *Tresor*; on civic rhetoric and ideals; and on the representation of souls in medieval otherworldly visions and travels. She has published articles on themes ranging from the representation of the blessed souls in the *Commedia* to aspects of Dante's ethical and political thinking.

Filippo Gianferrari is currently Visiting Lecturer in Italian at Smith College. He studied at the University of Bologna before receiving his doctorate in medieval studies from the University of Notre Dame, with a dissertation on 'Dante and Thirteenth-century Latin Education: Reading the *auctores minores*'. His research focuses primarily on Dante and medieval education and is informed by a thoroughly interdisciplinary approach, intersecting the fields of Latin palaeography, history of the book and historiography. He has published mostly on the topic of Dante's intellectual formation, with recent essays including '"Poca favilla, gran fiamma seconda" (*Par.* I 34): riscrivere un proverbio tra Cino, San Giacomo e San Girolamo' (forthcoming, *Le tre corone*, 2020) and '*Pro patria mori*: From the *Disticha Catonis* to Dante's Cato', *Dante Studies* (2017).

Claire E. Honess is Professor of Italian Studies at the University of Leeds, and Dean of the Leeds Doctoral College. Together with Matthew Treherne, she co-founded the Leeds Centre for Dante Studies in 2007 and was a co-investigator on the AHRC-funded project, 'Dante and Late Medieval Florence: Theology in Poetry, Practice and Society'. Her research focuses especially on political imagery and ideas in Dante and on medieval poetry. She is the author of the book *From Florence to the Heavenly City: The Poetry of Citizenship in Dante* (2006) and of a translation of, and commentary on, four of Dante's political epistles (*Dante Alighieri, Four Political Letters*, 2007). Honess has co-edited various volumes, including *Reviewing Dante's Theology* (2013) and '*Se mai continga ... ': Exile, Theology and Politics in Dante* (2013). She has been an editor of the journal *The Italianist* since 1996, and was Chair of the Society for Italian Studies from 2015–18.

Catherine Keen is Associate Professor in the Italian Department at University College London. She is Senior Co-Editor of the journal *Italian Studies*. Her research interests cover Dante's *Commedia* and his minor works, especially relating to his thought on politics and exile – themes addressed in her monograph on *Dante and the City* (2003). She has also published on the early Italian lyric tradition, with a special interest in the poetry of Cino da Pistoia, and on translation and reception of classical literature in Duecento and Trecento Italy, particularly the works of Cicero and of Ovid.

Giuseppe Ledda is Associate Professor in the Dipartimento di Filologia Classica e Italianistica at the University of Bologna. He is Co-Director of the peer-reviewed journal *L'Alighieri*, and a senior member of the committee of *Studi danteschi*. He also sits on the Governing Committee of the Italian Dante Society, and of several research centre committees inside and outside Italy. His research on Dante focuses on various topics, including rhetorical and narrative strategies, hagiography and the Bible, medieval bestiary lore and the reception of classical literature. His research interests also include Renaissance and modern authors, such as Pulci, Ariosto and Montale. He has published and edited numerous books, including the monographs *La Bibbia di Dante* (2015) and *La guerra della lingua. Ineffabilità, retorica e narrativa nella 'Commedia' di Dante* (2002).

Elena Lombardi is Professor of Italian Literature at Oxford and the Paget Toynbee Fellow at Balliol College. She is the author of *The Syntax of Desire. Language and Love in Augustine, the Modistae and Dante* (2007), *The Wings of the Doves. Love and Desire in Dante and Medieval Culture* (2012) and *Imagining the Woman Reader in the Age of Dante* (2018). She has also co-edited volumes on Dante and medieval culture, and published several essays on medieval literature (on the Sicilian Poets, Guido Cavalcanti, Dante and Petrarch).

Nicolò Maldina is Lecturer in Italian at the University of Edinburgh. He was previously Postdoctoral Research Fellow at the University of Leeds, within the AHRC-funded project 'Dante and Late Medieval Florence: Theology in Poetry, Practice and Society', and also worked as active member of the ERC-funded project, 'Italian Voices. Oral Culture, Manuscript and Print in Early Modern Italy (1450–1700)'. His research interests lie in medieval and early modern Italian Studies, and especially concern the study of how Dante's *Commedia* interacts with different textual forms produced within medieval religious movements (in particular the Dominicans and the Franciscans). He has also worked extensively on Boccaccio, Petrarch and Ariosto's *Orlando furioso*. Maldina recently published a monograph, *In pro del mondo. Dante, la predicazione e i generi della letteratura religiosa medievale* (2017), and his several articles on

Dante include: 'Le similitudini nel tessuto narrativo della Commedia di Dante. Note per un'analisi strutturale', *Studi e problemi di critica testuale* (2012); 'L'Oratio super Pater Noster di Dante tra esegesi e vocazione liturgica', *L'Alighieri* (2012); and 'Dante e l'immagine del buon predicatore nel *Paradiso*', *L'Alighieri* (2014).

Anna Pegoretti is Assistant Professor at Roma Tre University. Between 2010 and 2016 she held the positions of Frances Yates short-term Fellow at the Warburg Institute (2010), Newton International Fellow for the British Academy at the University of Leeds (2011–12), Postdoctoral Research Fellow at the University of Warwick, within the AHRC-funded project, 'Dante and Late Medieval Florence: Theology in Poetry, Practice and Society' (2012–16), Adjunct Professor at the University of Reading (2015–16). In 2016–17 Pegoretti was Research Fellow at the University Ca' Foscari, Venice. Her research interests range from Dante Studies and the reception of Dante's works to the relationship between geography and literature in medieval Italy and the history of the book and of education in medieval and early modern Italy. Among her recent publications are the monograph *Indagine su un codice dantesco. La 'Commedia' Egerton 943 della British Library* (2014), the journal article 'Filosofanti' in *Le tre corone* (2015) and the book chapter 'Early reception until 1481', in the new *Cambridge Companion to Dante's 'Commedia'* (2018).

Justin Steinberg is Professor of Italian Literature in the Department of Romance Languages and Literatures at the University of Chicago and Editor-in-Chief of the journal *Dante Studies*. He is the author of *Dante and the Limits of the Law* (2013) and *Accounting for Dante: Urban Readers and Writers in Late Medieval Italy* (2007). He is currently writing a book on Boccaccio and the law.

Matthew Treherne is Professor of Italian Literature and Head of the School of Languages, Cultures and Societies at the University of Leeds. Together with Claire Honess, he co-founded the Leeds Centre for Dante Studies and was Principal Investigator of the AHRC-funded project, 'Dante and Late Medieval Florence: Theology in Poetry, Practice and Society'. Dante and Tasso are his primary research interests, although he has also worked on the American novelist and Nobel Prize winner Toni Morrison. Treherne has co-edited several books, including *Reviewing Dante's Theology* (2013), *'Se mai continga ... ': Exile, Theology and Politics in Dante* (2013), *Dante's 'Commedia': Theology as Poetry* (2010) and *Forms of Faith in Sixteenth-Century Poetry* (2009).

Editions followed and abbreviations

a) Dante's works

Unless otherwise specified, all references within the volume are to the following editions of Dante's works:

Commedia:

Dante Alighieri, *La Commedia secondo l'antica vulgata*, ed. by Giorgio Petrocchi, 4 vols (Milan: Mondadori, 1966–7)

The Divine Comedy of Dante Alighieri, ed. and trans. by Robert M. Durling; intro. and notes by Ronald L. Martinez and Robert M. Durling, 3 vols (New York–Oxford: Oxford University Press, 1996–2011)

Opere minori:

Dante Alighieri, *Le Opere*, ed. by Marco Santagata, 2 vols (Milan: Mondadori, 2011–14). Vol.1: *Rime*, ed. by Claudio Giunta; *Vita nova*, ed. by Guglielmo Gorni; *De vulgari eloquentia,* ed. by Mirko Tavoni.

Vol.2: *Convivio,* ed. by Claudio Giunta and Gianfranco Fioravanti; *Monarchia,* ed. by Diego Quaglioni; *Epistole,* ed. by Claudia Villa; *Egloge,* ed. by Gabriella Albanese.

La Vita Nuova, trans. by Mark Musa (Bloomington and London: Indiana University Press, 1962).

Dante's Lyric Poetry, trans. by Kenelm Foster and Patrick Boyde, 2 vols (Oxford: Oxford University Press, 1967).

De vulgari eloquentia, ed. and trans. by Steven Botterill (Cambridge: Cambridge University Press, 1996).

The Banquet, trans. with intro. and notes by Christopher Ryan (Saratoga, CA: Anma Libri, 1989).

Monarchy, ed. and trans. by Prue Shaw (Cambridge: Cambridge University Press, 1996).

The Letters of Dante, trans. by Paget J. Toynbee, 2nd edn (Oxford: Clarendon Press, 1966); for the political epistles *Four Political Epistles*, trans. by Claire Honess (London: Modern Humanities Research Association, 2007).

Dante and Giovanni del Virgilio, trans. by Philip H. Wicksteed and Edmund G. Gardner (New York: Haskell House Publishers, 1970).

Title abbreviations

Cvo	*Convivio*
DVE	*De vulgari eloquentia*
Ecl.	*Egloge*
Ep.	*Epistole*
Inf.	*Inferno*
Mon.	*Monarchia*
Purg.	*Purgatorio*
Par.	*Paradiso*
Questio	*Questio de aqua et terra*
Rime	*Rime*
VN	*Vita nuova*

b) Bible references

The default reference for all Bible quotations in Latin is:

Biblia Sacra iuxta Vulgatam versionem, ed. by Robert Weber and Bonifatius Fischer, 2 vols (Stuttgart: Württembergische Bibelanstalt, 1969).

Unless otherwise specified, English translations are taken from the Douay-Rheims translation of the Vulgate, in the following edition:

The Vulgate Bible: Douay-Rheims Translation, ed. by Swift Edgar and Angela M. Kinney, 6 vols (Cambridge, MA: Harvard University Press, 2010–13).

Acknowledgements

The editors would like to thank our contributors very warmly for the commitment and energy they have shown in helping us to produce this volume, and for the insights and depth of expertise displayed in their essays. The volume is in part the outcome of meetings and discussions extended over several years between a group of Dante scholars with shared interests, especially in the themes outlined in our title: ethics, politics and justice. Inevitably, the essays gathered here represent only a part of the 'conversations about Dante' conducted within this group of collaborators; among those who were unable eventually to include work in this volume, we would particularly like to thank Stephen Milner and Paola Nasti for their contributions at earlier stages.

As members of the Department of Italian at University College London, we have been fortunate enough to benefit from the support of a generous group of departmental colleagues in numerous ways. Two of the most beloved and respected figures in the world of UK Italian Studies, Giulio Lepschy and Laura Lepschy, gave the project their blessing at an initial seminar meeting: the latter had been a dedicated head of the UCL Italian Department for many years. Leading Dante scholars Prue Shaw and John Took, both of our Department, were also important participants at the same event, while Tabitha Tuckett, the Rare Books Librarian in UCL Library's Special Collections, is another key member of our research community for her indefatigable work with the College's significant Dante collections. Another colleague, Sophie Fuller, currently completing her doctoral research on Dante at UCL, was of especial help in collaborating with Giuseppe Ledda in preparing his essay for publication and in contributing to the final phases of the book's preparation. We are very grateful for her expert assistance.

In working towards the volume's publication, we have benefited from financial support in various ways. Thanks to Anna Pegoretti, we received a subvention towards publication from the British Academy-Royal Society Newton Alumni Fund. Earlier seminar meetings organised by the editors have been supported by the Society for Italian Studies for the UK and Eire, and from within UCL by grants from the Joint Faculty Institute for Graduate Studies and the School of European Languages, Culture and Society. The Wolfson Foundation has been a generous supporter to Giulia Gaimari over the whole term of her doctoral research, which was funded by a Wolfson Postgraduate Scholarship in the Humanities.

Finally, we would like to thank UCL Press for their help and support in preparing the volume, especially Chris Penfold, Jaimee Biggins and Catherine Bradley for their patience and availability to answer our numerous questions while assembling the book. Feedback from the Press's anonymous peer reviewers has been invaluable in helping us to plan, collate and complete the collection.

Introduction: Justice in the Heart

Giulia Gaimari and Catherine Keen

> Molti han giustizia in cuore, e tardi scocca
> per non venir sanza consiglio a l'arco;
> ma il popol tuo l' ha in sommo de la bocca.
>
> (*Purg.*, VI. 130–32)
>
> [Many have justice in their hearts but loose the arrow
> late, so as not to come to the bow without counsel;
> but your people have it ready on their lips.]

Ethics, Politics and Justice in Dante: cultural contexts and literary ambitions

Anyone who embarks on studying Dante Alighieri's *oeuvre* will soon realise that it is fruitless, if not impossible, to attempt to keep the various facets of his speculation separate from one another. Indeed, the three conceptual domains on which we have chosen to concentrate in this volume – 'ethics', 'politics' and 'justice' – are virtually inextricable within Dante's thought and literary production. In the quotation that provides the title for these introductory reflections, Dante employs the telling image of holding justice in one's own heart. In *Purgatorio* VI, it occurs in the context of a bitingly satirical political invective, in which Dante rebukes his Florentine fellow-citizens' lack of consideration for justice, law and political equilibrium (the 'Ahi, serva Italia' passage, *Purg.*, VI. 76–151). However, the same image of holding, or seeking to hold, justice in the heart also opens the autobiographical and extremely enigmatic lyric *Tre donne intorno al cor mi son venute* [*Three women have come round my heart*] – the women of the poem's opening line being personifications of a three-fold conception of justice, in its divine, natural and civic iterations.

Thus at different moments in his literary career Dante turned to the same poetic image to explore his reflections on justice and morality in both the personal and the political sphere. He expressed himself in each instance with the varied tone and lexis appropriate to the form and occasion of writing. This rhetorical deftness, together with the scope and ambition of Dante's poetic imagination, marks the singularity of his contribution to medieval thinking about ethics, the political order and the domain of law and judgement. In the essays collected in this volume, particular stress is laid on Dante's self-presentation as both poet and prophet of justice. Such an emphasis brings to the fore the importance of his self-reflection on the medium and means of his communication, as well as on the ethical and political content of his writings, over the course of his literary career.

The heart's association with justice for Dante involves not only self-edification, but also the ways in which individuals relate to one another and participate in the conduct of public affairs. After all, as Aristotle pointed out in the fifth book of the *Nicomachean Ethics*, justice is a virtue 'ad alterum': that is, it is directed towards others.[1] Additionally, as was frequently repeated in thirteenth-century handbooks dedicated to the moral and rhetorical education of Italian civic governors – those holding the official title of *podestà* – 'diligere iustitiam' [loving justice] was essential in order to enforce civic justice righteously. Indeed, this principle had the unequivocal authority of scripture behind it, since the Book of Wisdom tells rulers explicitly: 'Diligite iustitiam, qui iudicatis terram' [Love justice, you that are the judges of the earth] (Wisdom 1.1).[2]

Dante's theorisation and poetic representation of justice cannot be detached from his speculations on human moral responsibility. Nor can they be separated off from his concern with the moral probity of those who are entitled to apply the law, and who should guide humanity towards earthly happiness; from his meditations on the fundamental role of education, which teaches people to be fully human – that is, to follow reason and thus become capable of recognising the true nature of things and of expressing their judgements accordingly; nor, ultimately, from his reflections on his own authority as a didactic and prophetic poet, capable of going above and beyond the boundaries of any medieval literary genre. Importantly, addressing the themes of ethics, politics and justice in Dante invites consideration of his beginnings, by investigating the historical and intellectual contexts in which Dante lived and operated as a writer, thinker and politician. To understand how his ideas evolved, it is crucial to take into account the historical events that marked Dante's life, the culture in which he was immersed and his access to sources giving instruction on political and spiritual morality. This can be done both by investigating the material transmission of the texts he might have read and by seeking to understand the contemporary oral practices by which ideas and values circulated.

In the Duecento Florence of Dante's youth, for instance, political manoeuvring entailed changes within the city's legal system, aimed at preserving peace and social justice and improving the townspeople's education in civic morality. In 1293, with some modification in 1295, the legislative programme known as the 'Ordinamenti di Giustizia' [Ordinances of Justice] was compiled and approved by the regime governing Florence at the time, the so-called 'Secondo Popolo'. The Ordinances aimed at restoring tranquillity and citizen welfare by restraining and punishing those individuals belonging to the civic elites whose violent behaviour was endangering public life. And Dante himself entered Florence's political arena in 1295, precisely in the aftermath of the promulgation of these new norms.

The political agenda of Florence's anti-elite, 'Popolo' movement was supported by a strong ideology revolving around ideals of greatness, peace, common good and justice, typical of ancient Rome's Republican era. These ideals stemmed especially from the re-elaboration, in contemporary Florence, of classical works by Cicero, Sallust and Seneca, often by means of translation and commentary that explained and updated the ancient works for the town's modern, communal readership. This interest in Roman political morality also found concrete expression within a specific didactic genre: the manuals dedicated to the moral, rhetorical and civic education of the *podestà* and his administrative entourage, mentioned above for their emphasis also on Scriptural doctrines touching justice in governance.[3] Historian Quentin Skinner states that, within these handbooks, 'the ideal of justice is accordingly seen as the bedrock. To act justly is the one and only means of promoting the common good, without which there can be no hope of preserving concord and hence of attaining greatness'.[4]

Dante would make his first acquaintance with the Roman authors precisely in an environment where they were read not only for their authority in matters of generalised moral and philosophical speculation, but also as works with immediate applicability to contemporary political organisation. The same goes for his introduction to Aristotle's works. It was in Florence, in fact, that Dante first encountered the Greek philosopher's ethical and political thinking. This was arguably thanks to the 'civic pedagogy' championed by two prominent Florentine intellectuals between the end of the thirteenth and the beginning of the fourteenth century: the lay statesman Brunetto Latini and the Dominican friar Remigio de' Girolami.

Brunetto's Old French encyclopaedia, the *Tresor*, soon translated into the Tuscan vernacular, offered a partial version of Aristotle's *Nicomachean Ethics* alongside a collection of moral precepts of both classical and biblical origin to its civic readerships. Alongside this work of secular scholarship, Fra Remigio's sermons and treatises *de iustitia, de bono comuni* and *de pace* [on justice, on the common good and on peace] often combined Aristotle's ethical and political speculation with that of the Church fathers, especially that of St Augustine. His aim was to prompt Florence's citizenry to love justice, to prefer the common good over private interests and to promote public peace.[5]

As these opening remarks suggest, an understanding of the context that provided Dante with his first intellectual formation is an important preliminary for the investigation of our discussion of 'Ethics, Politics and Justice in Dante'.[6] But, as the essays that follow show, the interest of these themes lies precisely in the fact that Dante developed in such original, unexpected and genuinely creative ways the culture that he shared with his fellow-citizens. Following the rupture of his political exile from Florence in 1302, Dante's adherence to the city's legal and political traditions, and its shared imaginary of justice, came under strain. The precise evolution of his political sympathies – and the nature of his political alliances – over the 20 years of his banishment are patchily documented, and consequently open to scholarly debate.[7]

What is clear is that, in exile, Dante began to develop a distinctive new sense of the ways in which, while excluded from participation in civic governance, he might still contribute to the peninsula's culture of justice and political morality through his role as a poet and, occasionally, propagandist; he maintained a public role now based exclusively on his literary and rhetorical talents. It is this story of Dante's evolution as poet and writer that our volume wishes to emphasise. Its essays do not engage extensively with questions about his specific political allegiances over the period of exile. Although some of our contributors touch on his so-called political *Epistles*, their chapters trace the intersection of these documents with passages of his Latin and Italian poetry. They focus on Dante's endorsement of Henry VII of Luxembourg's imperial campaign in Italy in relation to a much-coveted restoration of the ideals of justice, peace and prosperity throughout the peninsula – rather than on chronologies, campaign details or diplomacy and *realpolitik*.[8]

In a similar fashion, our readers will soon realise that none of the essays collected here is explicitly dedicated to exploring Dante's *Monarchia*. In this Latin treatise Dante, by means of sharp, logical reasoning, aims at demonstrating the necessity, divine origin and Roman legacy of the imperial office. As Dante's sole formal work of political theory, the *Monarchia* testifies to his extraordinary originality and ability to stand out from thirteenth- and fourteenth-century political analyses and juridical disputes concerning the relation between secular and ecclesiastical powers. The interpretation of the arguments that Dante develops is still a subject of intense scholarly debate.[9]

This, however, is not the primary focus of the following essays. Instead, the volume is conceived as a dialogic collection that investigates Dante's views on ethics, politics and justice by moving away from the issue of 'imperialism'. In fact, by presenting essays that range from exploring the Florentine context of Dante's early intellectual formation and literary endeavour to discussing Dante's role in fourteenth-century, pre-humanist Italy, at the climax of his poetic career, this volume's contributions put an all-embracing value on exploring how Dante approaches the themes of politics and justice as a poet – not limited to constitutional theory but ranging more broadly across moral and spiritual philosophy. Equally, our collection also stresses the relation between Dante's social and political perspectives and the importance of learning and of refining one's own judgement, in view of both eternal self-redemption and the reinstatement of justice within this world.

From Duecento Florence to Dante's last poetic works and beyond

With an essay *On Grammar and Justice: Notes on Convivio II. xii. 1–7*, Anna Pegoretti opens this volume's discussions by exploring Dante's own views on education and learning. She offers a reassessment of a much-debated portion of the *Convivio*, in which Dante briefly describes his intellectual development after the death of Beatrice. The essay focuses on three main issues: first, the connection between justice and the act of disseminating wisdom; second, the link that it is possible to establish between Dante's account and the underlying metaphor of the banquet; and third, the role played by Boethius's *Consolation of Philosophy* in the teaching of grammar within the explicitly moralised medieval educational framework – in the words of Paul Gehl, as a 'moral art'.[10] Finally, the essay argues for the prominence of Latinate and institutional education in Dante's account, reading this as a claim against the dominant, thirteenth-century Florentine vernacular culture. By presenting himself as rediscovering Boethius anew, thanks both to his Latin skills and to his personal moral energies, Dante offers his *Convivio* as an individual act of justice. In doing so he invites new audiences to share his refreshed, original vision of moral and political philosophy.

Equally attentive to the circulation of classical lore in the crucial years of Dante's Florentine formation, Nicolò Maldina presents a case study investigating how Servasanto da Faenza, a Franciscan friar active in the Florentine convent of Santa Croce during the last decades of the thirteenth century, addressed his audiences by employing and re-elaborating classical sources with edifying intent. Maldina highlights the importance of such a religious reading of the classics in relation to Dante's poetry. The essay, entitled *A Classicising Friar in Dante's Florence: Servasanto da Faenza, Dante and the Ethics of Friendship*, scrutinises Servasanto's use of Cicero's *De amicitia*, Valerius Maximus's *Facta et dicta memorabilia* and Seneca's *Epistulae ad Lucilium*, within a sermon on St Bartholomew dedicated to the theme of friendship. Maldina then moves towards considering how Servasanto's celebration of St Bartholomew as a true friend of Christ – an essential moral and spiritual attribute that should characterise anyone aspiring to become a true prophet – may have shaped Beatrice's presentation of Dante in *Inferno* canto II. Through the words of Beatrice depicting Dante as "'l'amico mio, e non de la ventura'" ['my friend, not the friend of fortune'] (*Inf.*, II. 61), the author of the *Commedia* starts to establish his prophetic and apostolic identity by emphasising the necessity of cultivating true friendship with God of whom Beatrice, as early as the juvenile *Vita nova*, is one of the tangible expressions.

Maldina's essay reveals some of the hinterland to Dante's statement of authorial ambition at the start of the *Inferno*. In the following four essays the *Commedia* is the primary focus of attention; in the next two we stay with the *Inferno*'s early canti, beginning with another take on the proemial episode. Giuseppe Ledda's discussion of *An Ethical and Political Bestiary in the First Canto of Dante's 'Comedy'* explores the animal imagery of *Inferno* canto I from an ethical and political perspective. By scrutinising a variety of medieval sources in detail – bestiaries, encyclopaedias, biblical commentaries and sermons – Ledda untangles the moral symbolism of the three beasts impeding Dante-character from ascending the 'dilettoso monte' [delightful mountain] (*Inf.*, I. 77): the *lonza*, the lion and the she-wolf. Ledda's thorough analysis of the sometimes ambivalent moral value of animal symbolism in medieval tradition helps cast new light on one of the best-known episodes of Dante's *Commedia*. As his study demonstrates, the familiarity of an episode should not deter further critical attention. Ledda shows that there is much more to be said about the way the scene illuminates the whole notion of the poem's journey, and its ethical and political scope. He shows how it offers new insights into the way that Dante-poet constructs the moral characterisation of his autobiographical *persona*, Dante the pilgrim, within the poem.

Like Ledda, Nicolò Crisafi and Elena Lombardi take on one of the *Inferno*'s best-known episodes, the meeting with Francesca and Paolo in canto V. Under the heading of *Lust and the Law: Reading and Witnessing in 'Inferno' V*, the two scholars investigate the interconnectedness of the act of witnessing and the act of reading (conceived as an act involving judgement), within Dante's discussion and representation of lust in *Inferno* V and *Purgatorio* XXVI. Having stressed how the medieval conception of lust involves different disciplines, from canon law to medicine, Crisafi and Lombardi draw attention to the *rima equivoca* 'legge': 'si legge' [law: it is read] that appears in both cantos, sparking an investigation of issues of interpretation, ethics, gender, political power and the law. The essay closes by considering the speech of Francesca in *Inferno* V as the confession and defence of a convicted adulteress in the context of contemporary legal practices. This discourse, as a reflection on the practices of reading and storytelling, also imposes the imperative for moral deliberation on the readers of the *Commedia*, in the present day just as much as in the Trecento.

A third essay focused on the *Inferno* addresses questions that likewise prompt Dante's readers to think anew about the morality of reading, and about the connections between literature and the law, embracing both ethics and jurisprudence. Justin Steinberg invites us to question just how systematic Dante's approach is when it comes to matters of judgement and reward in the afterlife. His essay, indeed – *More than an Eye for an Eye: Dante's Sovereign Justice* – takes on issues that pertain not only to Hell and punishment, but to the mode of thought that informs Dante's legal and ethical outlook as a whole. Steinberg challenges the nineteenth-century scholarly commonplace by which the alignment of sin and punishment, in Dante's *Inferno* and *Purgatorio*, has usually been described as *contrapasso* [countersuffering]. He re-scrutinises the thirteenth-century Latin translations and commentary reception of Aristotle's *Nicomachean Ethics*, in which the word *contrapassum* always denotes a limited conception of justice, as it fails to cover crimes against the sovereign and the body politic. Steinberg argues that when Bertran de Born, in *Inferno* XXVIII, depicts his punishment as *contrapasso*, he fails to recognise the public nature of his sin. As a consequence, Steinberg urges us *not* to consider countersuffering as the rigid law of all Dante's otherworldly justice, since Dante refers to the concept precisely in order to explore and discuss its limits.

After three chapters exploring the depths of Hell, our next essay provides a move high into the heavens and discusses *Paradiso* XXV. Filippo Gianferrari's essay – '*Ritornerò profeta': The 'Epistle' of St James and the Crowning of Dante's Patience* – opens by scrutinising how patristic and medieval exegeses transformed the interpretation of St James's *Epistle* from a severe condemnation against any form of pastoral teaching to a prescription on how to deliver morally fruitful and divinely inspired preaching. Gianferrari explores the ethical, political and prophetic echoes of James's letter within the works of Dante, and sheds light on how Dante employs and re-elaborates James's authority and imagery. This chapter persuasively stresses the role that James's biblical intertext played with regard to Dante's prophetic, poetic and didactic self-legitimisation – within both *Epistle* V, where Dante hails the restoration of justice and peace throughout Italy at the hands of Emperor Henry VII, and *Paradiso* XXV. In the latter Dante's self-definition as a *poeta* recalls James's instructions on how to become a good teacher, by asking God to use him as a medium for sowing the seeds of His divine wisdom.

The last essay in the main collection, fittingly, discusses Dante's last works: the Latin *Eclogues* that are among the least studied of his *oeuvre*. Sabrina Ferrara's essay on *Ethical Distance and Political Resonance in the 'Eclogues' of Dante* discusses Dante's poetic and ethical role within the cultural panorama of mid-fourteenth-century Italy, through close analysis of the exchange between Dante and the Bolognese professor Giovanni del Virgilio. Having shed light on their reciprocal, and irreconcilable, misunderstandings about the scope of vernacular poetry and the revival of classical literature, Ferrara shifts towards considering the ways in which Dante's *Eclogues* interact with selected passages from the *Commedia*. Her purpose is to show how Dante expands his reflections on the contemporary political scene within his exchange with Del Virgilio. She does so by demonstrating that Dante's establishment of an ethical distance between himself and his university interlocutor combines long-meditated political reflections with an innovative poetic programme that looks far beyond matters of language and style.

As this volume goes to press, Dante scholars find themselves in a particularly active moment of international and public-facing research engagement, highlighted by two important anniversaries: the 750th anniversary of Dante's birth in 2015 and the impending 700th anniversary of his death in 2021. This book also seeks to celebrate these high points by offering two chapters discussing the different modalities of the public reception and use of Dante's work both in Italy and Britain. In this way the volume's emphasis on morality, political philosophy and social justice is brought into the modern age of the nineteenth, twentieth and twenty-first centuries.

In the first of the two chapters, Catherine Keen reviews some of the ways in which ethical and political responses to Dante among popular, as well as scholarly, audiences have evolved over the centuries. The essay offers some brief reflections on the early decades of Dante's reception, considering both the enthusiasms and the reservations – even condemnations – generated by the provocative new poetry of a vernacular *Commedia* that presented reflections on politics, society and on both secular and divine justice to the widest of publics. Beyond this, the chapter offers a review of Dante's more recent nineteenth- and twentieth-century *fortuna*. It explores how modern audiences have accommodated reactions to the poet and his works within the new cultural horizon defined – for both Italians and international audiences – by the formal establishment of Italy as a nation-state, and by the vagaries of the national experience within the 150 years or so of its existence.

This chapter's broad, and necessarily partial, overview is complemented in the final chapter by a recent, focused case study, almost micro-historical in kind. Claire Honess and Matthew Treherne present the outputs of the public initiatives organised within the context of the collaborative research project 'Dante and Late Medieval Florence: Theology in Poetry, Practice and Society', which ran in the British Universities of Leeds and Warwick from 2011 to 2017. As Honess and Treherne stress, their project's emphasis on the local conditions in which Dante and his contemporaries could experience theology and religious cultures in late-medieval Italy and Florence offered new opportunities to engage twenty-first-century audiences, and to encourage fresh and creative approaches to Dante's works.

A dialogic collection: ethical and judicial learning, poetic authority and political perspectives

The essays collected in this volume cover a considerable span of Dante's works, from his early vernacular *Convivio* through the *Commedia* to the Latin poetry of the late *Eclogues*. Perhaps not surprisingly, in a volume that engages with themes of justice and politics, several essays focus on the *Inferno* – that part of the *Commedia* where Dante's thinking about societal and spiritual redemption finds expression in the creation of a vividly-imagined realm of suffering whose violence has proved especially challenging to both past and present audiences. These essays on the

Inferno, however, do not stand apart from the other contributions to the collection. Rather, a considerable and productive strand of dialogue runs between all the different chapters. This dialogue underlines the persistence Dante brings to his career-long commitment to explore the importance of ethics and politics in human society, and to urge the importance of *holding justice in the heart*.

As regards Dante's formative years, and the influence of early training, for instance, Maldina's exploration of how Servasanto da Faenza's religious reading of classical literature on friendship may have influenced Dante's poetry complements Pegoretti's emphasis on how Dante first accessed philosophical speculation, by applying his 'art of grammar' and his 'intellect' to the reading and understanding of Boethius's *Consolation of Philosophy*. After all, as Pegoretti recalls, a single passage in *Convivio* tells how, alongside the reading of Boethius, Dante also approached philosophy thanks to another fundamental text: namely, Cicero's *De amicitia*. Ledda's interdiscursive analysis uses an approach very close to Maldina's and Pegoretti's, whose research methods scrutinise the interaction between Dante's responses to formative cultural influences in Florence. In so doing Ledda brings to light the filtration, within *Inferno* canto I, of a broad horizon of biblical, classical and medieval sources that contributed to shaping the imagery and moral value of the *Commedia*'s poetry of moral and spiritual salvation.

Dante's early intellectual adventures thus responded to the emphases of a Florentine culture shaped by a particular civic pedagogy that blended lay and religious ethical traditions. However, they also remind us of the rapidity with which Dante evolved an independent and often polemical reaction to what he received through this semi-official culture. Nor did his originality or propensity to critical re-evaluation of contemporary scholarship fade over time: Ferrara's essay stresses how Dante expressed his intellectual and literary autonomy in the culture wars of much later decades. Her thorough discussion of the bucolic exchange between Dante and Giovanni del Virgilio, by highlighting the sophistication of the *Eclogues*, reinforces Pegoretti's acute comments on Dante's Latinity. In his last poetic production, Dante gives full rein to the Latin skills he had been determined to acquire, and extend beyond average parameters, some three decades before.

Ferrara emphasises Dante's awareness of his own achievements as a poet, both in vernacular and in Latin, and his sense of the political as well as moral and theological ends expressed in his commitment to a radical renewal of poetic culture. In reviewing the theme of poetic laureation, her discussion intersects with Gianferrari's. Where Ferrara reviews Dante's claims to a laurel crown as a second Virgil in his Latin poetry, Gianferrari shows that Dante advances similar or even stronger grounds for coronation, as a prophetic and apostolic poet of the mother-tongue, in *Paradiso*. Ferrara shows that Dante defends the excellence of the *Commedia* even while displaying a second and complementary range of talents as a ground-breaking Latin poet in the *Eclogues*; Gianferrari underlines how Dante cross-fertilises between his Latin and vernacular production in his self-presentation as a poet prophesying justice and hope – both in the secular realm of his Latin epistles on politics and through his engagement with broader moral reformation in the *Paradiso* cantos.

Along the same lines, Maldina's discussion of how the reception of classical culture in Duecento Florence nourished discourses on Christian friendship, originating in both religious and lay environments, offers new insights into the development of Dante's self-perception as a prophet of God.

As regards the chapters exploring Dante's infernal and purgatorial poetry (the two essays by Steinberg and by Crisafi and Lombardi), each addresses the field of law. In both essays this is conceived as covering not only universal conceptions of human moral righteousness, but also the systems of norms and practices regulating social life and the application of justice in medieval Italy. Both Steinberg's re-assessment of Dante's notion of countersuffering and Crisafi and Lombardi's exploration of the interactions between the law and the act of reading, within the cantos of lust populated by courtly poets and readers of courtly poetry, shed light on the relationship between literature and ethics.

Both essays draw the readers of the *Commedia* onto the stage. They in fact show how judgement is constantly tested by Dante-author's judicial poetry and its ability to challenge preconceptions by following the redemptive ascension of Dante-pilgrim from Hell, through Purgatory, up to the heights of Paradise. Though dedicated to investigating the moral significance of animal imagery in *Inferno* canto I, moreover, Ledda's study equally casts light on the ethical scope of the *Commedia* as a whole, as a poetic account of a journey to salvation embarked on by a poet who had suddenly lost the right path.

Above all, what brings all this volume's essays together is the contributors' consistent interest in exploring the medieval sources shaping the intellectual and historical panorama surrounding Dante and his literary experiences, as well as the ways that knowledge was made accessible to Duecento and Trecento lay audiences and thus to Dante. Thanks to close scrutiny of Aristotelian and biblical commentaries, encyclopaedic traditions, homiletic practices and civic statutes, the contributors to this volume provide new readings of multiple aspects of Dante's ethical, political and legal meditations. Their attention is focused not only on the moral challenges and juridical structures of the *Commedia*, but also on the ethical and political lore emerging from the so-called 'minor works'. In fact Dante's commitment to advocating justice – never detached from reflections on the best and most convenient literary and linguistic forms to adopt in order to convey his thoughts, as well as on his own didactic and prophetic authorship – extends over the whole range of his literary production, as the essays of the current volume show.

After all, in the letter addressed to his 'amico Florentino' [Florentine friend], having been offered conditions he considered totally unacceptable to return to Florence in 1315, Dante presents himself, in exile, as a 'viro praedicante iustitiam' [a man preaching justice] (*Ep.*, XII. iii. 7). Regardless of what beliefs we hold about Dante's self-depiction as 'exul immeritus' [undeservedly in exile], one of the most recurrent encouragements emerging from Dante's *oeuvre* as a whole concerns the urgency of keeping justice in the heart, and of guaranteeing equity by doing justice to others – in service of both worldly and otherworldly peace and happiness for the individual and the community alike. Without aspiring to offer a comprehensive account of the poetry of *Ethics, Politics and Justice in Dante*, we hope that the essays gathered in this volume may shed light on the fine interdependence between moral, political and legal perspectives within the thought and works of Dante. In so doing they will contribute to an open and lively dialogue between present and future readers.

Notes

1. See Aristoteles Latinus, *Ethica nicomachea translatio Roberti Grosseteste Lincolniensis (recensio pura)*, lib. V, cap. III, ed. René Antoine Gauthier (Leiden: Brill; Bruxelles: Desclée de Brouwer, 1972), 228–9.
2. See at least *Oculos pastoralis pascens officia et continens radium dulcibus pomis suis*, ed. Dora Franceschi (Turin: Accademia delle scienze, 1966), 36; Brunetto Latini, *Tresor*, ed. Pietro G. Beltrami et al. (Turin: Einaudi, 2007), 3. 75. 4 (794) and 3. 95. 2 (838).
3. See Quentin Skinner, *Visions of Politics*, 3 vols (Cambridge: Cambridge University Press, 2002), II, 10–38; Silvia Diacciati, *Popolani e magnati* (Spoleto: Fondazione Centro Italiano di Studi sull'Alto Medioevo, 2011), 309–37.
4. Skinner, II, 25.
5. On the structure and medieval sources informing Brunetto's *Tresor* see Pietro G. Beltrami, 'Introduzione', in Brunetto Latini, *Tresor*, vii–xxvi. The renewed scholarly interest in Brunetto's role as a vernacular divulgator in relation to the context of Dante's intellectual formation emerges from the recent workshop 'Reconsidering Dante and Brunetto Latini (and Bono Giamboni)', held at the University of Notre Dame Rome Global Gateway on 18–19 May 2017 and attended by various contributors to this volume. A collection of essays stemming from the workshop's discussions, edited by Zygmunt G. Barański, Theodore J. Cachey Jr. and Luca Lombardo, will be published by Salerno Editrice (Rome). On Remigio and Dante see at least the recent article by Delphine Carron, 'Remigio de' Girolami dans la Florence de Dante (1293–

1302)', *Reti Medievali Rivista* 18.1 (2017): 1–29, in the themed segment, *Dante attraverso i documenti. II. Presupposti e contesti dell'impegno politico a Firenze (1295–1302)*, ed. Giuliano Milani and Antonio Montefusco.

6. On past and present research strands focusing on Dante's intellectual formation, and on methodological problems related to them, see Zygmunt G. Barański, 'Sulla formazione intellettuale di Dante: alcuni problemi di definizione', *Studi e problemi di critica testuale* 90.1 (2015): 31–54. See also Lorenzo Dell'Oso, 'Per la formazione intellettuale di Dante: i cataloghi librari, le tracce testuali, il *Trattatello* di Boccaccio', *Le tre corone* 4 (2017): 129–61.

7. Some important recent contributions on these controversies include: Giuseppe Indizio, *Problemi di biografia dantesca*. Ravenna: Longo, 2013; Giorgio Inglese, *Vita di Dante. Una biografia possibile*. Rome: Carocci, 2015; Marco Santagata, *Dante. Il romanzo della sua vita*. Milan: Mondadori, 2012; Enrico Fenzi, 'Dante ghibellino. Note per una discussione', *Per leggere* 24 (2013): 171–98; Mirko Tavoni, 'La cosiddetta battaglia della Lastra e la biografia politica di Dante', *Nuova Rivista di Letteratura Italiana* 17.2 (2014): 51–87.

8. That is, while the *Epistles* are touched on in some essays (notably Gianferrari and Ferrara), they are not the primary focus of any. A recent collection of studies focused on Dante's involvement with Henry VII's Italian campaign explores the 'practical' aspect of his interest in imperial politics: *Enrico VII, Dante e Pisa*, ed. Giuseppe Petralia and Marco Santagata (Ravenna: Longo, 2016). See also Claire E. Honess, '"Ecce nunc tempus acceptabile": Henry VII and Dante's Ideal of Peace', *The Italianist* 33.3 (2013): 484–504. New research perspectives on Dante's *Epistles* have been recently presented at the conferences, 'Dante attraverso i documenti III. Contesti culturali e storici delle epistole dantesche' (Venice, 19–21 October 2016) and 'Dante attraverso i documenti IV. Contesti culturali e storici delle epistole dantesche' (Venice, 15–17 June 2017).

9. Recently discussions of Dante's political perspectives emerging from the *Monarchia* have been presented in the conference 'Dante as a Political Theorist: Historicizing Theology and Theologizing Power' (New York, 27 March 2015). For a recent overview of Dante's political thought, with up-to-date bibliography, see also Donatella Stocchi-Perrucchio, '*Dante Politico*: Toward a Mapping of Dante's Political Thought', *Mediaevalia* 38 (2017): 13–36.

10. Paul F. Gehl, *A Moral Art: Grammar, Society, and Culture in Trecento Florence* (Ithaca–London: Cornell University Press, 1993).

1
On Grammar and Justice: Notes on *Convivio*, II. xii. 1–7

Anna Pegoretti

Dante's ideas about education and learning can be traced primarily in the first two books of his *Convivio*. Here the poet develops a specific programme of dissemination of knowledge in the vernacular, presents a description of disciplines and provides autobiographical details concerning his own learning experience. The treatise clearly sets out its aims from the beginning, where Dante offers a rather peculiar elaboration of two themes that were topical in medieval philosophical writing: the desire for knowledge and the impediments to its fulfilment. The *incipit* of the *Convivio* notoriously quotes an Aristotelian adage, recurrent also in discourses in praise of philosophy delivered by masters in medieval university Faculties of Arts: 'Sì come dice lo Filosofo nel principio della Prima Filosofia, tutti li uomini naturalmente desiderano di sapere' (*Cvo*, I. i. 1) [As the Philosopher says at the beginning of the *First Philosophy*, all men by nature desire to know].[1] In line with the exegetical tradition on this passage, Dante immediately confronts the topic of the impediments that limit the acquisition of knowledge. Yet his approach is radically new. Proceeding in an unprecedented way, the poet plans with his *Convivio* to overcome at least some of the obstacles, which impede certain categories of men from learning.[2]

The complex dialectic between the universal character of the desire for knowledge and the actual identification of a limited audience to whom the treatise seems to be addressed is a matter for debate among scholars.[3] However, we can safely state that Dante's ground-breaking pedagogical programme, which he intends to realise through the auto-commentary on his doctrinal *canzoni*, marks a new step in the development of a vernacular philosophy created by lay authors for a lay public.[4] Dante's plan is to bridge the gap between the most learned, who enjoy the 'bread of angels', and at least a part of those who are doomed to 'share the food of sheep' (*Cvo*, I. i. 7). This aim has led him to set up his own 'banquet', whose main courses are his *canzoni*. Such a decision, Dante tells us, was inspired by friendship and mercy, which move both those who sit at the highest table and himself:

> Ma però che ciascuno uomo a ciascuno uomo naturalmente è amico, e ciascuno amico si duole del difetto di colui ch'elli ama, coloro che a così alta mensa sono cibati non sanza misericordia sono inver di quelli che in bestiale pastura veggiono erba e ghiande se[n] gire mangiando. E acciò che misericordia è madre di beneficio, sempre liberalmente coloro che sanno porgono della loro buona ricchezza alli veri poveri [...]. E io adunque, che non seggio alla beata mensa, ma, fuggito della pastura del vulgo, a' piedi di coloro che seggiono ricolgo di quello che da loro cade, [...] misericordievolemente mosso, [...] per li miseri alcuna cosa ho riservata.

(*Cvo*, I. i. 8–10)

> [But since man is by nature a friend of all men, and every friend is grieved by defects found in the one he loves, they who are fed at so lofty a table are not without compassion toward those whom they see grazing about on grass and acorns in animal pastures. And since compassion is the mother of generosity, they who possess knowledge always give liberally of their great riches to the truly poor [...]. Therefore I (who do not sit at the blessed table, but, having fled the pasture of the common herd, gather up a part of what falls to the feet of those who do sit there [...], and moved by compassion [...]) have set aside for those who are unfortunate something.]

In commenting on this passage, Sonia Gentili has pointed out that the concept of the benefit derived from mercy ('misericordia è madre di beneficio') relies on an Augustinian doctrine, which conceived mercy as strictly related not to charity (as in Aquinas), but to justice.[5] According to Augustine, the virtue of justice actualises itself in helping the wretched, 'in subveniendo miseris' (*De trinitate* XIV. ix. l. 38). This description, which originally appears as part of Augustine's discussion of the role of the four cardinal virtues in the afterlife, crystallises as a clear definition of the same virtues in the relevant chapter of the most widespread theological work of the late Middle Ages, Peter Lombard's *Sentences* (III. d. xxxiii. ch.1.2: 'iustitia est in subveniendo miseris'). Augustine's definition sparked a whole tradition according to which mercy towards *miseri* provides a *beneficium* that amends the imbalance in distributional justice created by greed and hoarding.[6] Hence we may conclude that the *Convivio* itself has to be seen as the product of an act of justice.

One could argue that such an ideological stance ought not tolerate any sort of restriction of the prospective audience. However, I do not see any insurmountable incongruity between acting with mercy and liberality and the identification of a specific group of recipients for a single act.[7] As a matter of fact, Dante sets up a banquet exclusively for those who are affected by external impediments to their pursuit of knowledge. What is more, this is a two-tier banquet, whose arrangement is based on a moral appraisal.[8] Those impeded by civic or domestic duties will sit at the table, while the indolent deserve only to sit at their feet:

> vegna qua qualunque è [per cura] familiare o civile nella umana fame rimaso, e ad una mensa colli altri simili impediti s'assetti; e alli loro piedi si pongano tutti quelli che per pigrizia si sono stati, ché non sono degni di più alto sedere.

> (*Cvo*, I. i. 13)

> [Let come here all those whose human hunger derives from domestic or civic responsibilities, and let them sit at the same table with others likewise handicapped; and at their feet let all those place themselves who do not merit a higher seat because of their indolence.]

The kind of indolence ('pigrizia') that Dante aims to overcome is that which frustrates any attempt to obviate the inconvenience of living far from an adequate intellectual environment. However generic, the explanation reveals a remarkable awareness of the importance of educational facilities and intellectual milieus: '[...] lo difetto del luogo dove la persona è nata e nutrita, che tal ora sarà da ogni studio non solamente privato, ma da gente studiosa lontano' [... the handicap that derives from the place where a person is born and bred, which at times will not only lack a university (*studio*) but be far removed from the company of educated persons] (*Cvo*, I. i. 4).[9] Such concern for the material and social aspects of learning resonates with Dante's renowned account of his own educational experience as an adult, in *Cvo*, II. xii. 7. Here he refers to his attendance at the 'scuole delli religiosi' and 'disputazioni delli filosofanti' [to the schools of the religious orders and to the disputations held by the philosophers], sometime after Beatrice's death. The process that led Dante to frequent these schools and disputes is described in some detail, in a passage that is well worth re-examining.

After the loss of 'lo primo diletto della mia anima' [the first delight of my soul], that is, after the death of Beatrice, the poet experiences an existential crisis – 'rimasi di tanta tristizia punto' [pierced by such sorrow] – which calls for support (*Cvo*, II. xii. 1). Hence, Dante approaches two prominent consolatory texts: the *Consolation of Philosophy*, in which Boethius searches for relief from his imprisonment and wretchedness, and the *De amicitia*, where Cicero elaborates Laelius's loss of his friend Scipio. The effects of these readings go well beyond consolation, and impact on Dante's intellectual experience in a twofold way. First, the desire to penetrate the meaning of the two texts (the 'sentenza') pushes the poet's interpretative abilities to their limits. It requires the best of both his grammatical skills – 'l'arte di gramatica ch'io avea' – and his personal *ingegno* [intellect]:

> E avegna che duro mi fosse nella prima entrare nella loro sentenza, finalmente v'entrai tanto entro, quanto l'arte di gramatica ch'io avea e un poco di mio ingegno potea fare; per lo quale ingegno molte cose, quasi come sognando, già vedea, sì come nella Vita Nova si può vedere.

> (*Cvo*, II. xii. 4)

> [Although it was difficult for me at first to penetrate their meaning, I finally penetrated it as deeply as my command of Latin and the small measure of my intellect enabled me to do, by which intellect I had perceived many things before, as in a dream, as may be seen in the *New Life*.]

Second, the two works open up to Dante a whole new intellectual world to explore:[10]

> E sì come essere suole che l'uomo va cercando argento e fuori della 'ntenzione truova oro, lo quale occulta cagione presenta, non forse sanza divino imperio; io, che cercava di consolar me, trovai non solamente alle mie lagrime rimedio, ma vocabuli d'autori e di scienze e di libri: li quali considerando, giudicava bene che la filosofia, che era donna di questi autori, di queste scienze e di questi libri, fosse somma cosa.

> (*Cvo*, II. xii. 5)

> [And just as it often happens that a man goes looking for silver and apart from his intention finds gold, which some hidden cause presents, perhaps not without divine ordinance, so I who sought to console myself found not only a remedy for my tears but also the words of authors, sciences, and books. Pondering these, I quickly

determined that Philosophy, who was the lady of these authors, sciences, and books, was a great thing.]

From this arises the decision to go to those 'places' – schools and disputations – where philosophy, that is knowledge, thoroughly unfolds. To sum up, we could say that an existential demand sparked a personal search in texts of moral philosophy. In turn these readings nurtured a desire for further in-depth learning, pursued through strenuous study and through attendance at institutions of higher education.

The position of this passage is of paramount importance for the overall project of the *Convivio*. At the beginning of book II, chapter xii, Dante embarks on the allegorical *and true* explanation of the *canzone* – 'esposizione allegorica e vera' (*Cvo*, II. xii. 1) – interpreting the conflict between the memory of the 'glorious lady' who had passed away and the interest in a new 'gentle' or 'noble' lady, as a tension between different intellectual stances, with the *donna gentile* in the role of Lady Philosophy.[11] The accounts of both personal and intellectual life fruitfully converge to complete the profile of the author himself. He was not allowed to eat the bread of angels at the noblest table of wisdom, but was able to sit at its foot and to 'collect' the crumbs that he now shares.[12] Indeed, there is no reason not to think that his mid-to-high position in the hierarchy of the banquet was granted first and foremost by his attendance at schools and disputations.[13] Not by chance, it was precisely after 30 months of attendance and of study that – Dante says – he started writing what is now the first 'main course' of the *Convivio, Voi che 'ntendendo* (*Cvo*, II. xii. 8). Hence Dante's presentation of his own personal intellectual experience and formation is perfectly attuned with both the underpinning metaphor of the banquet and his intermediate position in the intellectual hierarchy – one that allows him to recompose the leftovers of wisdom and to offer them to his prospective audience. At the same time, this portrait both sets the limits of Dante's educational project and legitimises it.[14] Finally, it paves the way for his description of the system of knowledge, which is the subject of the following chapters and was certainly perceived by the author as an essential element.[15]

Dante's declaration about the limits of his 'arte di gramatica' has raised substantial speculation. 'Grammar' could well refer either to his knowledge of Latin language or his expertise in the liberal art of grammar. The first interpretation is quite restrictive, even though it is supported by Dante's wide use of the term *gramatica* with such a meaning, in both Latin and vernacular works. Far from considering it a mere topos, some scholars read this passage as an explicit declaration of weakness in Latin. Most recently, Robert Black has gone as far as to list 'remnants of

Dante's imperfect Latin education [...] evident in his mature writings' to support this interpretation.[16]

Whatever we might think about Dante's Latin – whose excellence, in my view, thoroughly unfolds in the magnificent late *Eclogues*[17] – the poet's own career seems to outline the profile of a skilful, proud and valued *dictator*. In the *Vita nova*, he mentions an epistle that he supposedly sent to the city's governors to mark Beatrice's death (*VN*, 19. 8 [Barbi XXX. 1]); in the following decade, he acted as chancellor of the exiled Florentine *Universitas Alborum* [Association of the Whites]. Moreover, one could wonder why Dante should choose to declare such a deficiency while promoting himself as a competent mediator of wisdom and doctrine.

As regards the second possible interpretation of 'grammar', it should be pointed out that, since the grammar curriculum of the time was founded on the learning of the Latin language, this option *de facto* incorporates the first.[18] Not by chance, Mengaldo admitted the difficulty of interpreting this passage, stating that it is not possible to exclude that 'arte di gramatica' could actually mean 'knowledge of grammar rules', 'grammar technique', with the noteworthy comment that 'comunque il senso non cambia' [the ultimate meaning does not change anyhow].[19]

It is worth noting that the passage specifically refers to the '*art* of grammar'. *Arte* is another ambiguous term, employed by Dante mainly to describe an operational and practical expertise, based on the command of a technique.[20] The description of grammar as a discipline, which features in the following chapter, is not particularly helpful – primarily because in this section Dante labels the seven liberal arts as 'sciences', a term that undoubtedly points to theoretical knowledge.[21] What is more, he describes grammar as a 'science of language'. This includes lexicon, conjugations and constructions and, most notably, their changes over time (*Cvo*, II. xiii. 10). Certainly a historical linguistics of this kind could hardly find much space in late-medieval teaching of grammar, and in the pedagogy of literacy, which included prescriptive morphology and syntax. What is more, it is anything but useless in understanding either the 'art of grammar', on which Dante relied in his reading of Boethius and Cicero, or the kind of grammar education he could have acquired, either at school or independently.

Just as Mengaldo recognised the ultimate ambiguity of the term 'grammar', so we could well think that the boundaries of 'art' are equally blurred. We could thus state, as a provisional conclusion, that the 'art of grammar' refers to Dante's command of the Latin language, as well as a set of grammatical rules and techniques which pertained to the art of grammar as a discipline – and whose ultimate aim, at its highest levels, was a full mastery of writing and reading in Latin.[22]

The discussion about *gramatica* intersects with Dante's likewise troubling definition of the *Consolation* as a text 'non conosciuto da molti' [not known to many] (*Cvo*, II. xii. 2). In fact, Boethius's work was 'the most widely read [...] in Italian schools from 1300 to 1450'.[23] It featured in reading lists at the highest stages of grammatical education and was widely copied.[24] This is why most scholars understand Dante's statement as referring not to a poor dissemination of the text, but rather to superficial and partial understanding of it.[25]

Further light could possibly be shed on the gap between the surviving evidence and the poet's own experience – or his presentation of it – by properly framing the *Consolation* within the curriculum of grammar schools in late medieval Florence. According to Paul Gehl, Boethius's long and quite challenging text, hardly subject to cuts, 'could not have been a regular part of the early latinizing curriculum [...]. It must have been seen as an advanced special-case text, appropriate for the best and most promising students'.[26] And so Dante autonomously climbed the upper levels of the grammatical curriculum, relying on all the linguistic and literary knowledge he had acquired so far,[27] finally to take a step forward towards the whole new level of higher education represented by schools and disputations. In my opinion, what the account emphasises most is not the knowledge acquired at that time, but first and foremost the whole process of self-improvement. The reference to the 'arte di gramatica', therefore, has to be reframed within this context.

Moreover, Gehl demonstrates how, from around 1260–70 through to the end of the fourteenth century, the scope of grammar teaching extended well beyond the boundaries of literacy, Latin and literature, to promote an ambitious programme of moral education. Despite its professional marginalisation in favour of specific rhetorical skills (the *ars dictaminis*), grammar teaching in pre-university schools aimed to have a profound educational impact: 'both medieval and humanist grammar masters had assumed that practical moral philosophy was learned through the study of Latin school authors, and that these moral lessons were inseparable from the linguistic ones'.[28] Despite the conspicuous efforts that Dante scholars have made in interpreting this passage and in detecting the role played by the *Consolation* in Florentine education, it seems to me that Gehl's underlying assumption, epitomised by the title of his book, has been widely disregarded. The syllabus included both pagan and Christian 'classics', such as the *Consolation of Philosophy*, following a scheme that resonates significantly with Dante's reference to grammar in his account of his existential and profoundly philosophical search for relief after Beatrice's death.[29]

With these remarks, I do not want to suggest that Dante was deliberately hinting at something more than the 'art of grammar' as I previously defined it. I rather wish to point out that the actual practice of grammar teaching in his time included texts that *de facto* pertained to moral philosophy. This fact could help us better to explain the whole passage as a flowing account that traces an educational development, starting from an advanced art of grammar applied to texts of moral philosophy and finally approaching the higher level of teaching and learning provided by schools and disputations.

Recent publications have extensively retraced the reception of the *Consolation* in thirteenth-century Florence. Here the dissemination of the original text was complemented by literary production clearly modelled on Boethius's work, including both vernacular texts – such as Bono Giamboni's *Libro de' vizi e delle virtudi* – and Latin works that were vernacularised very quickly, for example Arrigo da Settimello's *Elegy* and the treatises by Albertano da Brescia, such as the *Liber consolationis et consilii*.[30] This impressive body of works clearly shows how deep the influence of the *Consolation* was, and is a further element appearing to contradict Dante's remark about its being scarcely known. Even before the rather belated attempts at vernacularisation of the original text, Boethius's lesson had a profound impact on Florentine civic culture through a vital vernacular literary production. Against this Dante could well claim his unmediated, integral and laborious reading of the original text. If the vernacular tradition aimed to lay the foundations of a civic culture, detached from the Latin one produced mainly by ecclesiastical institutions (particularly in Florence, where a university was still to come),[31] Dante apparently went in the opposite direction. He identified in the *scuole delli religiosi* (and possibly other *studia*) the source of a broad, direct and Latinate knowledge, mastered by professional teachers and by *filosofanti* well trained in the specialised exercise of the academic dispute.[32] However limited to crumbs, only direct access to such knowledge could legitimise Dante's own project of vernacular dissemination of a doctrinal, Latinate culture.[33]

The prominence of Latin in late medieval education emerges in a passage of the *Convivio* itself, where Dante clarifies the many reasons for his love for the vernacular. The third one points out the 'benefit' that his mother tongue provided in granting him access to Latin, and so allowing him to advance along the 'path of knowledge':

> questo mio volgare fu introduttore di me nella via di scienza, che è
> ultima perfezione [nostra], in quanto con esso io entrai nello latino

e con esso mi fu mostrato: lo quale latino poi mi fu via a più inanzi andare. E così è palese, e per me conosciuto, esso essere stato a me grandissimo benefattore.

(*Cvo*, I. xiii. 5)

[Moreover, this vernacular of mine was what led me into the path of knowledge which is our ultimate perfection, since through it I entered upon Latin and through its agency Latin was taught to me, which then became my path to further progress. So it is evident that it has been a very great benefactor to me, and this I acknowledge.]

As Fioravanti's commentary points out, this statement seems to support the evidence we have of a use of the vernacular in teaching Latin texts.[34] What is more important to my argument, however, is that, in Dante's view, the most advanced improvement in knowledge seems to have been granted to him exclusively by his Latin-based education. The author defines the service that the vernacular made in helping him to access Latin texts a 'grandissimo beneficio' [very great benefit] (*Cvo*, I. xiii. 3). Such a label ought not to be overlooked in the light of the 'benefit' that Dante himself seeks to provide to his readers with the *Convivio*. The recognition of the importance that Dante grants to the Latin training in his own education cannot but further enhance his role as founder of a new philosophy that he aims to convey in the new bread of his own vernacular ('luce nuova, sole nuovo' [a new light, a new sun], *Cvo*, I. xiii. 12). This would be a language eventually able to 'manifestare conceputa sentenza' [to make manifest the meaning conceived] (*Cvo*, I. x. 9).[35]

In justifying the use of the vernacular in his auto-commentary, Dante notoriously dismisses the previous philosophical vernacular culture. While the polemic against Taddeo Alderotti is explicit, Brunetto Latini's choice to write his *Tresor* in *langue d'oil* is addressed in more oblique, but rather unequivocal terms (*Cvo*, I. x. 10–11).[36] Most recently, Barański has fruitfully emphasised the relationship to Brunetto in Dante's development of an alternative intellectual profile. Lombardo has specifically pointed out the foundational role that the *Tesoretto*, as an unrealised *prosimetrum*, played for the mixture of lyric verse and prose that characterises both the *Vita nova* and the *Convivio*.[37] Brunetto's attempt, however, seems to impact on the *Convivio* in even wider ways. These involve not only matters of literary genre, but also of language, and the development of a vernacular poetry thoroughly able to convey philosophical doctrine. In several points of the *Tesoretto*, Brunetto declares his intention to open up the meaning of his poetry through vernacular prose,

on the basis of the fact that rhymes constrain writing, and to undermine
the understanding of the 'sentenza' [meaning]:

> Ma perciò che la rima
> si stringe a una lima
> di concordar parole
> come la rima vuole,
> sì che molte fïate
> le parole rimate
> ascondon la sentenza
> e mutan la 'ntendenza,
> quando vorrò trattare
> di cose che rimare
> tenesse oscuritate,
> con bella brevetate
> ti parlerò per prosa
> e disporrò la cosa
> parlando in volgare,
> ché tu intende ed apare.[38]

(*Tesoretto*, 411–26)

[Since rhyme constrains to make words match on its basis, in such
a way that rhymed words often hide their meaning and affect their
understanding, when I will deal with subjects that would remain
obscure in poetry, I will speak in a pleasantly brief prose, and I will
explain the whole thing in the vernacular, so that you will understand and learn.]

Brunetto's insistence on metaphors of light and obscurity is prominent:
he will use a 'pure' vernacular so as not to be obscure ("n bel volgare e
puro, | tal che non sia oscuro | vi dicerò per prosa', 1119–21); at the very
end, he announces the intention to switch to prose 'per dir più chiara-
mente' [to speak more clearly, 2901]. I have little doubt that Dante had
these lines in mind while announcing the 'luce nuova, sole nuovo' of his
new 'bread'.[39] What is more, Brunetto's remark about the constraints of
poetry is first embraced by Dante:

> per questo comento la gran bontade del volgare di sì [si vedrà];
> però che si vedrà la sua vertù, sì com'è per esso altissimi e novis-
> simi concetti convenevolemente, sufficientemente e aconciamente,
> quasi come per esso latino, manifestare; [la quale non si potea bene

manifestare] nelle cose rimate per le accidentali adornezze che quivi sono connesse, cioè la rima e lo tempo e lo numero regolato.

(*Cvo*, I. x. 12)

[by means of this commentary the great goodness of the vernacular of *sì* will be seen, because its virtue will be made evident, namely how it expresses the loftiest and the most unusual conceptions almost as aptly, fully, and gracefully as Latin, something that could not be expressed perfectly in verse, because of the accidental adornments that are tied to it, that is, rhyme and meter.]

This is then to be reformulated at the end of the first book as the vernacular's ultimate aim:

Ciascuna cosa studia naturalmente alla sua conservazione: onde, se lo volgare per sé studiare potesse, studierebbe a quella; e quella sarebbe aconciare sé a più stabilitate, e più stabilitate non potrebbe avere che [in] legar sé con numero e con rime. E questo medesimo studio è stato mio.

(*Cvo*, I. xiii. 6–7)

[Everything by nature pursues its own preservation; thus if the vernacular could by itself pursue anything, it would pursue that; and that would be to secure itself greater stability, and greater stability it could gain only by binding itself with meter and with rhyme. This has been precisely my purpose.]

As Ascoli has pointed out, rhythm and rhyme, 'previously dismissed as external adornments to be stripped away in order to reveal the true conceptualizing beauty and goodness of vernacular prose, are now recuperated as the instruments by which Dante-poet imposes unifying stability on the "volgare," a stability which echoes both the "nobility" and the "bellezza" earlier attributed to Latin'.[40]

As Dante scholars, we cannot but lament the laconic concision of Dante's account of his intellectual formation, as we painfully try to explain it better, step by step. Yet none of the words and parentheses of *Cvo*, II. xii. 1–7, which feature at a turning point of the book, is less than carefully chosen and crafted. It seems to me that Dante intentionally excludes the previous doctrinal vernacular culture from the account of his formation, in order to draw an intellectual self-portrait that proudly achieves the level of middle and higher education, up to the foot of the high table of wisdom. He does so by staging himself strenuously reading two key Latin texts. One of them, Boethius's *Consolation*, was leaving an imprint on Florentine vernacular culture in massive, but mainly oblique and mediated ways; the other, the *De amicitia*, had apparently disappeared from the curriculum of the schools and was generally disregarded by Florentine intellectuals in favour of Cicero's political and rhetorical works.[41] Once this position was acquired and his credentials were declared, Dante could finally and legitimately unfold his own project of founding a new lay philosophy in a new, strengthened vernacular. A project, which has to be understood as a *beneficio* and as an individual act of justice, that aims partially to amend the imbalances in the distribution of the 'bread of the angels'.

Notes

1. *Dante's 'Il Convivio'*, trans. by Richard H. Lansing (New York: Garland, 1990). The original text is that established by Ageno, with the minor amendments introduced by Gianfranco Fioravanti in his commented edition.
2. The remarkable novelty of such a move has been fully recognised by Francis Cheneval in his introduction to Dante Alighieri, *Das Gastmahl*, trans. by Thomas Ricklin, introduction and commentary by Francis Cheneval, Ruedi Imbach, Thomas Ricklin, 4 vols (Hamburg: Meiner, 1996), I, li–lii. See most recently, with full bibliography, Anna Pegoretti, '"Da questa nobilissima perfezione molti sono privati": Impediments to Knowledge and the Tradition of Commentaries on Boethius' *Consolatio Philosophiae*', in *Dante's 'Convivio': Or How to Restart a Career in Exile*, ed. Franziska Meier (Bern: Peter Lang, 2018), 77–97.
3. Some persuasively argue that Dante delimits its addressees to the 'principi, baroni, cavalieri e molt'altra nobile gente, non solamente maschi ma femmine' [princes, barons, knights and many other noble people, not only men but women] mentioned in *Cvo*, I. ix. 5. See Luca Bianchi, '"Noli comedere panem philosophorum inutiliter". Dante Alighieri and John of Jandun on Philosophical "Bread"', *Tijdschrift voor Filosofie* 75 (2013): 335–55; Gianfranco Fioravanti's introduction to his commentary on the *Convivio*: Dante Alighieri, *Opere*, dir. Marco Santagata, 2 vols (Milan: Mondadori, 2011–2014), II (2014): *Convivio, Monarchia, Epistole, Ecloghe*, 1–805 (53–59, and *ad loc.*); Gianfranco Fioravanti, 'La nobiltà spiegata ai nobili. Una nuova funzione della filosofia', in *Il Convivio di Dante*, ed. Johannes Bartuschat and Andrea A. Robiglio (Ravenna: Longo, 2015), 157–63; Mirko Tavoni, *Qualche idea su Dante* (Bologna: il Mulino, 2015), esp. 77–103.
4. The characteristics of a lay philosophy of this kind have been fully recognised and described by Ruedi Imbach, *Laien in der Philosophie des Mittelalters: Hinweise und Anregungen zu einem vernachlässigten Thema* (Amsterdam: Grüner, 1989); Imbach, *Dante, la philosophie et les laïcs* (Fribourg, Suisse: Éditions universitaires, 1996); Ruedi Imbach and Catherine König-Pralong, *La sfida laica. Per una nuova storia della filosofia medievale* (Rome: Carocci, 2016; first edition *Le défi laïque: existe-t-il une philosophie de laïcs au Moyen Age?* Paris: Vrin, 2013).
5. Sonia Gentili, *L'uomo aristotelico alle origini della letteratura italiana* (Rome: Carocci–Università degli studi di Roma La Sapienza, 2005), 141–6.
6. See Gentili, *L'uomo aristotelico*, 143–4. It is worth noting that Gentili develops her remarks in a substantially different direction and with partially different aims. On the basis of Aristotle's *Nicomachean Ethics*, she discusses the *Convivio*'s overarching combination of ethical and artistic values, and thus Dante's self-presentation as both benefactor and good *artifex*. What is most interesting for my argument is the connection between dissemination and justice. As Gentili effectively points out, the idea of dissemination as providing a benefit to an audience, identified on the basis of their moral constitution and potential, is widespread in thirteenth- and early

fourteenth-century Italian vernacular culture: Gentili, 'La filosofia dal latino al volgare', in *La filosofia in Italia al tempo di Dante*, ed. Gianfranco Fioravanti and Carla Casagrande (Bologna: il Mulino, 2016): 191–224 (196–8).

7. In *Cvo*, I. viii. 2, Dante presents his choice of writing the auto-commentary in the vernacular, and not in Latin, as a further act of liberality – a moral attitude that is characterised by giving to many, giving useful things and giving without being asked ('dare a molti; [...] dare utili cose; [...] senza essere domandato lo dono, dare quello'). In paraphrasing this passage, Gentili talks about the universality of the gift ('universalità del dono', *L'uomo aristotelico*, 146; 'La filosofia dal latino al volgare', 199) and about the endeavour of giving to as many as possible (*L'uomo aristotelico*, 157). Paolo Falzone writes: 'a beneficiare dei contenuti del trattato è ammesso in teoria chiunque sia libero dagli impedimenti suddetti [i.e. the internal impediments] [...]. Ciò esclude che i destinatari ideali dell'opera [...] possano essere identificati meccanicamente con un qualsivoglia gruppo sociale' [those who benefit from the contents of the treatise are in theory any who are free from the aforementioned impediments. [...] This excludes the possibility that the ideal addressees of the work [...] be mechanically identified with any given social group]: Falzone, 'Il *Convivio* di Dante', in *La filosofia in Italia*, 225–64 (231). Of course, Dante chose the vernacular in order to reach a wider, albeit regional, non-Latinate audience (*Cvo*, I. vii. 11–16). Yet I am not entirely persuaded that 'giving to *many*' immediately and necessarily means giving to *anyone* lacking internal impediments, or that the widening of the audience should automatically mean that Dante had in mind a universal act of dissemination. In his seminal article, '"Noli comedere panem philosophorum inutiliter"', Luca Bianchi persuasively compares Dante's strategy to Aristotle's identification of his audience in *Nic. Eth.* I. iii (340–43; see also 353–54). In her essay '"Miseri, 'mpediti, affamati": Dante's Implied Reader in the *Convivio*', in *Dante's 'Convivio'*, 207–21, Enrica Zanin rather perplexingly tries to keep everything together, identifying a progressive narrowing of the audience from 'those with the natural desire to know' (207), namely anyone, up to 'noblemen' (210).

8. Bianchi, '"Noli comedere panem philosophorum inutiliter"', 343: 'Dante devotes a specific passage of the introduction provided in the first book of his *Convivio* [...] to making clear that, however large, his own audience must also have certain physical and moral prerequisites'. Restriction of the audience had not involved the earliest dissemination of the *canzoni*, whose shameful previous interpretation by some is what compels the author to write his auto-commentary (*Cvo*, I. ii. 16).

9. However, the text could be over-interpreted as 'being far removed from institutions of higher education': that is why some editors print '*Studio*' with a capital 'S'. Dante Alighieri, *Il convivio*, ed. Maria Simonelli (Bologna: Pàtron, 1966), *ad loc.; Convivio*, ed. Giorgio Inglese (Milan: BUR, 1993), *ad loc*. Lansing's translation further narrows this interpretation, referring to the 'university', even though the title of *studium* was also conferred on religious institutions.

10. This is the most flexible and possibly safest explanation of Dante's reference to 'the words of authors, sciences, and books' that I am able to offer. A discussion of this passage is found in Zygmunt G. Barański, 'On Dante's Trail', *Italian Studies* 72.1 (2017): 1–15 (10–11), which emphasises especially the limits of Dante's 'intellectual formation' in Florence.

11. On the Boethian roots of this personification, see most recently Paola Nasti, '"Vocabuli d'autore e di scienze e di libri" (*Conv.* II xii 5): percorsi sapienziali di Dante', in *La Bibbia di Dante: esperienza mistica, profezia e teologia biblica in Dante. Atti del convegno internazionale di studi (Ravenna, 7 novembre 2009)*, ed. Giuseppe Ledda (Ravenna: Centro dantesco dei Frati minori conventuali, 2011), 121–78 (136–9); Luca Lombardo, '"In sembianza di donna". Reperti boeziani nei testi toscani delle origini: dal rifacimento al *Convivio* di Dante', *Le Tre Corone* 4 (2017): 11–46.

12. New light on the foundational role of the imagery of bread in the *Convivio* has been recently shed by Bianchi, '"Noli comedere panem philosophorum inutiliter"'; Nicolò Maldina, 'Raccogliendo briciole. Una metafora della formazione dantesca tra *Convivio* e *Commedia*', *Studi danteschi* 81 (2016): 131–64; Zygmunt G. Barański, '"Oh come è grande la mia impresa": Notes towards Defining Dante's *Convivio*, in *Dante's 'Convivio'*, 9–26; Albert R. Ascoli, '"Ponete mente almeno come io son bella": Prose and Poetry, "pane" and "vivanda", Goodness and Beauty, in *Convivio* I', in *Dante's 'Convivio'*, 115–43, who extensively discusses the 'slipping' referents of Dante's different breads. On this remarkable difficulty see also Laurence Hooper, 'Dante's *Convivio*, Book 1: Metaphor, Exile, Epochē', *Modern Language Notes* 127.5, Supplement (2012): 86–104. In an extremely interesting recent essay by Gianfranco Fioravanti, 'Il pane degli angeli nel *Convivio* di Dante', in *Nutrire il corpo, nutrire l'anima nel Medioevo*, ed. Chiara Crisciani and Onorato Grassi (Pisa: ETS, 2017), 191–200, Dante's bread is read in the light of the liturgy of the *Corpus Domini*.

13. Fioravanti points out that 'l'immagine della mensa [...] ha tutta l'aria di rimandare ad un contesto istituzionale. Per questo sembra plausibile che Dante stia pensando anche ad un sapere concreto e curriculare ed alle istituzioni che lo forniscono' [the image of the banquet [...] seems to recall an institutional environment. Thus, it is possible that Dante also has in mind an actual study curriculum and the institutions that provide it] (*ad Cvo*, I. i. 7). It is not possible here to discuss which *studia* Dante had in mind precisely. What is relevant to my discussion is that Dante claims an institutional training.

14. On the *Convivio* as an educational project, see Franziska Meier, 'Educating the Reader: Dante's *Convivio*', *L'Alighieri* 45 (2015): 21–33. Far from contrasting with my proposal, Meier's idea that Dante's *Convivio* offers 'an audacious counterproposal of philosophical education in opposition to a domineering and highly professionalized academic training' (23) could to some extent be seen as the other side of the same coin.

15. The tradition of the so-called *divisio scientiae*, through which knowledge was described as a hierarchical structure of disciplines and sub-disciplines, flourished throughout the Middle Ages, to reach a climax in the thirteenth century. Such descriptions can be found in all sorts of academic and encyclopaedic texts, including vernacular texts very close to Dante, such as the first book of Brunetto Latini's *Tresor* and his *Rettorica*. See at least James A. Weisheipl O.P., 'The Nature, Scope, and Classification of the Sciences', in *Science in the Middle Ages*, ed. David C. Lindberg (Chicago: University of Chicago Press, 1978), 461–82; Gilbert Dahan, 'La classificazione delle scienze e l'insegnamento universitario nel XIII secolo', in *Le Università dell'Europa: le scuole e i maestri. Il Medioevo*, ed. Jacques Verger and Gian Paolo Brizzi (Milan: Silvana Editoriale, 1994), 19–43; Olga Weijers, *Le maniement du savoir: pratiques intellectuels à l'époque des premières universités (XIIIe–XIVe siècles)* (Turnhout: Brepols, 1996).

16. Robert Black, 'Education', in *Dante in Context*, ed. Lino Pertile and Zygmunt G. Barański (Cambridge: Cambridge University Press, 2015), 260–76, 268.

17. In his commentary on the *Eclogues*, Marco Petoletti fully brings to light the exquisite resurgence of Latin bucolic poetry promoted by this work: see Dante Alighieri, *Egloge*, ed. Marco Petoletti, in Dante Alighieri, *Epistole. Egloge. Questio de aqua et terra* (Rome: Salerno, 2016), 489–650. On the *Eclogues*, and their rhetorical sophistication, see Sabrina Ferrara's essay in this volume.

18. This is how I understand Fioravanti's gloss *ad loc.*: 'qui "gramatica" indica tanto la lingua latina, quanto la disciplina che ne permette lo studio'.

19. Pier Vincenzo Mengaldo, 'Gramatica', in *Enciclopedia Dantesca* (*ED*) (Rome: Istituto dell'Enciclopedia Italiana, 1970–8), III (1971), 259–64 (260).

20. See, albeit with some caution, the entry 'Arte' by Fernando Salsano in the *Enciclopedia Dantesca*, I (1970), 397–99.

21. *Cvo*, II. xiii. 8: 'alli sette primi [i.e. *cieli*] rispondono le sette scienze del Trivio e del Quadruvio' [to the first seven [heavens] correspond the seven sciences of the Trivium and the Quadrivium]; see also §§ 14, 16–17, 26. On the identification of sciences on the basis of their object, see Fioravanti, *ad* xiii. 3. As Luca Bianchi has pointed out to me, the coincidence of liberal arts and sciences is not striking in Dante's time. Even in the *Convivio*, *perspettiva* is at first labelled as an art – *Cvo*, II. iii. 6: 'un'arte che si chiama perspettiva' [the art called optics] – and later on listed among the sciences as the 'handmaid' of geometry (xiii. 27).

22. For the levels of the grammar curriculum, see the effective summary provided by Black, 'Education', 262.

23. Robert Black, *Education and Society in Florentine Tuscany: Teachers, Pupils and Schools, c. 1250–1500* (Leiden: Brill, 2007), 151. The situation with regard to the thirteenth century is much more perplexing. However, even Black – whose scepticism about 'classical' education at that time is well known – admits the *Consolation* among the books of the grammar curriculum from the twelfth century onwards: see Black, *Education and Society*, 48–50.

24. A useful and extensive summary of available research on the *Consolation* in the Middle Ages is provided by Luca Lombardo, *Boezio in Dante: la 'Consolatio Philosophiae' nello scrittoio del poeta* (Venice: Edizioni Ca' Foscari, 2013), 13–136.

25. See in particular Thomas Ricklin, '" ... quello non conosciuto da molti libro di Boezio". Hinweise zur *Consolatio Philosophiae* in Norditalien', in *Boethius in the Middle Ages: Latin and Vernacular Traditions of the Consolatio Philosophiae*, ed. Maarten J. F. M. Hoenen and Lodi Nauta (Leiden: Brill, 1997), 267–86; Robert Black and Gabriella Pomaro, *La 'Consolazione della Filosofia' nel Medioevo e nel Rinascimento Italiano/Boethius's 'Consolation of Philosophy' in Italian Medieval and Renaissance Education: Schoolbooks and Their Glosses in Florentine Manuscripts*

(Florence: Sismel-Edizioni del Galluzzo, 2000), 1–50; Giuseppina Brunetti, 'Guinizzelli, il non più oscuro Maestro Giandino e il Boezio di Dante', in *Intorno a Guido Guinizzelli, Atti della Giornata di studi (Università di Zurigo, 16 giugno 2000)*, ed. Luciano Rossi and Sara Alloatti Boller (Alessandria: Edizioni dell'Orso, 2002), 155–91; Paola Nasti, '"Vocabuli d'autore"', 142; Luca Lombardo, '"Quasi come sognando". Dante e la presunta rarità del "libro di Boezio" (*Convivio* II xii 2–7)', *Mediaeval Sophia* 12 (2012): 141–52; Lombardo, *Boezio in Dante*, 164–9. Paola Nasti has analysed the manuscript tradition of the *Consolation* in Dante's time, fruitfully pointing out a diversified and scattered transmission of commentaries to the text which could explain Dante's statement, in 'Storia materiale di un classico dantesco: la *Consolatio Philosophiae* fra XII e XIV secolo tradizione manoscritta e rielaborazioni esegetiche', *Dante Studies* 134 (2016): 142–68. See also Luca Lombardo, '"Ed imaginava lei fatta come una donna gentile". Boezio, Brunetto Latini e la prima formazione intellettuale di Dante', *Le Tre Corone* 5 (2018): 39–71 (66–70).

26. Paul F. Gehl, *A Moral Art: Grammar, Society, and Culture in Trecento Florence* (Ithaca and London: Cornell University Press, 1993), 156.

27. See Fioravanti, *ad Cvo*, II. xii. 4.

28. Gehl, 26. See also Ronald G. Witt, *In the Footsteps of the Ancients: The Origins of Humanism from Lovato to Bruni* (Leiden: Brill, 2000), 197.

29. The most widespread Boethian commentary at that time was the profoundly philosophical one by William of Conches, whose influence is clearly detectable in several passages of Dante's *oeuvre*. On the diffusion of William's commentary in thirteenth-century Florence, see Black and Pomaro, *La 'Consolazione della Filosofia'*, 85–88; Brunetti, 'Guinizzelli, il non più oscuro maestro Giandino'. As regards its influence on Dante, see Claudio Giunta, 'Dante: l'amore come destino', in *Dante the Lyric and Ethical Poet. Dante lirico e etico*, ed. Zygmunt G. Barański and Martin McLaughlin (London: Legenda, 2010), 119–36 (this essay substantially informs Giunta's commentary on *Amor che movi* in Dante Alighieri, *Opere,* dir. by Santagata, I (2011): *Rime, Vita nova, De vulgari Eloquentia*, 384–409); Nasti, '"Vocabuli d'autore"',136–53; Lombardo, *Boezio in Dante, ad ind.*; Bianchi, '"Noli comedere panem philosophorum inutiliter"'.

30. Nasti, '"Vocabuli d'autore"', 136–53; Johannes Bartuschat, 'La littérature vernaculaire et la philosophie en Toscane dans la deuxième moitié du 13ème siècle', *Tijdschrift voor Filosofie* 75 (2013): 311–33; Lombardo, '"In sembianza di donna"' and '"Ed imaginava lei"'. In the first of his two articles, Lombardo provides the transcription of a thirteenth-century letter in the vernacular (44–5), written by a certain Tepertus (possibly Tiberto Galliziani da Pisa, 29), which vernacularises extensive portions of Boethius's work. A further early partial vernacularisation is the one found in a manuscript in Florence's *Biblioteca Medicea Laurenziana*, MS Laur. Plut. 23 dex. 11, pointed out by Black and Pomaro, 85–8; Brunetti, 'Guinizzelli, il non più oscuro maestro Giandino', identified the author with the Giandino 'master at the *studium*', named by Giovanni Villani alongside the Franciscan friar Arlotto da Prato in relation to the death of Charles I of Anjou in January 1285. This attempt, which consists principally of a vernacular paraphrase of the poetic metres, could possibly be related to teaching techniques: see below, note 34.

31. See Lombardo, '"In sembianza di donna"', 26–7.

32. The meaning of the word 'filosofanti' is discussed in Anna Pegoretti, 'Filosofanti', *Le tre corone* 2 (2015): 11–70.

33. Ascoli aptly states that 'initially "pane" is used to figure the philosophical content currently available only to an intellectual elite fluent in "grammatica," that is, Latin' (19). More complex is Barański's focus on the table of Wisdom as a 'supernatural feast […] a rare privilege that needs to be undertaken with the utmost humility', one which deals with Dante's concept of 'true Wisdom' that 'resides exclusively in God'. However, there is no doubt that Dante's intermediate position actually is 'a mark of great personal merit' (Barański, "Oh come è grande"', 25). On the limits and consequences of Dante's 'recollection', see Zygmunt G. Barański, 'Sulla formazione intellettuale di Dante: alcuni problemi di definizione', *Studi e problemi di critica testuale* 90 (2015): 31–54 (47–8).

34. Fioravanti, *ad loc*. See Gehl, 27, 30. See also Black, *Education and Society*, 48: 'From the thirteenth century, […] teachers began to offer synonyms for Latin words to explain their meaning to pupils'. Evidence is provided by several Tuscan manuscripts of Boethius's *Consolation*: see Robert Black, *Humanism and Education in Medieval and Renaissance Italy: Tradition and Innovation in Latin Schools from the Twelfth to the Fifteenth Century* (Cambridge: Cambridge University Press, 2001), 275–81.

35. On Dante's foundation of a new philosophical culture, which overcomes mere dissemination and vernacularisation, see Imbach and König-Pralong, *La sfida laica*, 64–8. On Dante's dismissal of Brunetto's compilatory strategy, see Nasti, '"Vocabuli d'autore"', 153–9.
36. See Gentili, 'La filosofia dal latino al volgare', 201.
37. Barański, 'On Dante's Trail', 8; Lombardo, '"Ed imaginava lei"'.
38. Brunetto Latini, *Poesie*, ed. Stefano Carrai (Turin: Einaudi, 2016): 5–155.
39. This hypothesis does not undermine the prominent importance of the sustained biblical imagery in Dante's presentation of his project: for the people illuminated by a new light see Is. 9, 1–2 and Matth. 4, 16. See Fioravanti, 'Il pane degli angeli', 200.
40. Ascoli, 137. On Dante's foundation of a vernacular poetry, worthy of being named as such, see Tavoni, 295–334. On the development of rhyme in Dante's *Commedia*, see most recently the acute observations by Franco Suitner, 'Sul condizionamento della rima in Dante: primi appunti', *Letteratura Italiana Antica* XX (2019). *Studi in onore di Antonio Lanza*, forthcoming.
41. On the rhetorical-political preferences of thirteenth-century Ciceronianism, see for instance *The Rhetoric of Cicero in its Medieval and Early Renaissance Commentary Tradition*, ed. Virginia Cox and John O. Ward (Leiden: Brill, 2006), especially the essays by Cox, Johnston and Milner (I would like to thank Catherine Keen for pointing me in the right direction). The impact of Cicero's philosophical works in Dante's time is not something that I could even try to touch on here, and that deserves extensive investigation. My focus on the *Consolation of Philosophy* is justified by the wide and documented impact that this work had on Florentine vernacular culture. The use of the *De amicitia* in grammar teaching (alongside the *De senectute*) is attested in the twelfth century: see Black, *Humanism and Education*, 192 and Robert Black, 'The Origins of Humanism, its Educational Context and its Early Development: a Review Article of Ronald Witt *In the Footsteps of the Ancients*', *Vivarium* 40.2 (2002): 272–97 (277–8). Manuscripts containing both the *Consolatio* and the *De amicitia* have been traced by Nasti, 'Storia materiale'.

2

A Classicising Friar in Dante's Florence: Servasanto da Faenza, Dante and the Ethics of Friendship*

Nicolò Maldina

The aim of this essay is rather limited, and perhaps the title may look ambitious when compared to its actual content. I shall not offer here a comprehensive discussion of the role of classical antiquity in shaping religious culture in Dante's Italy, nor shall I presume definitively to solve any of the many problems related to the topic. On this occasion I shall not even try to sketch a well-rounded profile of the classicising friar mentioned in the title. Hence the subtitle: I propose to limit myself to posing a few still unaddressed questions on the reception of classical culture in Dante's intellectual context. I shall do so by discussing a sermon preached on an unknown occasion (presumably in Florence during the last decades of the thirteenth century) by the Franciscan Servasanto da Faenza and later collected in the so-called *De proprio sanctorum* collection of his sermons, with a specific focus on the use made by the preacher of classical sources.[1] Only towards the end of this brief discussion shall I touch on the importance to our understanding of Dante's poetry of such a religious reading of classical culture.

The definition 'classicizing friar' comes from Beryl Smalley's pioneering study on *English Friars and Antiquity*. The term 'points to fondness for classical literature, history and myth' displayed in sermons, preaching aids and biblical commentaries written by a group of early fourteenth-century English friars centred mostly in Oxford and Cambridge 'without suggesting that the group played any special part in the rise of humanism',[2] insofar as they do not aim to produce a scholarly type of classicism but rather to use classical sources 'for the furtherance of the Gospel through the art of preaching'.[3] To the best of my knowledge, to date only a few attempts have been undertaken to investigate the presence of a similar attitude in late medieval Italy. This, even though Billanovich's seminal studies on Italian pre-humanism have long since established that an English friar was active as commentator of classical texts (including Seneca, Boethius and Livy) in central Italy, most notably between Pisa and Florence at the end of the thirteenth and the beginning of the fourteenth centuries: the Dominican Nicholas Trevet.[4] In what follows I shall argue that Servasanto can also be listed among these Italian classicising friars, in light of the high number of quotations and references to classical literature and culture in his surviving sermons. My discussion will focus on his role as mediator of classical texts to Dante's intellectual context.

Among Servasanto's many sermons rich in quotations from classical authorities, one worthy of special consideration is the first of two on St Bartholomew. It is based on a verse from the Gospel of Luke, 'Amice, ascende superius' [Friend, go up higher],[5] and it develops an articulated discourse on friendship that aims to comment on this biblical authority by means of constant references to Cicero's *De amicitia*. Although no such use of the *De amicitia* can be found in standard exegesis on the Gospel of Luke,[6] the use of references to Cicero's treatise to comment on that verse is not peculiar to Servasanto's sermon. It can also be found in other sermons from the thirteenth and fourteenth centuries.[7] However, references to the same verse in late medieval preaching often occur in support of discourses on knowledge. Sermons based on Luke 14. 10 are thus peculiar to university preaching. Here the focus is less on the first word (*amice*) than on the last two (*ascende superius*), so as to support a line of reasoning intended to celebrate study as true friendship to knowledge, i.e., the only activity that can elevate men on earth.[8] By contrast, Servasanto's sermon does offer a slightly different interpretation of the second half of the biblical verse, by reading (as we shall see towards the end of this essay) the adverb *superius* in a moral sense. This consists in a demonstration that Bartholomew was a good friend of Christ ('verus ergo amicus Bartholomeus fuit, quando Christo non diviti, sed summe pauperi se conjunxit' [Bartholomew was in fact a good friend, when he joined Christ not for riches but for great poverty]).[9] Such a reading is based on an articulated set of references to the notion of friendship as developed by classical, rather than biblical,[10] authorities and including, in addition to the aforementioned *De amicitia*, Valerius Maximus, Seneca, Boethius and Macrobius.[11]

Surprisingly enough, no extant manuscript of any of the classical authorities quoted by Servasanto can be found in the ancient catalogue of the library of Santa Croce.[12] Nonetheless, excerpts from the majority of them (Valerius Maximus, Macrobius and Seneca) are present in a manuscript now held in Florence's Biblioteca Medicea Laurenziana, MS Plut. 6 sin. 10, which had been housed in the Franciscan convent since the late thirteenth century.[13] A closer look into this collection of *notabilia* is essential to a better understanding of Servasanto's reading of classical culture in this sermon. Let us, for instance, consider an *exemplum* concerning Alexander the Great that Servasanto intended using to demonstrate that good friends are as united as if they were one, as well as to exhort his listeners to be good friends to each other, given that even pagans could be champions of friendship:[14]

Nam, postquam Alexander, rex Macedonum, regem Darius devicisset et regnum Persarum suo dominio subjugasset, et ad quemdam locum, ubi erat mater Darii, devenisset, illa quemdam militem videns, quem propter elegantiam formae, et magnitudinem personae Alexandrum esse credidit, ipsum tanquam regem salutavit. Cumque audiret, quo ille quem salutaverat, rex non esset, timens, verba querebat, quibus se excusaret. Cui rex: Nihil est, quod in hac re debeas formidare: quia et hic Alexander est, et ego sum id quod ipse est.[15]

Quod ita esse rex Alexander sensit. Darei castris, in quibus omnes necessarii eius erant, potitus Hephaestione gratissimo sibi latus suum tegente ad eos adloquendos uenit. Cuius aduentu mater Darei recreata humi prostratum caput erexit Hephaestionemque, quia et statura et forma praestabat, more Persarum adulata tamquam Alexandrum salutauit. Admonita deinde erroris per summam trepidationem excusationis uerba quaerebat. Cui Alexander 'nihil est' inquit 'quod hoc nomine confundaris: nam et hic Alexander est'.[16]

[In fact, after Alexander, king of the Macedonians, defeated King Darius and conquered the Persian kingdom, and came to a certain place where Darius's mother was, she, seeing a certain soldier and believing he was Alexander because of his graceful and magnificent appearance, welcomed him as the king. When she realised that he whom she welcomed was not the king, full of fear she asked to be excused. The king said to her: There is nothing to be afraid of, because he is Alexander too and I myself am what he himself is.]

[King Alexander realised that this was the case. He captured the camp of Darius, and with his favourite friend Hephaestion by his side, he came to speak to the relatives of Darius, who were all in the camp. The mother of Darius was cheered by his arrival and lifted up her head from the ground where she had lain prostrated. Since Hephaestion was more impressive in height and appearance, she bowed down before him in the Persian way, greeting him as if he were Alexander. When her mistake was pointed out, she was absolutely terrified and tried to find words with which to excuse herself. But Alexander said to her, 'There is no need to get upset just because of a name: he is Alexander too'.]

Here is Servasanto's *exemplum* (on the left) alongside its most probable source (on the right): an anecdote narrated in Valerius Maximus's *Facta et dicta memorabilia*. Although the *exemplum* is quite clearly a rewording of this text, Servasanto does not mention the name of the soldier mistaken for Alexander, who in the ancient versions of the anecdote is always named as Hephaestion; instead he narrates the story as if it occurred simply to 'quemdam militem' [a certain soldier]. Apart from this difference, which is indeed a major one, the *exemplum* shows strong links with the *Facta et dicta*: the most notable similarity is not the wording of the sentence attributed to Alexander ('hic Alexander est' [Alexander is here as well]), which may well come from any of the other ancient versions of the story,[17] but the simple fact that both Servasanto and Valerius Maximus link the anecdote to the theme of friendship: the first by narrating it in a sermon on friendship and the second by including it in his collection's section on friendship. Whereas the other accounts put their stress on the magnanimity of Alexander himself, these both focus on the fact that such magnanimity is a clear sign of his close friendship with Hephaestion.

Servasanto's use of Valerius Maximus as a source for *exempla* from ancient history is not surprising, considering that such use is constant in his sermons.[18] What is surprising is that this specific *exemplum* is not at all common in late medieval preaching: to the best of my knowledge the story is not included in any existing medieval sermon or collection of *exempla*. Yet the substitution of a character as essential as Hephaestion seems to point out that Servasanto is not copying the story directly from Valerius's text. To date, I have not found any medieval version of the anecdote that fails to mention Hephaestion.

However, some observations on Servasanto as reader of the *Facta et dicta* become possible by considering the list of *notabilia* from Valerius Maximus's texts present in the aforementioned manuscript from the library of Santa Croce. This list is alphabetical, and tends to group the *exempla* according to their relevance to the development of different moral themes. Under the letter 'a', the anonymous compiler also lists some passages from the *Facta et dicta* on friendship, introduced by the title 'De amicitia l. iiii c. vii',[19] written in red characters. The title echoes precisely the chapter on friendship of the *Facta et dicta* (Book IV, chapter 7), and is followed by a list of *exempla*. Here is the list, transcribed in bullet points and contrasted with the actual table of contents of Valerius's text (in square brackets):

1. Comendatio amicitiae
2. Gracco et Blosio   [4.7.1]
3. Pomponio et Lectorio amicis G(aii) Gracci   [4.7.2]
4. Lucio Regio et Scipione   [4.7.3]
5. Volupnio et Lucullo   [4.7.4]
6. Lucio Petronio et Celio   [4.7.5]
7. Terentio Servo et Decimo Bruto   [4.7.6]
8. Decimo Lelio cum Agrippa   [4.7.7]
9. Damone et Phytia   [4.7.ext. 1]
10. Amicitie effectibus magnis et plenis
11. Alexander et Ephestione   [4.7.ext. 2]
12. Pompeio et Valerio
13. Felicitate quo invidiam patiam

[1. Commendation of friendship; 2. On Gracchus and Blosius; 3. On Pomponius and Lectorius, friends of Gaius Gracchus; 4. On Lucius Regius and Scipio; 5. On Volupnius and Lucullus; 6. On Lucius

Petronius and Celius; 7. On Terentius Servus and Decimus Brutus; 8. On Decimus Laelius with Agrippa; 9. On Damon and Pythias; 10. On the great and copious effects of friendship; 11. On Alexander and Hephaestion; 12. On Pompey and Valerius; 13. On felicity from enduring envy]

The list of *notabilia* follows the sequence of *exempla* in Valerius's text quite closely, as they are listed in the same order. Moreover, the first of the *notabilia* (*comendatio amicitiae*) probably refers to the introduction of this section of *exempla* in the *Facta et dicta* (4. 7. Intr.), so that the first item on the list also reflects a passage in the classical source. The text which the list refers to, however, must have been slightly different from the modern standard edition, as it seems to contain three extra chapters: two on friendship itself (numbers 10 and 13 on the list), plus one extra *exemplum* (*Pompeio et Valerio*). Besides this difference, significant as it is, what matters most is that the list of *notabilia* testifies to the circulation in late thirteenth-century Florence of the anecdote on Alexander and Hephaestion as a good example relating to friendship.

The manuscript does not offer any suggestion that would explain why Servasanto fails to mention Hephaestion. However, its importance must not be underestimated, as it appears to be one of the most rich and complete collections of classical *excerpta* and authorities available at the library of Santa Croce during Servasanto's stay in that convent.[20] In this regard it is important to consider that the manuscript contains numerous quotes and *exempla* on friendship derived from ancient philosophers and writers. For instance, on the very first page there is a discussion of friendship drawn from Aristotle's *Nicomachean Ethics*, which focuses on the distinction between true and false friendship (ff.1r–2v).[21] The presence of such a discussion testifies to the circulation of this theme in the Florentine environment, and of a distinction between different types of friendship that offers Servasanto the argument with which to begin his sermon by distinguishing between selfish and unselfish friendship (as we shall see later on).

This latter discussion is far less articulated than the Aristotelian one, but it is still significant that it reflects the same interests shown by the anonymous compiler of these *notabilia*. However, Servasanto does not follow the Aristotelian theory of friendship, and tends rather to ground his argument on the authority of Seneca's *Epistulae ad Lucilium*, which are quoted twice in the sermon.[22] This is a rather unusual choice. However, it makes complete sense once we take into account that the Florentine manuscript also contains an anthology of passages from Seneca's works, mostly from the *Espistulae* themselves. These are transcribed according to their relevance to different themes, among which there is also a comprehensive series of passages on friendship. It is thus quite clear that in the intellectual environment of Santa Croce, Seneca was also perceived as an authority *de amicitia*: this makes Servasanto's choice more understandable.

His first quotation from Seneca's letters appears in support of the discussion of the long-standing *tòpos* of unselfish friendship, and reads as follows:

> Seneca: Ergo amicum quaero cui serviam, pro quo mori valeam, non a quo munera ulla recipiam. Nam qui in amicitia non amici, sed sua commoda pensat, non bene cogitat, quia sicut coepit, sic desinet, et cum amicum viderit afflictum, discedet.[23]

> [Seneca: therefore, I seek a friend to serve, for whom it is worth dying, not from whom to receive any reward. In fact, anyone who, being a friend, cares not about his friend but about his own convenience, does not reflect properly, because as it began so it will end, and when he sees his friend suffering he will leave.]

What is to be stressed about this quote is, first and foremost, its originality. During the thirteenth century Seneca was used as an authority on friendship, albeit a minor one, also in other texts related to preaching (most notably in Peraldus's *Summa*), but with reference to different passages from the Senecan *corpus*, from both the *De beneficiis* and the *Epistulae ad Lucilium*.[24] However, while Peraldus follows his sources quite closely, Servasanto's quote does not appear in any work by Seneca, even though its content seems to echo a paragraph of a letter entirely devoted to the theme of friendship ('In quid amicum paras? Ut habeam pro quo mori possim, ut habeam quem in exilium sequar, cuius me morti et opponam et impendam' [For what purpose, then, do I make a man my friend? In order to have someone for whom I may die, whom I may follow into exile, against whose death I may stake my own life, and the pledge, too]).[25] This letter is transcribed among other Senecan passages *de amicitia* in the Florentine manuscript: 'Amici paro ut habeam pro quo mori possim, ut habeam quem in exilium sequar, cui me morti opponam et impendam' [I make friends so as to have someone for whom I may die, to have someone to follow into exile, for whose death I may stake my own life, and the pledge, too].[26]

What I am suggesting is not necessarily that Servasanto is here putting into his own words a sentence that he found in this collection of *notabilia*. Besides the fact that there is no positive evidence that Servasanto knew and used this manuscript, it might well be the case that the sentence worded as in his sermon also circulated in another, still unknown, *florilegium*.[27] Still, it is worth observing that the rewording of Seneca's passage (most notably its beginning: 'In quid amicum paras?') is similar both in Servasanto's sermon ('Ergo amicum quaero') and in the Florentine collection ('Amici paro'): the latter uses the same verb as Seneca (*paro*), but in a sentence syntactically closer rather to Servasanto than to Seneca (i.e., not phrased as a rhetorical question, but as a simple affirmation, 'verb + direct object'). However, what I want to stress is that the manuscript Plut. 6 sin. 10 must have conveyed into the Florentine cultural context themes, authorities and *exempla* that at a first sight seem peculiar to Servasanto's preaching style.

Whether or not this manuscript was a point of reference for Servasanto in terms of classical authors and motifs, the sermon on St Bartholomew, as mentioned, is an articulated discourse on friendship based on classical authorities. It is worth now moving on to consider the nature of such a discourse itself – or, to put it more precisely, to consider the ethics of friendship displayed in this sermon. Servasanto takes his starting point from a double reference to Cicero and Valerius Maximus, to make a point that echoes quite precisely the first observation made by Peraldus in his *summa*'s chapter on friendship: 'Unde concludit Tullius, quod omnibus rebus humanis est amicitia praeponenda' [Therefore Cicero concludes that friendship is to be preferred above all human things].[28]

Such a statement leads into a very traditional distinction between true and false friendship, and to the following, equally conventional, statement: 'Non est enim credendus amicus, qui beneficiis cessantibus, amicitia divideretur, eo quod tales omnes amici fortunae sunt, non perso-nae' [In fact, he should not be considered a friend who, once the advantages cease, breaks friendship, for these are friends to fortune not to the person].[29] The notion of *amici fortunae* is a long-standing *tòpos*, present in many ancient and medieval texts including Ovid's *Tristia* ('Vix duo tresve homini […] superestis amici, | cetera fortunae, non mea, turba fuit' [Barely you two or three of so many friends are left me: the rest were Fortune's crew, not mine]) and Brunetto Latini's *Favolello* ('ch'amico di ventura | come rota si gira' [because a friend of fortune turns like a wheel]).[30] One might also add to the list Boncompagno da Signa's chapter *De amico fortune*, in his treatise on friendship[31] – as well as words from Dante himself, who at the beginning of the *Commedia* makes Beatrice define his relationship with her as follows: '"l'amico mio, e non de la ventura"' ['My friend, not the friend of fortune'] (*Inf.*, II. 61).[32]

This line of the poem has been read most often with reference to the just-mentioned passages from Ovid and Brunetto, as well as to a few lines from Abelard's commentary to St Paul's Letter to the Romans: 'tale profecto homines, fortunae potius dicendi sunt amici quam hominis' [certainly men of this sort are to be defined friends of fortune rather than of men].[33] However, although these texts (especially the *Tristia*) clearly use the same wording as Dante, none of them offers a solid reference to the real sense of Dante's verse. Beatrice is celebrating a true friendship. By contrast Ovid laments the lack of true friends and Brunetto describes a false friend, while Abelard uses the *iunctura* to distinguish between those who love God unselfishly and those who do so because of their desire to be saved in the afterlife.[34] This latter use of the *amici fortunae* motif is particularly close to that of Servasanto: he celebrates St Bartholomew as a good friend of Christ, so as to exhort his audience to cultivate good friendship with God in order to be saved in the afterlife. Both texts present the same idea, but Servasanto's sermon also helps to locate this form of discourse in Dante's Florence. This latter circumstance is essential, especially when we try to read Dante's verse in light of the theology of friendship displayed in a text not so widely circulated and well known as Aberlard's commentary.[35]

Moreover, a closer look at other Florentine developments of this idea might help to shed some further light on the verse on friendship in *Inferno* II. Scholarship tends to offer two different interpretations of Beatrice's definition. The first dates back to Jacopo della Lana, and reads the line as meaning 'friend of mine, and not of fortune', and thus, 'my unfortunate friend'. The second, already present in Benvenuto da Imola's commentary on Dante's poem, reads 'friend of mine, despite bad fortune' and thus 'my true friend'. The latter reading seems preferable. However, both readings interpret the verse as if Dante meant that he was a good friend to Beatrice, with reference to the relationship between the two as described in the *Vita nova* rather than in the *Commedia* itself. This is most probably because Dante himself stated that his reading of Cicero's *De amicitia* after Beatrice's death helped him conceive their relationship, and thus shape it poetically, in a completely different way towards the end of the *Vita nova*.[36] I do not by any means want to suggest that this interpretation is groundless or, worse, wrong.[37] In what follows I simply want to add a new shade to Beatrice's definition that might well coexist with the traditional reading in the polysemy of Dante's verse, by arguing that the development of the theme of friendship in Servasanto's sermon leads to a better understanding of the traditional interpretation.

Beforehand, however, it is worth observing that Beatrice's definition is, to say the least, ambiguous. Conceived as a periphrasis to indicate Dante-the-character, in the expression 'l'amico mio' [my friend], it is not clear whether the stress is on Dante being a friend to Beatrice (as in nearly all the commentaries) or on Beatrice being a friend to Dante. The distinction might look deceptive, and most probably the verse contains both the senses, according to the mutuality intrinsic to friendship itself. However, while the first reading makes complete sense when compared to the link that ties Dante to Beatrice from the *Vita nova* to the *Commedia*, the latter might help to shape an interpretation of the verse that also takes into account the context of the poem's opening. In fact, the theme of friendship – or, to put it more precisely, the necessity for any good Christian to have good friends in order to walk the path that leads to Paradise – is developed by Bono Giamboni in a passage of his *Libro de' vizi e delle virtudi*. He describes a situation particularly close to that in which Dante-the-character finds himself in the first two cantos of the *Commedia*:

> E poi disse [*scil.* Philosophy]: Il regno di cielo è molto forte a conquistare, perché è posto molto ad alti, e vavisi per una stretta via, e per una piccola porta vi s'entra, secondo che t'ho detto di sopra. E ha ne la detta via molti nimici, i quali die e notte assaliscono altrui e non dormono niente, e se truovano alcuno in questa via che ben guernito e armato non sia e acompagnato, sì il fanno sozzamente a dietro tornare. E però fa bisogno a coloro che vi vanno che sian forniti di fedeli amici; e in altra guisa sarebber malamente traditi e ingannati.[38]

> [And then she said: the kingdom of heaven is very hard to conquer, because it is built in a high place, and one reaches it by a narrow path, and one enters here through a small door, as I told you before. And in this path there are many enemies, who attack day and night, and who do not sleep at all, and if they find someone on this path who is not well supplied and armed and who is not accompanied they make him turn back so badly. And thus it is necessary to those who walk this path to be supplied with trustworthy friends; and otherwise they would be badly betrayed and deceived.]

In this brief passage we find a path that leads to Salvation that cannot be easily walked because of the presence of enemies that push back whoever aims to reach the summit. Hence the need for good friends ('fedeli amici'), in order to conquer those enemies and be saved. I do not want to downplay the differences between Bono's text and the magnificent opening of the *Commedia*. It is significant, however, that Giamboni's *Libro* introduces the theme of good friendship within a scene common to that late medieval Florentine didactic literature that has already been studied as a precedent for *Inferno* I and II (for instance, one cannot fail to see the similarities with the content of the *Detto del gatto lupesco*).[39] In light of this passage from the *Libro de' vizi e delle virtudi*, one might argue that Beatrice's periphrasis is conceived to stress that Dante will be saved (i.e., will not be stopped by the enemies encountered on his path to Salvation) *also* because he has a good friend to help him. In this regard it is worth observing not only that by specifying that Dante is a friend '"non de la ventura"' ['not of fortune'] Beatrice means that Dante and herself are good friends (i.e. not simply friends), but also that the verse '"l'amico mio, e non de la ventura"' is the first of a tercet (*Inf.*, II. 61–63) in which Beatrice establishes an explicit connection between this friendship and her intervention to save him because he has found himself stuck ('"ne la diserta piaggia è impedito"') after having been pushed back in trying to walk a path beset by fearful enemies ('"sì nel cammin, che volt'è per paura"').

This said, we shall now turn back to Servasanto's sermon. The preacher discusses St Bartholomew's friendship as an example of a more general form of friendship that every Prophet and Apostle must have with Christ. In other words, the point that Servasanto makes is that the capacity to be a good friend of Christ is an essential feature of every Prophet – or to put it more precisely, that it is not possible for anyone to be a Prophet (or Apostle, which in medieval terms is the same thing)[40] except by being a good friend to Christ. Servasanto clarifies this point by reporting the lack of true friends of Christ, and thus of Prophets, in his contemporary world:

> Sed quis hodie Christi amicus? Ubi sunt hodie, quibus pandantur divina secreta? Ubi sunt hodie divina miracula? Ubi propheta, cui hodie pandantur divina secreta? Unde potest hodie dicere cum Propheta religio Christiana: Signa nostra non vidimus, iam non est propheta, et nos non cognoscet amplius [Psalms 73. 9]. Et illud: Prophetae nostri non invenerunt visionem a Domino [Jeremiah 2. 9]. Quis hodie, juxta Apostolum, cognovit sensum Domini? Aut quis consiliarius eius fuit? Sed quare, o fratres, haec omnia? Quare sic exclusi sumus a Domini nostri praesentia?

Numquid non sunt in Ecclesia Dei, qui digni essent hac gratia? Sunt quidem plurimi, sed ad hac gratia exclusi sunt propter peccata populi. Non sumus, fratres mei, hac gratia digni, quia non sumus Dei amici, sed potius inimici.[41]

[But who nowadays is a friend of Christ? Where nowadays are those to whom divine secrets are opened? Where nowadays are divine miracles? Where a Prophet, to whom divine secrets are opened? Hence nowadays one can say with the Prophet of Christian religion 'we see not our signs, there is no more any Prophet, neither is there any among us that knoweth how long'. And that 'our Prophets did not receive a vision from God'. Who nowadays as the Apostles knows the thoughts of God? Or who has been his counsellor? But why, brothers, all this? Why are we excluded from the presence of our God? Are there not in the Church of God men worthy of this grace? There are many, but they are excluded from this grace because of the sins of the community. We are not, brothers, worthy of this grace, because we are not friends of God but rather his enemies.]

Interpreted as such, the theme of good friendship (at this stage it is vital to remember that, as mentioned, Servasanto defines this feeling as not being a friend of fortune) reaches a more complex conclusion that that developed in Abelard's commentary: returning to his tag from Luke, being a good friend of Christ (*Amice*) helps one to ascend (*ascende superius*) not only to otherworldly salvation ('Ad subtilitatem excellentissimi premii' [to the refinement of an excellent reward]), but also 'ad dignitatem apostolici officii' [to the dignity of the Apostolic office].[42] While the first interpretation of Beatrice's words in *Inferno* corroborates what we have said in relation to Bono's conception of friendship, by supporting the idea that the ability to be a good friend is essential to gain Salvation, the latter adds a new shade to Beatrice's periphrasis. The definition of Dante as a good friend of a lady who, by virtue of her otherworldly condition, is part of a trio including St Lucy and the Virgin Mary herself,[43] implies that being her friend means, to a certain extent, also being a friend of the Divine.[44] If we then consider this point bearing in mind that, as is well known, in the first two cantos of the poem explicit references to David and to St Paul set the ground, albeit implicitly, for the recognition of the prophetic and apostolic nature of Dante's own poetry,[45] it appears quite clearly that being defined as a good friend by Beatrice adds another reference to the qualities that make Dante suitable to undertake the task of becoming a Prophet of God.

Notes

* This paper is part of a project that has received funding from the UK Arts and Humanities Research Council (AHRC), within the project 'Dante and Late Medieval Florence. Theology in Poetry, Practice and Society', based in the Universities of Leeds and Warwick.

1. The classic study on this preacher is Livarius Oliger, 'Servasanto da Faenza O.F.M. e il suo *Liber de virtutibus et vitiis*', in *Miscellanea Francesco Ehrle*, 5 vols (Rome: Biblioteca Apostolica Vaticana, 1924), I (*Per la storia della filosofia e della teologia*), 148–89. On Servasanto and Dante, see Nick R. Havely, *Dante and the Franciscans. Poverty and the Papacy in the 'Commedia'* (Cambridge: Cambridge University Press, 2004), 33–4, and Nicolò Maldina, *In pro del mondo. Dante, la predicazione e i generi della letteratura religiosa medievale* (Rome: Salerno, 2017), *ad indicem*.

2. See Beryl Smalley, *English Friars and Antiquity in the Early Fourteenth Century* (New York: Barnes & Noble, 1961), 1.

3. John T. Slotemaker and Jeffrey C. Witt, *Robert Holcot* (Oxford: Oxford University Press, 2016), 134. Further evidence of the non-scholarly attitude towards classical literature lies in the fact that these friars generally drew their quotations from secondary sources. See Smalley, 151–2.

4. See Giuseppe Billanovich, *La tradizione del testo di Livio e le origini dell'Umanesimo*, 2 vols (Padua: Antenore, 1981), I (*Tradizione e fortuna di Livio tra Medioevo e Umanesimo*), 34–40. See also Giuseppina Brunetti, 'Nicolas Trevet, Niccolò da Prato: per le tragedie di Seneca e i libri dei classici', *Memorie domenicane* 44 (2013): 345–71.

5. Luke 14. 10. Here and elsewhere quotes from the Bible follow the *Biblia Sacra iuxta Vulgatam versionem*, ed. Robert Weber (Stuttgart: Deutsche Bibelgesellschaft, 1983³), and English translations are taken from the King James version. Quotes from Servasanto's sermons are from *Bonaventurae opera omnia*, ed. Adolphe C. Peltier, 15 vols (Paris: Ludovicus Vives, 1864–71), XIII (1868), 493–636 (= Servasanto da Faenza, *Sermones de proprio sanctorum*, hereafter referred to as *PS*), and translations from the texts are mine. For the attribution to Servasanto of the sermons here published under the name of Saint Bonaventura see Johannes B. Schneyer, *Repertorium der lateinischen Sermones des Mittelalters für die Zeit 1150–1350*, 11 vols (Münster: Aschendorff, 1969–90), V, 376–99. See also *Repertorium edierter Texte des Mittelalters aus dem Bereich der Philosophie und angrenzender Gebiete*, ed. Rolf Schönberger, Andrés Quero Sánchez, Brigitte Berges and Lu Jiang (Berlin–Boston: Akademie Verlag, 2011), 3571.

6. See for instance Hugh of Saint Cher's comment, largely drawing on the so-called *Glossa ordinaria*: *Postilla Hugonis de Sancto Charo*, 7 vols (Venice: apud Nicolaum Pezzana, 1703), VI, 218v.

7. See for instance Schneyer, *Repertorium*, IV, 102 and Meister Eckhart, *Sermones*, ed. Ernst Benz, Bruno Decker and Joseph Koch (Stuttgart: W. Kohlhammer Verlag, 1987), 325. In addition, it is worth noting that Peraldus's *Summa* refers constantly to Cicero's treatise in its chapter on friendship. See *Summa virtutum ac vitiorum*, 2 vols (Paris: apud Ludovicum Boullenger, 1648), I, 180a–182a. On the importance of this *summa* as a source for Servasanto, see Antonio Del Castello, *La tradizione del 'Liber de virtutibus et vitiis' di Servasanto da Faenza. Edizione critica delle 'distinctiones' I–IV* (unpublished PhD thesis, University of Naples Federico II-École nationale des Chartes, 2011–13), xv–xxiii.

8. On the use of this verse in Franciscan preaching in this regard, see Joshua C. Benson, 'Matthew of Aquasparta's Sermons on Theology', in *Franciscans and Preaching. Every Miracle from the Beginning of the World Came about through Words*, ed. Timothy J. Johnson (Leiden–Boston: Brill, 2012), 145–74 (156–60).

9. *PS*, 591a.

10. It goes without saying that this does not exclude the presence of constant references to the Bible itself, and/or to patristic texts. See, for instance, *PS*, 590b: 'Unde dicitur: Si possides amicum, in tentatione posside illum, et non facile credas ei' [For it is said: If thou wouldst get a friend, try him before thou takest him, and do not credit him easily]; *PS*, 592a: 'Unde erat de dicentibus illud: Ecce nos reliquimus omnia' [Whence it is said: Behold, we have forsaken all]; *PS*, 591a: 'Amicitia enim, ut dicit Ambrosius, virtus est, et non quaestus' [For as Ambrose says: Friendship is a virtue, and not an acquisition]. It is nonetheless significant that the sermon mentions only briefly (*PS*, 592b) the biblical verse that clearly offers the key idea developed by Servasanto, i.e., that saints are good friends of Christ: 'Vos amici mei estis si feceritis quae ego praecipio vobis' [Ye are my friends, if ye do whatsoever I command you] (John 15. 14).

11. All quotes from classical texts follow the Teubneriana editions, unless otherwise stated, and were consulted via the database 'Bibliotheca Teubneriana Latina (BTL) und Thesaurus linguae Latinae (TLL) Online', accessed via: https://www.degruyter.com/view/db/btltll.

12. This can be easily checked thanks to the list published in Anna Pegoretti, '"Nelle scuole delli religiosi": materiali per Santa Croce nell'età di Dante', *L'Alighieri* 50 (2017): 5–55 (44–55).

13. The codex is item 96 in Pegoretti's catalogue (52), described as a *Florilegium* of moral and historical texts, with *notabilia* from *Nic. Eth.*, Seneca (*Epist.* and other), Orosius, Valerius Maximus, Pompeius Trogus, Solinus, Macrobius, *Institutiones* of *Corpus Iuris Civilis*. The presence of this manuscript in the ancient library of Santa Croce has been pointed out and investigated in the study by Giuseppina Brunetti and Sonia Gentili, 'Una biblioteca nella Firenze di Dante: i manoscritti di Santa Croce', in *Testimoni del vero: su alcuni libri in biblioteche d'autore*, ed. Emilio Russo (Rome: Bulzoni, 2000), 21–55 (36–8), with a focus on the importance of this manuscript for the Aristotelian features of the *Convivio*.

14. This is a use of classical *exempla* peculiar to Servasanto's preaching style. See Maldina, *In pro del mondo*, 222–5.

15. *PS*, 592b.

16. Valerius Maximus, *Facta et dicta*, IV. vii. ext. 2.

17. See for instance Curtius Rufus, *Historiae Alexandri Magni*, III. xii. 17: 'Quam manu allevans rex: "Non errasti", inquit, "mater: nam et hic Alexander est"' [The king, taking her hand and raising her to her feet, said: 'You were not mistaken, mother; for this man too is Alexander']. The English translation is taken from the Loeb edition: Quintus Curtius, *History of Alexander*, trans. John C. Rolfe (Cambridge, MA: Harvard University Press, 1971).

18. Moreover, in the sermon on St Batholomew, Valerius Maximus is quoted as one of the most reliable authorities on friendship. See *PS*, 590b, which is the beginning of the sermon: 'Docet Tullius, et Valerius Maximus, quod amicitia propinquitati praefertur. [...] Unde concludit Tullius, quod omnibus rebus humanis est amicitia praeponenda. [...] Dicit quoque Valerius, quod amicitiae bonum non est a quocumque facile assumendum, sed semel assumptum nunquam est deponendum, quia, qui semel fit amicus, est omni tempore diligendus' [Cicero and Valerius Maximus teach that friendship is to be preferred to proximity. [...] Therefore Cicero concludes that friendship is to be preferred above all human things. [...] Valerius says also that friendship is a good not easy to obtain, but once obtained never to be deposed, because he who has once been a friend is to be loved forever].

19. Florence, BML, MS Plut. 6 sin. 10, f. 62v.

20. As regards the classical authorities quoted by Servasanto and present in the manuscript, it should be observed that Macrobius is quoted in the sermon as the author of the *Saturnalia* (see *PS*, 593b: 'Narrat et Marcrobius, quod multi fuerunt servi, et pagani, qui pro dominis suis temporalibus se tradiderunt morti' [Also Macrobius narrates that there were many servants, even pagan ones, who gave themselves up to death for their earthly lords], with reference to *Saturnalia*, I. xi), but the list of *notabilia* in the Florentine manuscript refers to the commentary on the *Somnium Scipionis* only.

21. See, on this section of the manuscript Brunetti and Gentili, 'Una biblioteca', 37, note 41.

22. Seneca must have been perceived as an authority on friendship within the Florentine environment beyond Servasanto's preaching as well: Bono Giamboni also refers to his work to set up a moral discourse on that theme in his *Libro de' vizi e delle virtudi*: 'onde dice Seneca: Aiuta e consiglia l'amico tuo in su' bisogni, acciò che àl possi ritenere e vogliati bene, perché sanza amici non s'ha mai vita gioconda' [therefore Seneca says: Help and advise your friend in his needs, so that you can keep him and so that he may love you, because without friends you will never have a happy life], quoted from the edition by Cesare Segre (Turin: Einaudi, 1968), 64; translation mine. In jointly discussing passages from Servasanto's sermons and Giamboni's treatises, it must be observed that no documentable links tie the two Florentine authors besides the fact that they shared and helped shape the same intellectual environment. There is no evidence that Bono's *Della miseria dell'umana generazione* is a re-elaboration of Servasanto's works, as has been stated on several different occasions: see for instance St Alfonso Maria De Liguori, *Opere ascetiche*, ed. Oreste Gregorio, Giuseppe Cacciatore and Domenico Capone (Rome: Edizioni di Storia e Letteratura, 1960), 261; or as clearly appears also in the discussion offered in *Della miseria dell'uomo, Giardino di consolazione, Introduzione alle virtù di Bono Giamboni*, ed. Francesco Tassi (Florence: Guglielmo Piatti, 1836), xliv–xlv.

23. *PS*, 591a.

24. See for instance Peraldus, *Summa*, I, 181b: 'Senec. in libro de beneficiis: Dic illis non quod volunt audire; sed quod velint semper audisse. Idem in epistolis: Amici vitia frangenda sunt:

non amo illum, nisi offendero' [Seneca in his book on benefits: Tell them not what they want to hear, but what they would like to hear always. The same author in his letters: One should break the sins of one's friends: I do not love him if I don't displease him] (translation mine). References are to Seneca, *De benificiis*, VI. 32 and *Epistulae ad Lucilium*, III. 25. 1. On Peraldus's use of Seneca as authority on friendship, see *'Das büch der tugenden'. Ein Compendium des 14.Jahrhunderts über Moral und Recht nach der 'Summa theologiae' II–II des Thomas Aquin und anderen Werken der Scholastik und Kanonistik*, ed. Klaus Berg and Monika Kasper (Tübingen: Max Miemeyer Verlag, 1984), 233. The study, however, fails to recognise that the quote from Seneca's *Epistulae* is worded differently from its original, according to a version that must have circulated within the Dominican environment as part of a *florilegium*: the sentence is worded as in Peraldus also in Humberti de Romanis, *Opera de vita regulari*, ed. Joachim J. Berthier, 2 vols (Rome: Typis A. Befani, 1888–9), II, 522.

25. Seneca, *Epistulae ad Lucilium*, I. 9. 10. English translation from the Loeb edition: Seneca, *Epistulae morales ad Lucilium*, trans. Richard M. Gummere (Cambridge, MA: Harvard University Press, 1917–25).

26. Florence, BML, MS Plut. 6 sin. 10, f. 21v. English translation mine.

27. In this regard, it is worth noting the other reference to Seneca (see *PS*, 591a: 'Non enim debemus amicitiam contrahere cum divite, quia dives est, sicut Seneca docet: quia, sicut mel muscae sequuntur cadavera lupi, frumenta formicae, sic et falsi amici praedam sequuntur, non hominem, et fortunam potius, quam personam' [In fact, we should not become friends with a rich man because he is rich, as Seneca teaches: as flies seek honey, wolves dead bodies and ants wheat, so false friends follow plunder, not men, and fortune rather than persons]). This reference also does not come directly from the Senecan corpus, but must have circulated among preachers, given that one can find it also in Antoninus of Florence's *Confessionale*: see *Confessionale di Santo Antonino [...]* (Venice: Girolamo Scotto, 1566), 116: 'Onde non è amicitia quella ch'è fondata in amor carnale, o in parentado, o in guadagno; ma come dice Seneca, Sicut formicae grana, mel muscae, cadavera lupi, sic turba ista amicorum praedam sequitur' [Therefore it is not friendship if it is based on carnal love, or on kinship, or on profit; but as Seneca says: as ants seek wheat, flies honey, wolves dead bodies, so this crowd of friends follows plunder]. Translations mine.

28. *PS*, 590b. See Peraldus, *Summa*, I, 180a: 'Tullius in lib. De Amicitia: Omnibus rebus humanis anteponenda est amicitia' [Cicero in his book 'On Friendship': friendship is to be preferred above all human things]. See also *PS*, 590b: 'Docet Tullius, et Valerius Maximus, quod amicitia propinquitati praefertur, eo quod ex propinquitate removeri amor potest, sed ex amicitia nunquam' [Cicero and Valerius Maximus teach that friendship is to be preferred to proximity, insofar as one can remove love from proximity, but never from friendship]; and Peraldus, *Summa*, I, 180a: 'Idem [scil. Cicero] in eod [scil. *De amicitia*] In hoc praestat amicitia propinquitati, quod ex propinquitate benevolentia tolli potest: ex amicitia non potest' [The same author in the same book: in this friendship is better than proximity, because benevolence can be removed from proximity; [but] not from friendship].

29. *PS*, 591a.

30. On Brunetto's discussion of friendship see in particular Patrizia Gasparini, 'L'amitié comme fondement de la "concordia civium". Le *Favolello* de Brunet Latin (et une nouvelle source du *Tresor*)', *Arzanà* 13 (2010): 55–108.

31. See *Amicitia di maestro Boncompagno da Signa*, ed. by Sarina Nathan (Rome: La Società, 1909), XXVII (64–6), which is the source for Brunetto's *Favolello*: 'Amicus fortune tamquam rota volvitur et iudicat secundum casum' [A friend of fortune turns like a wheel and judges according to circumstance] (64); and for further references to other texts on the same theme (19).

32. The problem of how to translate this line is further disussed below.

33. References to Ovid, Brunetto and Abelard are taken from existing scholarship on *Inferno*, II. 61. See, in particular, Mario Casella, 'L'amico mio e non de la ventura', *Studi danteschi* 27 (1943): 117–34 and Francesco Mazzoni, *Saggio di un nuovo commento alla 'Divina Commedia': Inferno canti I–III* (Florence: Sansoni, 1967), 256–68. The translations of Brunetto and Abelard are mine; Ovid is quoted from Anthony S. Kline's translation, available at: https://www.poetryintranslation.com/PITBR/Latin/OvidTristiaBkTwo.php.

34. On Dante's notion of friendship as influenced by a Christian reading of classical sources on the subject see Filippa Modesto, *Dante's Idea of Friendship: the Transformation of a Classical Concept* (Toronto: University of Toronto Press, 2015), 58–77.

35. Only a few manuscripts of Abelard's comment to St Paul's Letter to the Romans survive: see Friedrich Stegmüller, *Repertorium Biblicum Medii Aevii* (Madrid: Consejo Superior de Investigaciónes Cientificas, 1949–61), nr. 6378, 741.

36. See *Convivio*, II. xii. 2–4, quoted following Franca Brambilla Ageno's text (Florence: Le Lettere, 1995): 'Tuttavia, dopo alquanto tempo, la mia mente, che si argomentava di sanare, provide, poi che né 'l mio né l'altrui consolare valea, ritornare al modo che alcuno sconsolato avea tenuto a consolarsi; e misimi a leggere quello non conosciuto da molti libro di Boezio, nel quale, cattivo e discacciato, consolato s'avea. E udendo ancora che Tulio scritto avea un altro libro, nel quale, trattando dell'Amistade, avea toccate parole della consolazione di Lelio, uomo eccellentissimo, nella morte di Scipione amico suo, misimi a leggere quello. E avegna che duro mi fosse nella prima entrare nella loro sentenza, finalmente v'entrai tanto entro, quanto l'arte di gramatica ch'io avea e un poco di mio ingegno potea fare; per lo quale ingegno molte cose, quasi come sognando, già vedea, sì come nella Vita Nova si può vedere' [Nevertheless, after some time my mind, which was endeavouring to heal itself, resolved (since neither my own consolation nor that of others availed) to resort to a method which a certain disconsolate individual has adopted to console himself; and I began to read that book of Boethius, not known to many, in which, while a prisoner and an exile, he had found consolation. And hearing further that Tully had written another book in which, while discussing Friendship, he had addressed words of consolation to Laelius, a man of the highest merit, upon the death of his friend Scipio, I set about reading it. Although it was difficult at first for me to penetrate their meaning, I finally penetrated it as deeply as my command of Latin and the small measure of my intellect enabled me to do, by which intellect I had perceived many things before, as in a dream, as may be seen in the *New Life*]. English translation from: *Dante's 'Il Convivio'*, trans. Richard H. Lansing (New York: Garland, 1990). For further discussion of this passage, see also Anna Pegoretti's essay in this volume.

37. For an interpretation of the presence of the theme of friendship in the first two cantos of the *Commedia*, in relation to Dante's moral salvation, see Modesto, 93–114.

38. Bono Giamboni, *Libro de' vizi e delle virtudi*, XI, p.83.

39. See Antonio Lanza, *Primi secoli. Saggi di letteratura italiana antica* (Rome: Archivio Guido Izzi, 1991), 41–59 and Franco Suitner, 'Le tre fiere di Dante, la *Queste* e il *Gatto lupesco*', in *Dante e il mondo animale*, ed. Giuseppe Crimi and Luca Marcozzi (Rome: Carocci, 2013), 34–48.

40. See Maldina, *In pro del mondo*, 60–80.

41. *PS*, 593a. I have added in square brackets the biblical passages quoted by Servasanto. It is worth observing that Servasanto builds the entire sermon around the contrast between the true friendship of which the Apostles were capable and the false friendship to Christ that characterises his contemporary world. See *PS*, 593b: 'O stultitia christiana, et amicitia falsa, sub christiano nomine palliata, quae sub pelle ovi lupium animum gerit' [O Christian foolishness, and false friendship, covered under the name of Christian, that bears the soul of a wolf under the skin of a sheep].

42. *PS*, 593b–594a: 'Quia ergo sic Christi fuit amicus, ideo audire meruit: Amice, ascende superius. Nam ascendit primo ad dignitatem apostolici officii; secundo, ad excellentiam singularis martyrii, tertio vero, ad subtilitatem excellentissimi premii' [Because he who has been this sort of friend to Christ thus deserves to be addressed as follows: Friend, go up higher. In fact, he ascended first to the dignity of the Apostolic office; secondly, to the excellence of martyrdom; thirdly to the refinement of an excellent reward].

43. See *Inferno*, II. 94–108 and 124–6.

44. This has to be considered since, in the very same canto, Dante is qualified as 'fedele' [faithful one] of St Lucy: *Inferno*, II. 98.

45. See also for other bibliographical references Maldina, *In pro del mondo*, 34–48.

3
An Ethical and Political Bestiary in the First Canto of Dante's *Comedy**

Giuseppe Ledda

Recent studies on animal imagery in the *Comedy* have shown how the poet draws on the reader's knowledge of the symbolic values ascribed to animals in medieval tradition, and how he uses similar allegorical techniques in new ways. In the past I have mostly examined the spiritual and religious meanings of these images. In this essay, my intention is instead to study animal imagery from a moral perspective, in order to show how this repertory of images nourishes the ethical dimension of the poem. In particular, I will focus on the animals of the first canto: *lonza*, lion, wolf and hound.

> Ed ecco, quasi al cominciar de l'erta,
> una lonza leggera e presta molto,
> che di pel macolato era coverta;
> e non mi si partia dinanzi al volto,
> anzi 'mpediva tanto il mio cammino,
> ch'i' fui per ritornar più volte vòlto.
> Temp' era dal principio del mattino,
> e 'l sol montava 'n sù con quelle stelle
> ch'eran con lui quando l'amor divino
> mosse di prima quelle cose belle;
> sì ch'a bene sperar m'era cagione
> di quella fiera a la gaetta pelle
> l'ora del tempo e la dolce stagione;
> ma non sì che paura non mi desse
> la vista che m'apparve d'un leone.
> Questi parea che contra me venisse

con la test'alta e con rabbiosa fame,
sì che parea che l'aere ne tremesse.
    Ed una lupa, che di tutte brame
sembiava carca ne la sua magrezza,
e molte genti fé già viver grame,
    questa mi porse tanto di gravezza
con la paura ch'uscia di sua vista,
ch'io perdei la speranza de l'altezza.

(*Inf.*, I. 31–54)

[And behold, almost at the beginning of the steep, a *lonza*, light and very swift, covered with spotted fur; | and it did not depart from before my face but rather so impeded my way that I was at several turns turned to go back. | The time was the beginning of the morning, and the sun was mounting up with those stars that were with it when God's love | first set those lovely things in motion; so that I took reason to have good hope of that beast with its gaily painted hide | from the hour of the morning and the sweet season; but not so that I did not fear the sight of a lion that appeared to me. | He appeared to be coming against me with his head high and with raging hunger, so that the air appeared to tremble at him. | And a she-wolf, that seemed laden with all cravings in her leanness and has caused many peoples to live in wretchedness, | she put on me so much heaviness with the fear that came from the sight of her, that I lost hope of reaching the heights.]

Identifying the *lonza*

The *lonza* is a feline yet to be clearly identified by Dante scholars. I believe that in the context of medieval zoology it is a *pardus*, not a lynx, leopard or panther. Dante evidently modelled his triad of beasts on the episode in which the prophet Jeremiah warns of three beasts that threaten the populace in its sinful rebellion against the Lord: *pardus, leo* and *lupus*:

> Idcirco percussit eos leo de silva, lupus ad vesperam vastavit eos, pardus vigilans super civitates eorum; omnis qui egressus fuerit ab eis capietur, quia multiplicatae sunt praevaricationes eorum, confortatae sunt aversiones eorum.

(Jeremiah 5. 6)

[Wherefore a lion out of the wood hath slain them, a wolf in the evening, hath spoiled them, a leopard watcheth for their cities: every one that shall go out thence shall be taken, because their transgressions are multiplied, their rebellions are strengthened.]

As the lion and wolf in Jeremiah correspond to the other two beasts in the first canto, the *lonza* should correspond to the *pardus*. The *pardus* also has many other relevant biblical occurrences, most of them in association with the lion or the wolf, sometimes with both.[1]

For that matter, the term *lonza* seems to be an alternative to *pardo*, which is a very rare term in old Italian.[2] Dante could have chosen the form *lonza* so as to begin the names of all three beasts with the letter *L*, perhaps in a subtle reaffirmation that the evil manifested in the beasts is in fact a parodic reversal of good – for, as Dante recalls, *El* was God's name in Hebrew.[3] Medieval encyclopaedias describe the *pardus* as having a spotted pelt, great speed and ferocity, all qualities that Dante ascribes to the *lonza*. For instance, the influential encyclopaedia of Isidore of Seville says: 'Pardus [...] genus varium ac velocissimum et praeceps ad sanguinem. Saltu enim ad mortem ruit' [The pard, a beast of many colours, is very swift, likes blood, and kills with a leap].[4]

The spotted coat is also typical of the panther (Latin *panthera*), but this animal has completely different characteristics in respect to Dante's *lonza*. It is a gentle beast, particularly celebrated for the sweet smell of its breath, and it always carries very positive symbolic values, being interpreted usually as an allegory of Christ.[5] For these reasons, Dante's *lonza* cannot be a panther. For other Dante commentators the *lonza* has to be identified as a leopard (Latin *leopardus*). But it is necessary to remember that in medieval zoology the leopard is nothing other than the offspring of a mating between a lion and a *pardus*: for this reason, it shares some properties with the *pardus*.[6] The lynx too (Latin *lynx*), although more similar to a wolf than a lion, has a spotted coat like the *pardus*. No single bestiary or encyclopaedia attributes to the lynx the swiftness and agility that are two of the main characteristics of Dante's *lonza*. Instead the lynx is well known for other properties, especially the fact that its urine changes into a hard, precious stone.[7] The *pardus*, on the contrary, is always described as extremely swift ('velocissimus' for Isidore, and 'bestia velocissima' in Bartholomaeus Anglicus),[8] just as Dante's *lonza* is 'light and very swift' ('leggera e presta molto').

A close look at the few appearances in old Italian of the term *lonza* reinforces its identification with the *pardus*.[9] Apart from an early, not very clear occurrence in the verse *Proverbia quae dicuntur supra natura feminarum*,[10] a more interesting presence of the *lonza* is that found later, in the poem entitled the *Detto del gatto lupesco*. Here the *lonza* appears in a list of the beasts gathered to obstruct the protagonist's way. With the *lonza* (line 127: 'e una lonça'), the poem mentions also 'four leopards' (line 125: 'quattro leopardi') and 'the panther' (line 131: 'la pantera').[11] Thanks to this text, we can also definitively exclude the possibility of identifying the *lonza* with the leopard or the panther. Some very interesting occurrences can be found also in a pair of satirical sonnets by Rustico Filippi, which make evident the *lonza*'s nature: ferocious and courageous, but also wild and brutal.[12] Likewise, in a sonnet by Folgore da San Gimignano (the introductory sonnet to the '*Corona*' *della settimana*), the sentence 'Leggiero più che lonza o liopardo' [lighter than a *lonza* or a leopard] makes it clear that the *lonza* is not the same creature as a leopard.[13] It also presents the adjective 'leggero' [light], used by Dante too, and by the biblical tradition for the *pardus* ('levis').

Other evidence for the identification of the *lonza* with the *pardus* can be found in the use of the French term *lonce* in Brunetto Latini's *Tresor*. Here, in a passage where the Florentine encyclopaedist translates a passage by Isidore, the term that Brunetto translates with *lonce* is *pardus*.[14] Another proof comes from Giovanni Boccaccio, as reported in Benvenuto da Imola's Dante commentary. After having examined all the other candidates, Benvenuto concludes by arguing for the identification of the *lonza* with the *pardus*, partly on the basis of Boccaccio's testimony.[15]

Lonza as pardus: a symbol of fraud

In medieval culture the *pardus* always has a negative allegorical value. It is commonly associated with diabolic symbolism or with the image of the sinner. As Eucherius of Lyon said, 'Pardus diabolus vel peccator moribus varius' [The pard is the devil or the sinner, fickle in his customs].[16] The biblical presences of the *pardus* confirm the negative and primarily diabolical meaning usually attributed to this animal. References to the *pardus* can be found in several biblical passages in which such negative values are evident,[17] and are widely confirmed by medieval biblical exegesis.

From a moral viewpoint, the *pardus* is commonly associated with fraud, or with various vices in which fraud is implicated. So, for instance, one of the marginal notes in *De proprietatibus rerum* interprets the entry on the *pardus* with a 'Nota contra dolosos et malitiosos' [Note against tricksters and malicious people].[18] The connection with fraud is extremely common in patristic literature and quotations could easily be multiplied.[19] Patristic and medieval exegesis of the biblical presences of the *pardus* also confirms this value. This is true for the interpretation of Jeremiah 5. 6:

> Wherefore a lion out from the wood hath slain them, a wolf in the evening, hath spoiled them, a leopard [*pardus*] watcheth for their cities: every one that shall go out thence shall be taken, because their transgressions are multiplied; their rebellions are strengthened.

Aquinas, among others, considers the *pardus* in that passage a figure of Nebuchadnezzar, in consideration of his fraudulent nature ('Quantum ad obsidionem urbis, pardus vigilans, idest Nabuchodonosor propter fraudulentiam').[20] Aquinas makes the same connection with fraud for the occurrence of *pardus* in Jeremiah 13. 23: 'difficiliter potestis converti, Aethiops, propter naturalem infectionem peccati, pardus, propter dolositatem, vel diversitatem peccatorum' [It is difficult for you to be changed, Ethiopian, due to the natural corruption of sin, pard, due to deceitfulness or the diversity of sinners].[21]

Another significant passage is Isaiah 11. 6: 'Habitabit lupus cum agno, et pardus cum haedo accubabit; vitulus, et leo, et ovis, simul morabuntur' [The wolf shall dwell with the lamb: and the leopard [*pardus*] shall lie down with the kid: the calf and the lion, and the sheep shall abide together]. Exegesis of this text, although often more generic,[22] can sometimes be oriented towards fraud, as it is in Isidore of Seville's *De fide catholica*: 'In cuius ovili pardus cum haedo accubat permisti scilicet subdoli cum simplicibus' [The pard lies down with the kid in its sheepfold, namely the deceitful mixed among the innocents];[23] or in a sermon by Aelredus Rievallensis: 'Pardus est animal quoddam plenum varietate: tales fuerunt aliqui vestrum, per calliditatem, per deceptionem, per fraudem' [The pard is a particular animal that is full of changeability: just as some of you were, through cunning, through deceit, through fraud];[24] or in Aquinas: 'pardus, astutus, cum haedo, simplice' [the pard, cunning, with the kid, innocent].[25] The same can be said of exegesis concerning the passage in Hosea 13. 7, although the evidence in this case is less clear.[26]

There are some quite generic interpretations for the passage from Daniel 7. 6: 'et ecce alia quasi pardus et alas habebat avis quattuor super se, et quattuor capita erant in bestia; et potestas data est ei' [After this I beheld, and lo, another like a leopard, and it had upon it four wings as of a fowl, and the beast had four heads, and power was given to it]. But a more precise reading is also common, which attributes the moral symbolism of fraud to the *pardus* – as can be seen in *De eruditione* by Richard of Saint Victor, where the bear is interpreted as a figure of envy and the *pardus* as a symbol of hypocrisy and fraud.[27] Patristic and medieval exegetes devote considerable attention, of course, to the passage from the Book of Revelation 13. 2. In this case too generic interpretations can be found, as well as references to heretics without a precise moral interpretation, but the standard exegesis again connects the beast to fraud.[28]

Among the biblical references to the *pardus*, the most frequently commented in patristic and medieval literature is the strange passage in the Song of Solomon about the 'montes pardorum', that is, the mountains of the pards: 'Veni de Libano, sponsa, veni de Libano, ingredere; respice de capite Amana, de vertice Sanir et Hermon, de cubilibus leonum, de montibus pardorum' [Come from Libanus, my spouse, come from Libanus, come: thou shalt be crowned from the top of Amana, from the top of Sanir and Hermon, from the dens of the lions, from the mountains of the leopards [*pardorum*]] (4. 8). In this case too, besides some readings in a figural-historical sense, some allegorisations as a symbol of the devil or of heretics and some generic moralisations,[29] the *pardus* is very frequently associated with fraud or with sins connected with fraud.[30] On the other hand the lion, with which the *pardus* is paired in this passage, is usually viewed as an image of violence or of pride. Gregory the Great explains it in this way, for instance; as does the Venerable Bede: 'cubilia etenim leonum ad montes sunt pardorum, hi qui acriore spirituum malignorum furore instigati, ad nocendum Christi gregem, et vi et fraude praevalent' [For the dens of lions and the mountains of leopards are those incited by the more violent fury of evil spirits to inflict injury on Christ's flock, who gain the upper hand by force and deceit].[31] Sometimes the *pardus*'s form of fraud can be specified as hypocrisy, as in the *Allegoriae in universam sacram scripturam* by Rabanus Maurus: 'Per pardum hypocritae, ut in Cantico'.[32]

Finally, the *pardus*'s speed and ferocity, added to its spotted pelt, made it an emblem of malice and trickery in medieval culture, not only in biblical exegesis, but also in naturalistic literature.

The *lonza*'s spotted pelt

The moral values most often imputed to the *lonza* in commentaries on the *Comedy* are lust, envy and fraud. Among these interpretations only the last, as we have seen, has a broad and solid historical basis in medieval culture, both in biblical exegesis and in naturalistic literature.

Let us now turn to evidence found further along in the poem. The participle *maculato* recurs only once in the poem, for the damned souls of the final bolgia, the counterfeiters 'di schianze macolati' [spotted with scabs] (*Inf.*, XXIX. 75). This ties the *lonza* to the theme of fraud. Furthermore, the only other animal with a spotted skin is the monstrous Geryon, the 'sozza imagine di froda' [filthy image of fraud] (XVII. 7), which serves both as guardian of the eighth circle and as emblem of the sins of fraud punished there. Early in canto XVII the monster is said to have 'lo dosso e 'l petto e ambedue le coste | *dipinti* […] di nodi e di rotelle' [back and breast and both sides *painted* with knots and little wheels] (lines 14–15, italics mine). And right at the end of canto XVI the poet had recalled the *lonza* when, at Virgil's request, Dante handed his master the cord he had 'intorno cinta, | e con essa pensai alcuna volta | prender la lonza a la pelle *dipinta*' [girding me, and with it I had thought at times to capture the *lonza* with the spotted (*dipinta*) hide] (XVI. 106–08, italics mine). So, only a few verses apart, the *lonza* and Geryon are defined with the same adjective, *dipinto*. And Virgil uses the cord to tame a painted-skinned beast, just as Dante had intended: only instead of the *lonza* the beast is Geryon. So we have a marked correlation between the *lonza* and Geryon; it is extremely probable that the *lonza* bears a symbolic meaning of fraud, like Dante's Geryon and like the *pardus* of the bestiaries.

In light of this correlation, I believe that the three beasts of *Inferno* I may correspond to the three forms of sin punished in Hell:[33] fraud (the *lonza*), violence (the lion) and incontinence (the she-wolf). Here they are presented not in order of objective seriousness (as in the subdivision of Hell itself), but in order of the threats they pose to the subjective disposition of the protagonist – hardly at all inclined to fraud, rather more to violence and most to incontinence. From the first canto alone, however, the reader cannot draw a precise idea of all this. The elements that suggest this interpretation only appear later on in the poem, with the subdivision of Hell in canto XI and the association of the *lonza* with fraud in cantos XVI–XVII.

Three beasts for three-fold sin

The three beasts are instead understood, by medieval commentators of Dante's *Comedy*, as symbols of the three capital vices: the *lonza* representing lust, the lion pride and the she-wolf *avaritia*, in the particular sense of *cupiditas*.[34]

The idea that the *lonza* could be a symbol of lust is already very common in early commentary on the *Comedy*, but it has no foundation in medieval symbolism associated with the animals. Indeed, there are only faint traces of the *pardus* as a supposed medieval symbol of lust. Nor should conclusions be drawn from the allusion to Virgil proposed along those lines by many commentators: 'maculosae tegmine lyncis' [in the pelt of the spotted lynx] (*Aen.*, I. 323). The quotation is irrelevant, because it refers to the lynx, not to the *pardus*. For that matter the lynx's spotted pelt is part of a trick played by Venus when she pretends to be a Spartan huntress. Rather than an element of iconography associated with Venus, it is a detail meant to characterise a life devoted to the hunt. Sometimes the commentators who sustain the symbolism of lust support their position by reference to the pervasive and undeniable symbolism of fraud; they argue that the beast, with its spotted coat, symbolises the fraudulent and deceitful enticement of lust.[35] This is, obviously, a poor proof that rather confirms the strength and inescapability of the *lonza*'s interpretation as an image of fraud.[36] It must be added that Geryon, the 'sozza imagine di froda' to which the *lonza* is in various ways connected, has nothing to do with erotic-lustful fraud of this kind.

Another proof often alleged by scholars in favour of such an interpretation is a passage from the *Bestiario toscano*, published by Milton Stahl Garver and Kenneth McKenzie. Here an animal named *loncia* is said to be a lustful beast[37]– but in this case it is an amplification of a common property usually attributed to the *leopardus*. Here the *leopardus* is indicated with the term *loncia*. If we scrutinise this text more broadly and attentively, we can note that the alternative term *lonça* is here used for the she-*pardus*, or *parda*, who, after mating with a lion, gives birth to a *loncia*, that is a *leopardus*.[38] The term *leopardo* is here used for male *pardus*. As can be seen, it is an extremely confused text from a lexical point of view. In any case such a text, among so much confusion, confirms that Dante's *lonza* can be a she-*pardus* or a she-*leopardus*, but does not offer any decisive evidence for the interpretation of the *lonza* as a symbol of lust.[39]

The term *pardo* is almost totally absent in thirteenth- and fourteenth-century Italian, but the term *leopardo* is widely attested. By contrast, in the Bible the term *leopardus* is almost absent, but there are several extremely important occurrences of the term *pardus*, which I have discussed above. The same can be said for patristic and medieval literature, especially when connected with biblical exegesis.

If the biblical-exegetical tradition paid great attention to the *pardus* and almost ignored the *leopardus*, it seems extremely implausible that – when taken together with two of the most relevant beasts of the biblical-exegetical tradition, the lion and the wolf – the animal indicated by Dante with the term *lonza* could be identified with an animal with an extremely weak literary and biblical tradition, the *leopardus*, rather than with the extremely important *pardus*, so pervasively present in the Bible and in the exegetical tradition, where it also regularly accompanies the lion. Moreover, the fact remains that nowhere else in the *Comedy* is there an echo of the series lust, pride and avarice: this hypothetical series would therefore be totally isolated within the poem.

A similar series does in fact recur in the cantos that tackle Florence, namely pride, avarice and envy. The double repetition of this triad could tempt the reader retrospectively to interpret the three beasts of the first canto in this way;[40] but medieval tradition does not support a reading of the *lonza* as a symbol of envy. Nor is the *pardus* ever a symbol of envy, which is instead ascribed to the lynx.[41] But, as we have seen, the *lonza* is not a lynx.

The nineteenth century introduced a political reading of the three beasts as personifications of political entities: the *lonza* represents Florence, the lion the royal house of France and the she-wolf Rome's Papal Curia.[42] Today nobody would propose such an interpretation in an absolute and exclusive way, but some scholars have suggested that a political level may be present, without precluding the existence of a stronger, moral sense.[43] This would also accord with the way in which biblical visions were interpreted in the Middle Ages: that is, with both a moral or allegorical sense and at the same time also a historical or political one.

The lion and the wolf

As for the lion, its many appearances in the Bible imbue it with different meanings. The principle of symbolic ambivalence is fundamental for the interpretation of the biblical and medieval bestiary. The lion is emblematic of this double-edged symbolism, as it can represent both Christ and the devil.[44] Naturally, the lion in the first canto can only be read in a negative sense, as a diabolic adversary, and enemy of humanity's pursuit of happiness.

Countless medieval texts state explicitly that the lion represents the devil by its force and cruelty.[45] Biblical exegesis insists on its diabolical symbolism also when associated with the *pardus*.[46] In moral terms, the lion is associated with wrath in the bestiary of vices proposed by Boethius (*Cons. Phil.*, IV. 3). Pride is also at times ascribed to the lion, and the lion's posture in canto I with its head held high does encourage the reader to think of pride. Nonetheless, the lion's evident pride does not contradict its possible symbolic value of violence: for the proud in Hell, in particular Farinata and Capaneus, are all punished among the violent. While the posture *con la testa alta* could be indicative of pride, the 'rabbiosa fame' [raging hunger] suggests other vices, such as gluttony or avarice, while the adjective *rabbiosa* calls to mind wrath.

After the *lonza* and the lion comes a she-wolf. The noun *magrezza* [leanness] appears at only three points in the poem, first here and then twice in the depiction of the gluttonous in *Purgatorio* (XXIII. 39 and XXIV. 69). It constitutes an evident link between the wolf and the vice of gluttony. In the Bible the wolf always has a negative value, and in medieval culture it is chiefly a symbol of the devil.[47] In moral terms it is widely linked with avarice,[48] but also with other vices, such as gluttony and lust.[49]

Let us examine the other occurrences of wolf imagery in the poem. The second occurrence, 'maladetto lupo' [cursed wolf] (*Inf.*, VII. 8), refers to Pluto, the diabolic monster-guardian of the fourth circle, the place of misers and spendthrifts. Then in *Purgatorio* the wolf represents the three vices of excessive love for worldly goods, vices which correspond to the sins of incontinence in Hell: 'Maladetta sie tu, antica lupa, | che più che tutte l'altre bestie hai preda | per la tua fame sanza fine cupa!' [A curse be on you, ancient she-wolf, that more than any other beast find prey for your endlessly hollow hunger!] (*Purg.*, XX. 10–12). To me, this seems to reinforce the identification of the three beasts with the three types of sin (fraud, violence and incontinence).[50]

In *Inferno* I, meanwhile, Virgil notes the she-wolf's 'bramosa voglia' [greedy desire], so greedy that 'dopo 'l pasto ha più fame che pria' [after feeding she is hungrier than before] (*Inf.* I. 98–9). The food metaphors and the reference to desire or appetite place the she-wolf within the semantic sphere of incontinence, which overwhelms rational choice with disproportionate desire (e.g. in *Inf.*, V. 38–9).

On another note, recurrences of the *lupo* (the masculine form of 'wolf') throughout the poem are almost all concentrated around two entities: the people of Florence (*Purg.*, XIV. 50–1, *Par.*, XXV. 1–6) and the simoniac popes (*Par.*, IX. 127–36, XXVII. 55) who, in a reversal of the good pastor image, are seen as wolves who rip apart the flocks entrusted to them.[51] Hence wolf imagery also has a strong political valence. And in *Paradiso* XXV the animal emblem of the wolf is soldered onto the theme of autobiography, when Dante explicitly presents himself as 'nimico ai lupi' [enemy of the wolves] (line 6). A scene similar in some aspects to that in the poem's first canto plays out in the Earthly Paradise, concluding in the prophecy of the 'cinquecento diece e cinque' [five hundred ten and five, *Purg.*, XXXIII. 43], which corresponds to the hound that will drive the wolf-beast into Hell. If a political reading of the symbols is undeniable in the

Earthly Paradise, it is hard to imagine that a similar reading should be irrelevant in the first canto of *Inferno*.

Another important aspect of the first canto is that the three beasts are never present on stage at the same time, but each one appears after the other: the *lonza* disappears when the lion appears, just as the lion disappears when the she-wolf appears. Beyond this, Virgil speaks of "'questa bestia, per la qual tu gride'" ['this beast at which you cry'] (line 94). For these reasons some scholars propose that it is a single diabolical beast – taking the form now of a *lonza*, now a lion and finally a she-wolf, in an everlasting metamorphosis of evil. Guglielmo Gorni has effectively defined this beast as the 'bestia una e trina' [one and triune beast]. A correspondence between this diachronic trinity, in which evil presents itself at the beginning of the poem, will be found in a synchronic trinity at the bottom of Hell – that is, in Lucifer, as represented in the last canto of the first canticle (XXXIV. 37–45).[52]

The *veltro*

Coherently with the animal imagery employed thus far, the person who will defeat the she-wolf-beast and everything she represents is, in turn, presented via an animal image: that of the *veltro*, the hound, known for its great speed. If scholars have long disagreed on how to interpret the symbolic value of the three beasts, the interpretation of the hound has been no less contentious; it has possibly been even more so.[53] There are two main theories that read the hound either as an emperor, who will re-establish imperial power over an Italy devastated by corruption and civil wars, or as a saintly pope, who will conduct the Church back to its original purity and rightful, purely spiritual jurisdiction. Some readers have looked for a specific historical personage, be it an emperor or imperial vicar (Henry VII or Cangrande della Scala) or a pope (the Dominican Benedict XI). Another interpretation worth mentioning sees in the hound the Second Coming of Christ on Judgement Day. Finally, some readers consider the hound to be an allusion to Dante himself or, more precisely, to his poem, destined to restore justice to the world. As this variety of interpretations indicates, the open, indeterminate character of this image might indicate an essential polysemy – inviting the reader to interpret the hound via multiple discourses that may include, besides the moral and political, the rich metaliterary vein that runs through the poem.

The first canto of *Inferno* thus employs two typical modes for the use of animal imagery: firstly as moral symbols of vices or sinful dispositions, and secondly as political emblems. The canto also demonstrates the author's tendency to construct symbolic systems that combine multiple animals, and to complicate this rhetorical device with the ambiguity of prophetic language and the polysemy of symbols.

Notes

*   The author and editors would especially like to thank Sophie Fuller for her assistance in preparing this essay for publication and in providing translations into English for the quotations in Latin, Italian and Old French. References to the *Patrologia Latina* (*PL*) refer to the 'Patrologia Latina Database'.

1.   The three animals appear together in Isaiah 11. 6. For the frequent association with the lion, see Song of Solomon 4. 8; Ecclesiasticus (Sirach) 28. 26–7; Daniel 7. 3–7; Book of Revelation 13. 2. For the association with the wolf, Habakkuk 1. 8. Among the other occurrences of the *pardus*, see Jeremiah 13. 23.

2.   The earliest occurrences of *pardo* in the 'Tesoro della lingua italiana delle origini–Opera del vocabolario italiano' (TLIO–OVI) *corpus* of ancient Italian can be found only in the *Tesoro di Brunetto Latini volgarizzato*, V. 41, where it translates the French term *parde* from *Tresor*, I. 174. 9, so is provoked by the French term; Fazio degli Uberti, *Dittamondo*, IV. 11. 68; IV. 12. 77; and Petrarch, *Canzoniere*, 330. 5.

3.   See, for instance, Isidore of Seville, *Etymologiae*, VII. i. 3. Dante, *DVE*, I. iv. 4; *Par.*, XXVI. 136. See also Guglielmo Gorni, *Dante nella selva. Il primo canto della 'Commedia'* (Florence: Cesati, 1995).

4.   *Etymologiae*, XII. ii. 10. Here and throughout, English translations from Isidore follow *The Etymologies of Isidore of Seville*, ed. Stephen A. Barney, W. J. Lewis, J. A. Beach and Oliver Berghof (Cambridge: Cambridge University Press, 2006); whereas Isidore's Latin text follows Isidoro di Siviglia, *Etimologie o Origini*, ed. Angelo Valastro Canale (Turin: UTET, 2004). Isidore's text is repeated also in the *De bestiis* by Ps.-Hugh of Saint Victor, III. 2 (*PL*, 177. 83). See also Bartholomaeus Anglicus, *De proprietatibus rerum*, XVIII. 81: 'Pardus […] est bestia velocissima, colore vario orbiculata' [The pard […] is an extremely swift beast, with circular markings of differing colour], in Bartholomaei Anglici *De genuinis rerum coelestium, terrestrium et inferarum rerum Proprietatibus, Libri XVIII* (Frankfurt: apud Wolfangum Richterum, 1601; anast. reprint, Frankfurt a. M.: Minerva, 1964).

5.   For the panther's spotted pelt see, for instance, Isidore of Seville, *Etymologiae*, XI. ii. 8 or Bartholomaeus Anglicus, *De proprietatibus rerum*, XVIII. 80. The information about the panther's sweet smell is extremely common: see for instance Aristotle, *Historia animalium*, IX. 612a, in the edition Aristote, *Histoire des animaux*, ed. Pierre Louis (Paris: Les Belles Lettres, 1964–9); Pliny, *Naturalis Historia*, XXI. 39, in the edition Gaio Plinio Secondo, *Storia naturale*, ed. Alessandro Barchiesi, Chiara Frugoni and Giuliano Ranucci (Turin: Einaudi, 1982); Aelian, *De Natura Animalium libri XVII*, ed. Rudolf Hercher (Leipzig: Teubner, 1864–6), XIII. 6; Brunetto Latini, *Tresor*, ed. Pietro G. Beltrami et al. (Turin: Einaudi, 2007), I. 193. For the Christological interpretation of this information, see *Phisiologus Latinus Versio B Is*, XXIV, in *Bestiari medievali*, ed. Luigina Morini (Turin: Einaudi, 1996), 54–60; *Phisiologus. Versio Y*, XXIX, in *Bestiari tardoantichi e medievali*, ed. Francesco Zambon (Milan: Bompiani, 2018), 162–4; Philippe de Thaün, *Bestiaire*, lines 461–580, in *Bestiari medievali*, 136–42; Gervaise, *Bestiaire*, lines 139–238, in *Bestiari medievali*, 298–304; *Bestiario moralizzato*, XV, in *Bestiari medievali*, 500. Such a property was also interpreted in an erotic sense, in Richart de Fornival's *Bestiaire d'amours* (*Bestiari medievali*, 390), and in many lyric poems of the Italian Duecento. Dante alludes to this property of the panther, with notable symbolic freedom, when in *De vulgari eloquentia* he compares the 'volgare illustre' to the panther whose perfume is smelled everywhere but that hunters can find nowhere (*DVE*, I. xvi. 1). For a synthetic survey, see Maria Pia Ciccarese, *Animali simbolici. Alle origini del bestiario cristiano*, 2 vols (Bologna: Edizioni Dehoniane, 2007), II, 112–17.

6.   See Pliny, *Naturalis historia*, VIII. 42; Isidore of Seville, *Etymologiae*, XII. ii. 11: 'Leopardus ex adulterio leaenae et pardi nascitur'; Rabanus Maurus, *De universo*, VIII. 1 (*PL*, 111. 220); Ps.-Hugh of Saint Victor, *De bestiis*, III. 2 (*PL*, 177. 83); Bartholomaeus Anglicus, *De proprietatibus rerum*, XVIII. 65.

7. See for instance Isidore of Seville, *Etymologiae*, XII. ii. 20: 'Lyncis dictus, quia in luporum genere numeratur; bestia maculis terga distincta ut pardus, sed similis lupo [...]. Huius urinam convertere in duritiam pretiosi lapidis dicunt, qui lyncurius appellatur, quod et ipsas lynces sentire hoc documento probatur. Nam egestus liquorem harenis, in quantum potuerint, contegunt, invidia quadam naturae ne talis egestio transeat in usum humanum' [The lynx is so called because it is reckoned among the wolves [...] in kind; it is a beast that has spotted markings on its back, like a pard, but it is similar to a wolf; [...] People say that its urine hardens into a precious stone called *lyncurius*. That the lynxes themselves perceive this is shown by this proof: they bury as much of the excreted liquid in sand as they can, from a sort of natural jealousy lest such excretion should be brought to human use]. See also Pliny, *Naturalis Historia*, VIII. 57. 137. Rabanus Maurus, *De universo*, VIII. 1 (*PL*, 111. 222) repeats the words found in Isidore's text and adds the animal's moralisation as a symbol of envy. Isidore's text is repeated also in the *De bestiis*, III. 3, but without the additional moralisation (*PL*, 177. 84). Bartholomaeus Anglicus also repeats Isidore (*De proprietatibus rerum*, XVIII. 67), and the marginal gloss at this point makes explicit the moralisation of the animal as example of envy: 'Nota contra invidiam' (Troyes, Bibliothèque de Troyes, MS 979, f. 192r).
8. See the passages quoted above.
9. Such searches are now possible thanks to the TLIO–OVI database.
10. *Proverbia quae dicuntur supra natura feminarum*, 461: 'La onça è una bestia mala e perigolosa' [The *onça* is an evil and dangerous beast]. Quotation from *Poeti del Duecento (PD)*, ed. Gianfranco Contini, 2 vols (Milan: Ricciardi, 1960), I, 542.
11. Quotations from *PD*, II, 292.
12. Rustico Filippi, *Ne la stia mi par essere col leone*, which brings to the fore the animal's strong and unbearable smell: 'E' sente tanto di viverra fiato | o di leonza o d'altro assai fragore, | mai nessun ne trovai sì smesurato' (lines 9–11), in Rustico Filippi, *Sonetti satirici e giocosi*, ed. Silvia Buzzetti Gallarati (Rome: Carocci, 2005). In this passage the *lonza* cannot be identified, as Contini proposes, with a panther ('pantera'), for the latter is well known in the bestiaries for its sweet breath. In the sonnet *D'una diversa cosa ch'è aparita*, Rustico ironically defines a very timid and fearful person as 'fiery and courageus as a *lonza*' ('come una lonza sì fiera e ardita'). On these occurrences see also Romano Manescalchi, 'Osservazioni sulla "lonza" in Rustico Filippi e in Dante', *Studi danteschi*, 74 (2009): 127–47.
13. *Poeti giocosi del tempo di Dante*, ed. Mario Marti (Milan: Rizzoli, 1956).
14. See Brunetto Latini, *Tresor*, I. 190. 3: 'Une autre maniere de loups sont que l'en apele cervie[rs] ou luburne, qui sont pomelés de noires taiches come lonce, mes des autres choses est il sembla-bles au loup' [There is another type of wolf called a lynx, and others call it a luberne (luperne), and it is spotted with black spots like a *lonce*, but in other respects it is like a wolf]. Here and throughout, English translations follow Brunetto Latini, *The Book of the Treasure–Li livres dou tresor*, trans. Paul Barrette and Spurgeon Baldwin (New York: Garland, 1993). Compare with Isidore of Seville, *Etymologiae*, XI. ii. 20: 'Lyncis dictus, quia in luporum genere numeratur; bestia maculis terga distincta ut pardus, sed similis lupo' [The lynx is so called because it is reckoned among the wolves [...] in kind; it is a beast that has spotted markings on its back, like a pard, but it is similar to a wolf]. Isidore's words are repeated, almost unvaried, by Rabanus Maurus, *De universo*, VIII. 1 (*PL*, 111. 222), Ps.-Hugh of Saint Victor, *De bestiis*, III. 3 (*PL*, 177. 84) and Bartholomaeus Anglicus, *De proprietatibus rerum*, XVIII. 67.
15. Benvenuto da Imola, *ad loc.*: 'istud vocabulum florentinum lonza videtur magis importare pardum, quam aliam feram. Unde, dum semel portaretur quidam pardus per Florentiam, pueri concurrentes clamabant: vide lonciam, ut mihi narrabat suavissimus Boccatius de Certaldo' [That Florentine word, *lonza*, seems to mean the pard rather than any other beast. Therefore, when once a certain pard was being carried through Florence, the children came running along together shouting, 'See the *lonza*', as was told to me by that most agreeable Boccaccio from Certaldo].
16. See Ciccarese, *Animali simbolici*, I, 46. See also Rabanus Maurus, *De universo* VIII. 1 (*PL*, 111. 220): 'Pardus autem mystice significat diabolum diuersis uitiis plenissimum uel peccatorem quemlibet maculis scelerum et diuersorum errorum aspersum' [Symbolically, however, the *pardus* signifies the devil, overflowing with differing vices, or any sinner defiled by the stains of their crimes and various sins], Rabanus Maurus, *Commentaria in Ecclesiasticum* (*PL*, 109. 972). Antonius, *Vita S. Simeonis*, XIII (*PL*, 73. 331) and Flodoardus Remensis, *De triumphis Christi Antiochiae* (*PL*, 135. 577).
17. Song of Solomon 4. 8: 'Veni de Libano, sponsa, [...] de cubilibus leonum, de montibus pardorum' [Come from Libanus, my spouse, [...] from the dens of the lions, from the mountains

of the leopards [*pardorum*]]; Isaiah 11. 6: 'Habitabit lupus cum agno, et pardus cum haedo accubabit; vitulus, et leo, et ovis, simul morabuntur' [The wolf shall dwell with the lamb: and the leopard [*pardus*] shall lie down with the kid: the calf and the lion, and the sheep shall abide together]; Jeremiah 13. 23: 'Si mutare potest Aethiops pellem suam. Aut pardus varietates suas, et vos poteritis benefacere, cum didiceritis malum' [If the Ethiopian can change his skin, or the leopard [*pardus*] his spots: you may also do well, when you have learned evil]; Ecclesiasticus 28. 27: 'quasi leo et quasi pardus laedet illos' [and it shall be sent upon them as a lion, and as a leopard [*pardus*] it shall tear them]; Daniel 7. 6: 'et ecce alia quasi pardus et alas habebat avis quattuor super se, et quattuor capita erant in bestia; et potestas data est ei' [After this I beheld, and lo, another like a leopard [*pardus*], and it had upon it four wings as of a fowl, and the beast had four heads, and power was given to it]; Hosea 13. 7: 'Et ego ero eis quasi leaena, sicut pardus in via Assyrorum' [And I will be to them as a lioness, as a leopard [*pardus*] in the way of the Assyrians]; Habakkuk 1. 6–8: 'Quia ecce ego suscitabo Chaldeos, gentem amaram et velocem, [...], leviores pardis equi eius, et velociores lupis vespertinis' [For behold, I will raise up the Chaldeans, a bitter and swift nation, [...] Their horses are lighter than leopards [*pardis*], and swifter than evening wolves]; Revelation 13. 2: 'Et bestia, quam vidi, similis erat pardo' [And the beast, which I saw, was like to a leopard [*pardo*]].

18. See for instance Copenhagen, Kongelige Bibliotek, MS 213, f. 335r.

19. See for instance Athanasius, *Vita B. Antonii Abbatis* (*PL*, 73. 131): 'pardus discolor auctoris sui calliditates varias indicabat' [the many-hued pard showed the fickle cunning of its nature]; Rupertus Tuitiensis, *Commentarius in librum Ecclesiastes* (*PL*, 168. 1257); Henricus de Castro Marsiaco, *Epistolae*, XXIX (*PL*, 204. 236–7); Rupertus Tuitiensis, *De victoria Verbi Dei* (*PL*, 169. 1398): 'astutum atque versutum secundum pardi varietatem' [sly and full of wily cunning like the mottled appearance of the pard].

20. Aquinas, *In Jeremiam*, 5. 3, in S. Thomae de Aquino *Opera omnia*, recognovit ac instruxit Enrique Alarcón (automato electronico Pompaelone ad Universitatis Studiorum Navarrensis: aedes a MM A.D.), available online at http://www.corpusthomisticum.org.

21. Aquinas, *In Jeremiam*, 13. 2. The same reading can be found in Thomas à Becket, *Epistolae*: 'pardus varietates suas, sic fallaciam et fraudem exuere nesciunt' [like the pard its spots, they do not know how to cast off deceitfulness and fraud] (*PL*, 190. 498); Jacobus de Benevento, *De adventu Antichristi*, in S. Thomae de Aquino *Opera omnia*: 'Assimilatur autem pardo propter varietatem fraudulentiarum suarum fraudulentus valde erit' [Yet he is comparable to the pard, because of the variety of his deceits, he will be very deceitful].

22. In these generic interpretations, the *pardus* is connected to the multiplicity of sins. See for instance Rabanus Maurus, *Allegoriae in universam sacram scripturam* (*PL*, 112. 1022); Peter Damian, *Dialogus inter Iudaeum et Christianum, ad Honestum* (*PL*, 145. 62).

23. *PL*, 83. 466.

24. *Sermones de tempore* (*PL*, 195. 215). See also Martinus Legionensis, *Sermones*: 'Pardus quia in se colores habet varios, significat subdolos' [The pard because it has upon it many colours, signifies the treacherous] (*PL*, 208. 33).

25. Aquinas, *Super Isaiam*, 11, in S. Thomae de Aquino *Opera omnia*, available online at http://www.corpusthomisticum.org.

26. See for instance Guibert of Nogent, *Tropologiae in prophetas Asee et Amos ac Lamentationes Ieremiae* (*PL*, 156. 407).

27. 'Quid enim aliud est fraudolentia, quam astuta malitia, ad omnem fraudem tam prona quam prompta? Recte hypocritarum fraudolentia in pardo figuratur qui per totum corpus maculis quibusdam respergitur' [For what else is deceitfulness than cunning wickedness, as much prone as eager for every fraud. Rightly the deceitfulness of the hypocrites is figured in the pard, which is spattered with certain spots over its whole body] (*PL*, 196. 1358–9).

28. See for instance Bruno of Asti, *Expositio in Apocalypsim*: 'Pardus est animal multa macularum varietate depictum; merito ergo haec bestia pardo similis dicitur, quia ut infida, instabilis, versipellis, omnibus mentitur et in omnes deceptionis se vertit figuras' [The pard is an animal painted with a wide variety of spots; deservedly, therefore, this beast is called similar to a pard, because as it is treacherous, inconstant, double-dealing, it lies to everyone and turns itself to all forms of deception] (*PL*, 165. 674); Haymo Halberstatensis, *Expositio in Apocalypsin*: 'In varietate siquidem pardi, [...] ostenditur [...] omnium hypocritarum, atque omnium reproborum fictae actiones' [Accordingly, in the pard's changeability is shown the feigned actions of all hypocrites and all reprobates] (*PL*, 117. 1093). See also the Uncertain Author's *Expositio in Apocalypsin* (*PL*, 17. 883).

29. See for instance Bede, *Allegorica expositio in Cantica canticorum*: 'Leones quippe sunt daemonia, propter superbiam; pardi, propter crudelitatem sive varietatem artium malignarum' [Obviously, the lions are devils because of their pride; the pards, because of their cruelty or the variety of their malign deceits] (*PL*, 91. 1138); Anselm of Laon, *Enarrationes in Cantica canticorum*: 'quia distincti sunt variis sectis et haeresibus, sicut pardus variis maculis' [because they are distinguished by their various sects and heresies, just as the pard by its various spots] (*PL*, 162. 1208); Onorius of Autun, *Expositio in Cantica canticorum*: 'Pardi vero sunt haeretici in dogmate erroris varii' [In truth the pards are the heretics, differing in their doctrine of error] (*PL*, 172. 418–20).

30. See also Uncertain Author, *Expositio in Cantica Canticorum* (attributed to Cassiodorus): 'Coronatur [scil. Ecclesia] et de cubilibus leonum et montibus pardorum, quando superbos et quosque saevos ac dolosos convertit' [She [i.e. the Church] is crowned both by the dens of lions and the mountains of pards, at which time she converts the proud and those who are savages and the treacherous] (*PL*, 70. 1076); Gregory the Great, *Expositio super Cantica canticorum*: 'Pardi quippe maculas in cute semper portant, per quos qui alii quam hypocritae vel discordes significantur?' [The pards, of course, always wear spots on their skin, by which who other than the hypocrites or the inconsistent could be signified?] (*PL*, 79. 511–12); Gillebertus de Hoilandia, *Sermones in Canticum Salomonis*: 'Nescio enim quid asperum, quid ferum, quid fraudulentum in his vel nominibus, vel naturis datur intelligi' [For I do not know any rough, any savage, any deceitful thing that is given to be undersood in either these names or natures] (*PL*, 184. 151); Thomas Cisterciensis, *Commentaria in Cantica canticorum*: 'Quia pardus est animal distinctum variis maculis, designantur duplices et deceptores' [Because the pard is an animal distinguished by various spots, they are marked out as duplicitous and betrayers] (*PL*, 206. 291); Martinus Legionensis, *Sermones*: 'Pardi quippe maculas in cute semper portant, per quos quam hypocritae vel discordes significantur?' [The pards, of course, always wear spots on their skin, by which the hypocrites or the inconsistent are signified] (*PL*, 208. 1208); Alanus de Insulis, *Distinctiones dictionum theologicalium*: 'Pardus proprie. Dicitur etiam haereticus qui diversis fraudibus decipit' [The pard, specifically. It is said also [to be] the heretic who deceives by his different frauds] (*PL*, 210. 891); Peter Damian, *Sermones*: 'pardi autem, quia hoc animal varii coloris est, propter deceptionis ac fraudis multimodam varietatem' [pards, however, because this animal is of differing colour, on account of the multiplicitous variety of deception and fraud] (*PL*, 144. 688; passage repeated by Peter in his *Collectanea in Vetus Testamentum*, *PL*, 145. 1147); Wolbero Sancti Pantaleoni, *Commentaria in Cantica canticorum* (*PL*, 195. 1160); Richard of Saint Victor, *In Cantica canticorum explicatio*: 'Leones quoque et pardi sunt daemones; quia nunc, aperta iniquitate, saevientes quosdam decipiunt, nunc blandis consiliis et variis fraudibus rectos seducunt' [Also lions and pards are devils; because now by open iniquity they deceive certain raging men, now by flattering counsel and by various frauds they seduce the upright] (*PL*, 196. 482); Philip of Harveng, *Commentaria in Cantica canticorum* (*PL*, 203. 383–4).

31. Bede, *Allegorica expositio in Cantica canticorum* (*PL*, 91. 1138). English translation from *The Venerable Bede: On the Song of Songs and Selected Writings*, translated, edited and introduced by Arthur Holder (New York: Paulist Press, 2011),120.

32. *PL*, 112. 1022. See also Gilbert Foliot, *Expositio in Cantica canticorum* (*PL*, 202. 1259).

33. This interpretation has been proposed by some commentators, including Carlo Steiner, Isidoro Del Lungo, Carlo Grabher and Luigi Pietrobono, and more recently by Charles S. Singleton, Robert Hollander and Nicola Fosca (for the sake of convenience, commentaries are cited wherever possible following the Dartmouth Dante Project (DDP): https://dante.dartmouth.edu/). Daniele Maria Pegorari brings new arguments and evidence to support the interpretation, in 'La lonza svelata. Fonti classiche, cristiane e "interne" dell'allegoria della frode', *Giornale storico della Letteratura italiana*, 192 (2015): 523–41.

34. This interpretation is maintained by Fernando Salsano and Gaetano Ragonese, 'Fiera', in *Enciclopedia Dantesca* (*ED*), 6 vols (Rome: Istituto dell'Enciclopedia Italiana, 1970–8), II (1970), 857–61, which also provides references to the ancient commentary tradition. Other references and arguments supporting this position are offered by Francesco Mazzoni, who considers the three beasts 'il simbolo concreto di tre impedimenti radicali (cioè connaturati all'uomo) propri della natura umana vulnerata dal peccato d'origine (e quindi comuni a tutti gli uomini)' [the concrete symbol of the three radical (i.e. of second nature to men) impediments [that are] characteristic of human nature wounded by Original Sin (and therefore common to all men)]: *Saggio di un nuovo commento alla 'Divina Commedia': Inferno canti I–III* (Florence: Sansoni, 1967), *ad Inf*. I. 21. These three impediments are understood to be the same that St John also speaks of: 'Omne quod est in mundo, concupiscentia carnis est, et concupiscentia oculorum, et superbia vitae, quae non est ex patre, sed ex mundo est' [For all that

is in the world, is the concupiscence of the flesh, and the concupiscence of the eyes, and the pride of life, which is not of the Father, but is of the world] (1 John 2. 16). The same position is supported in the commentaries by Umberto Bosco and Giovanni Reggio; Anna Maria Chiavacci Leonardi; Giorgio Inglese (Rome: Carocci, 2016); Saverio Bellomo (Turin: Einaudi, 2011). Inglese's argumentation is especially clear: after quoting the passage from Jeremiah 5. 6, he appends a reference to Hugh of St Cher, that has become a commonplace in the commentary tradition since the early nineteenth-century essay by Giovanni Busnelli, *Il simbolo delle tre fiere dantesche: ricerche e studi intorno al prologo della Commedia* (Rome: Civiltà Cattolica, 1909), 35. Inglese's contribution reads: 'Ugo di San Caro (m. 1263) vede in queste belve il diavolo in tre forme: "mystice leo est diabolus inquantum est superbus, lupus [...] inquantum de luxuria [temptat] [...] pardus [...] inquantum de avaritia" (ed. Colonia 1621, t. IV, c. 190v). In D. le tre fiere, che impediscono l'ascesa al bene, hanno appunto il ruolo di tentazioni diaboliche, più o meno forti: "lussuria, superbia, avarizia" [...]. Determinante I Io. 2, 16: "omne quod est in mundo concupiscentia carnis [desiderio carnale] et concupiscentia oculorum [brama di possesso] est et superbia vitae"' [Hugh of St Cher (d.1263) sees in these beasts the devil in three forms: 'symbolically the lion is the devil in as much as he is proud, the wolf [...] in as much as he tempts by lust [...], the pard [...] in as much as by avarice' (ed. Colonia 1621, vol. IV, fol. 190v). In D. the three beasts, which block the ascent to righteousness, have exactly the role of the devil's temptations, whether stronger or weaker: 'lust, pride, avarice' [...]. As I John 2. 16 avers: 'For all that is in the world, is the concupiscence of the flesh (carnal desire), and the concupiscence of the eyes (desire for worldly goods), and the pride of life']. This exegetical tradition suggests a connection between Hugh of St Cher's gloss to Jeremiah and the passage from St John's epistle. But no trace of such a connection can be found in Hugh's text. The two traditions are entirely separate, connected only in Dantean exegesis. Nor could the complete passage of Hugh of St Cher on Jeremiah be used as proof for the interpretation of the three beasts as symbols of lust, pride and avarice: 'Mystice. Leo est diabolus, in quantum est superbus, et in quantum de superbia tentat. Lupus, ipse idem de luxuria, quia lupus gaudet de effusione sanguinis. Pardus in quantum de avaritia, quia variat, et turbat cor, et in quantum de dolositate, et fallacia' [Symbolically: the lion is the devil, in as much as he is proud, and in as much as he tempts by pride; the wolf, [the devil] as he tempts by lust, because the wolf rejoices in the spilling of blood; the pard, in as much as [he tempts] by avarice, because he fluctuates and disturbs the heart, and in as much as [he tempts] by trickery and by deception]: Hugonis Cardinalis, *Opera Omnia in Universum Vetus, et Novum Testamentum*, 8 vols (Venice: apud Nicolaum Pezzana, 1703), IV, 190. As can be seen, while in Hugh there are the three vices of pride, lust and avarice, the correspondence between animals and vices is different from that proposed by Dante commentators. Only the meaning of the lion is the same. The she-wolf, instead, is interpreted as a symbol of lust, not of avarice, and the *pardus* as a symbol of avarice, not of lust. Moreover, a connection with fraud is also suggested for the *pardus*: 'Pardus [...] et in quantum de dolositate, et fallacia' [The pard [...] in as much as [he tempts] both by trickery and by deception]. So Hugh's passage cannot be used as a proof for the traditional interpretation of the three beasts as symbols of lust, pride and avarice. On the contrary, it adds another proof in favour of the interpretation of the *lonza/pardus* as a symbol of fraud.

35. See for instance the commentaries of Giorgio Padoan, *Inferno (canti I–VIII)*, ed. Giorgio Padoan, in *Opere di Dante: IX*, ed. Vittore Branca, Francesco Maggini and Bruno Nardi, (Florence: Le Monnier, 1967), (DDP).

36. See for instance, Pietro Alighieri's commentary, third redaction.

37. Milton Stahl Garver and Kenneth McKenzie, 'Il bestiario toscano secondo la lezione dei codici di Parigi e di Roma', *Studj romanzi* 8 (1912): 1–100. See also for instance 'Fiera', in *ED*.

38. This section of the *Bestiario toscano* is present only in appendices to the text witnessed in just two manuscripts out of a total of 16. See *Bestiari medievali*, 426–30, where this section is excluded.

39. The only property of the *loncia* here connected to lust is taken from Bartholomaeus Anglicus's chapter on the *pardus*, an animal for which the symbolism of fraud is absolutely prevalent. The *leopardus* too, on the other hand, is presented by Bartholomaeus and by the *Bestiario toscano* as a cunning, astute and fraudulent animal.

40. See *Inf.*, VI. 74–5: 'superbia, invidia e avarizia sono | le tre faville c'hanno i cuori accesi' [pride, envy, and greed are the three sparks that have set hearts ablaze]; XV. 68: 'gent'è avara, invidiosa e superba' [they are a people avaricious, envious, and proud]. The entry 'Lonza' in

the *ED* attributes this proposal originally to Castelvetro: 'Lonza', *ED*, III (1971), 691. For a strong reaffirmation, see Gorni.

41. The medieval bestiary tradition that the lynx's urine changes into a hard, precious stone, sometimes concealed by the animal to impede its pursuers, can make it a symbol of envy: see the sources in note 7 above, plus Ps.-Hugh of St Victor, *De bestiis*, III. 3 (*PL* 177. 84).

42. For bibliographical references, see 'Lonza', in *ED*.

43. See for instance the commentaries of Mazzoni and Chiavacci Leonardi.

44. See Gregory the Great, *Moralia in Iob*, V. 21. 41, ed. Marcus Adriaen (Turnhout: Brepols, 1979–85), in *Corpus Christianorum Latinorum*, 143: 'Habet quippe leo virtutem, habet et saevitiam. Virtute ergo Dominum, saevitia diabolum signat' [Of course the lion has strength, and has ferocity. By its strength, therefore, it represents the Lord, and by its ferocity it represents the devil]. See also Ciccarese, *Animali simbolici*, II, 13–19.

45. The diabolical symbolism of the lion is frequently underlined by Augustine, who associates the lion and the dragon. See, for instance, *Enarratio in Psalmum*, LXIX. 2 (*PL*, 36. 867): 'Diabolus ille biformis est. Leo est in impetu, draco in insidiis' [The devil himself is two-formed. He is the lion in his attack, the dragon in his ambushes]; *Enarratio in Psalmum*, XC. 9 (*PL*, 37. 1168): 'Leo aperte saevit; draco occulte insidiatur: utramque vim et potestatem habet diabolus' [The lion rages openly; the dragon lies in ambush secretly: just as the devil has both force and power]. See also Rabanus Maurus, *De universo*: 'Leo, Diabolus ob fortitudinem et crudelitatem' [The lion, the devil on account of his strength and cruelty] (*PL*, 111, 219).

46. See the numerous texts quoted above.

47. See Augustine, *Tractatus in Iohannis Evangelium*, XLVI. 7: 'Quis est lupus nisi diabolus?' (*PL* 35, 1731) [What is the wolf if not the devil?]; Ps.-Hugh of St Victor, *De bestiis*, III. 20 (*PL*, 177. 67): 'eius figuram diabolus portat' [the devil bears the figure (of the wolf)]. The encyclopaedic tradition underlines the proprieties of ferocity, anger and rapacity. See Isidore of Seville, *Etym.*, XII. ii. 24: 'Rapax autem bestia et cruoris appetens' [It is a violent beast, eager for gore].

48. See Boethius, *De consolatione philosophiae*, ed. Karl Büchner (Heidelberg: Editiones Heidelbergenses, 1960²), IV. iii. 17: 'Avaritia fervet alienarum opum violentus ereptor: lupi similem dixeris' [The violent despoiler of other men's goods, enflamed with covetousness, surely resembles a wolf].

49. Morton W. Bloomfield, *The Seven Deadly Sins* (East Lansing, MI: Michigan State College Press, 1952), 244; Mireille Vincent-Cassy, 'Les animaux et les péchés capitaux: de la symbolique a l'emblématique', in *Le monde animal et ses représentations au Moyen Âge*, ed. Francis Cervan (Toulouse: Université de Toulouse-Le Mirail, 1985), 121–32 (126–9). Bartholomaeus Anglicus: 'Rapax autem bestia et cruoris appetens, qui rabie rapacitatis quemcumque invenerit trucidat' [It is a violent beast, eager for gore, which by the madness of rapacity slaughters whomever it comes across]. Glosses such as: 'Nota contra luxuriosos' [Note against the lustful], and 'Nota contra gulosos' [Note against the gluttonous] appear in the manuscript tradition. In the third book of the *De bestiis* can be found an interesting reference to the she-wolf: 'Unde et meretrices lupas vocitamus, quia amatorum bona devastant' [Whence we also call prostitutes she-wolves, because they lay waste to the possessions of their lovers], Ps.-Hugh of St Victor, *De bestiis*, III. 20 (*PL*, 177. 67). On the lustful nature of the she-wolf see also Brunetto Latini, *Tresor*, I. 190: 'Et quant li tens de sa luxure vient, plusors loups ensivent par route une lieue; mes a la fin ele resgarde entre touz et eslit le plus laide qui gise o li' [When it is time to mate, several males follow a female, and they all go around her, and finally the she-wolf looks them all over and selects the puniest and the ugliest and lies with him].

50. The mention of the she-wolf in *Purg.* XX is usually interpreted as referring to avarice. Yet in this passage it does not seem possible to distinguish the image of the she-wolf – given its radical negativity – from that of the 'femmina balba' of the protagonist's dream in the previous canto (*Purg.* XIX, 10–60) who, as Virgil explicitly indicates, represents the three vices punished on the three last terraces of Purgatory: avarice, gluttony and lust. These vices are interpreted in Hell as sins of incontinence, therefore this reference is not incompatible with the interpretation of the three beasts as fraud, violence and incontinence.

51. Though the male wolf bears a different value in Ugolino's dream, *Inf.*, XXXIII. 29.

52. See Gorni.

53. See Sergio Cristaldi, *La profezia imperfetta. Il veltro e l'escatologia medievale* (Caltanissetta: Sciascia, 2011).

4
Lust and the Law: Reading and Witnessing in *Inferno* V

Nicolò Crisafi and Elena Lombardi

Witnessing plays an important role in the storytelling of the *Commedia*. The poem is structured as a first-hand account of an otherworldly journey whose protagonist and narrator is keenly aware of the importance and problematic nature of testimony. At different stages in the poem, Dante calls attention to his role as eyewitness, defends his character and the credibility of his testimony, makes direct appeals to his audience and, in one notable instance, even swears by his poem that his story, as unbelievable as it may seem, is true:[1]

> Sempre a quel ver c'ha faccia di menzogna
> de' l'uom chiuder le labbra fin ch'el puote,
> però che sanza colpa fa vergogna;
>   ma qui tacer nol posso; e per le note
> di questa comedìa, lettor, ti giuro,
> s'elle non sien di lunga grazia vòte,
>   ch'i' vidi per quell'aere grosso e scuro
> venir notando una figura in suso,
> maravigliosa ad ogne cor sicuro.

(*Inf.*, XVI. 124–32)

[Always, to every truth that looks, in face, | like lies, one ought (quite firmly) bar the lip | lest, guiltless, what one says should still bring shame. | I cannot, though, be silent here. Reader, | I swear by every rhyme this comedy | has caused to chime (may it not lack long favour) | that now, through dark and fatty air, I saw – | to strike sheer wonder in the steadiest heart – | approaching us a figure swimming up.]

Confronted with an unbelievable 'fictional' truth ('quel ver c'ha faccia di menzogna'), Dante fulfils the formalities of witnesses at medieval trials by swearing his truthfulness.[2] Thus the poet-witness exacts the reader-juror's attention by taking an oath on his poem. The 'comedìa', invoked here for the first time with its (probable) title, is presented as a rather extraordinary textual object: while swearing by it evokes a stable, written, bound and even 'sacred' idea of the book,[3] its 'notes' evoke its oral, aural, continuous and, importantly, poetic aspects. The reader who believes his truth-claims is entrusted with the task of verifying Dante's words, by upholding the future fame of his work ('s'elle non sien di lunga grazia vòte', 129).[4] This paradox takes a more imperceptible form late in the poem, when the 'poema sacro' [sacred poem] itself performs the aspiration of this oath that the grace of Dante's readership may overcome adverse historical conditions in Florence to reinstate him to his rightful place in the city (Par., XXV. 1–9).[5]

Dante is not the only witness in the Commedia, nor is this the first time that he calls the reader's attention to the act of reading as involving a judgement – not only of the stylistic or narrative success of a work of literature, but of its very truthfulness, or rather of its performativity of truthfulness. Inferno V, the first canto of Hell proper and the first to host what we might read as a testimony, is, among many other things, also a reflection on the role of the related practices of reading and storytelling. Dante dramatises these in several important ways – from Francesca's transformative glossing of courtly love (lines 100–7) and her reading of the Lancelot (127–38) to the involvement of the extra-diegetic reader, captured in a hall of mirrors, where lovers and readers repeatedly exchange places.[6] In this essay we focus on a particular aspect of such dramatisation – the ways in which witnessing and judging call into question two different aspects of the issue, reading and the law – as suggested by the rima equivoca 'legge': 'si legge' [law: it is read] (Inf., V. 56–8, and Purg., XXVI. 83–5) that links the representations of lust in the first two cantiche. Because of the gender of Dante's first witness and of the other characters who are variously involved in reading and the law (Semiramis and Pasiphae), the cantos of lust also have something specific to say about the experience of women as witnesses in charge of their own story – and, importantly, how 'we', readers of all times, 'read' them.

Medieval discourses of lust

It is not by chance that issues of interpretation, law and gender come to react together in the circles of lust. Dante's position on lust is ambiguous: the apparently plain 'subjecting reason to desire' [che la ragion sommettono al talento] (*Inf.*, V. 39) can be interpreted as a definition of sin in general (as a blinding of rationality), but also of *cupiditas*, the inordinate desire at the heart of all human evil. More problematically, lust can also be a very fitting description for love: both earthly (as Teodolinda Barolini has shown by gathering many examples in the love lyrics of Dante's time) and divine (the bride of the *Song of Solomon* famously exclaiming, in Bernard of Clairvaux's words, that she is carried by desire, not reason – 'desiderio feror non ratione'); and it is tied, eclectically yet inextricably, to written texts that talk about love.[7]

Dante's ambivalent position on lust reflects a similar attitude in medieval culture, where lust is the unstable and destabilising interface between many discourses. In the Middle Ages lust is constructed in different ways in theological, monastic and pastoral environments, and involves such different disciplines as canon law and medicine.[8] Lust is the only sin of incontinence of concern for medieval canonists due to its societal consequences. Like theologians, canonists broke down lust into 'natural' lust and lust that was 'against nature', and looked closely at those cases which intersected most with marriage law. Any sexual behaviour that deviated from marriage and reproduction (or threatened the celibacy of the religious) was perceived as a menace to society. Strikingly, adultery was considered the most relevant sexual crime, even the 'benchmark' of major sexual offences, and sexual offences committed by women were regarded as more reprehensible than those committed by men. As James Brundage points out, 'where medieval canonical records have been published and analyzed, they show with monotonous regularity that a major part of the routine business of the canonical courts consisted in routine prosecutions of fornicators and adulterers, many of them recidivist, interspersed with occasional actions against perpetrators of other sexual offences'.[9]

Dante, as is well known, treated lust with a relatively light and original touch in *Inferno* V,[10] and a unique, if heavier, touch in *Purgatorio* XXVI. Women and courtly poetry/poets are the central characters in the two cantos, which feature authority (literary and otherwise), social agency, adultery and the law as fundamental themes. Moreover, the question of the fame, or rather *infamia*, of lustful women, and its relation to the written text, is presented in rather dramatic ways in the two cantos. Perhaps not by chance a woman (Cunizza da Romano), a courtly poet barely disguised as a crusading bishop (Folquet de Marseille) and the (counterfactual) writing of history by Emperor Charles Martel resurface in the consciously inconsistent wrapping up of the theme of earthly desires in *Paradiso* VIII and IX.

Reading and being read: the cases of Semiramis and Pasiphae

In *Inferno* V, shortly after defining lust through the broad categories of 'ragione' and 'talento', Dante both rarefies and narrows them down in a long passage, the so-called catalogue of the ancients. Here, through a clever and intentional funnelling of the terminology of lust and the rhetoric of love, Dante guides the reader through the transition and indeed continuity between the sin of lust and the poeticised experience of love, poignantly illustrated by the rhyme 'lussurïosa': 'amorosa' in lines 61–3. The inveterate vice of lechery ('vizio di lussuria', 55) enters one side of this funnel and love exits on the other ('amor', 69). The traditional catalogue of the ancients in these lines lists exemplary texts and characters that form the 'background library' of this episode, as well as providing an illustration of the historical significance and societal consequences of lust. These tales of love are, as Amilcare Iannucci and Teodolinda Barolini have pointed out, also tales of power and war.[11] History, myth, lust, love and love poetry conflate here around a mostly female display of authority, both positing and shifting the parameters for interpretation.

> 'La prima di color di cui novelle
> tu vuo' saper', mi disse quelli allotta,
> 'fu imperadrice di molte favelle.
>   A vizio di lussuria fu sì rotta,
> che libito fé licito in sua legge,
> per tòrre il biasmo in che era condotta.
>   Ell'è Semiramìs, di cui si legge
> che succedette a Nino e fu sua sposa:
> tenne la terra che 'l Soldan corregge.
>   L'altra è colei che s'ancise amorosa,
> e ruppe fede al cener di Sicheo;
> poi è Cleopatràs lussuriosa.
>   Elena vedi, per cui tanto reo
> tempo si volse, e vedi 'l grande Achille,
> che con amore al fine combatteo.
>   Vedi Parìs, Tristano'; e più di mille
> ombre mostrommi e nominommi a dito,
> ch'amor di nostra vita dipartille.

> (*Inf.*, V. 52–69)

['The first of those whose tale you wish to hear,' | he answered me
without a moment's pause, | 'governed as empress over diverse
tongues. | She was so wracked by lust and luxury, | licentiousness
was legal under laws she made – | to lift the blame that she herself
incurred. | This is Semiramis. Of her one reads | that she, though
heir to Ninus, was his bride. | Her lands were those where now the
Sultan reigns. | The other, lovelorn, slew herself and broke | her vow
of faith to Sichaeus's ashes. | And next, so lascivious, Cleopatra. |
Helen. You see? Because of her, a wretched | waste of years went by.
See! Great Achilles. | He fought with love until his final day. | Paris
you see, and Tristan there.' And more | than a thousand shadows he
numbered, naming | them all, whom Love had led to leave our life.]

Words such as 'lussuria', 'libito' and 'lussurïosa' recall the traditional
legal-theological lexicon of lust. Indeed, the law itself is called into question
in a rather enigmatic manner. Semiramis 'made lust licit in her law' ('libito
fé licito in sua legge', 56) – a line that plays on the replacement of a single
letter, which paradoxically turns the most singular caprice of lust ('libito')[12]
into what is legitimate for all ('licito'). Semiramis's legislation coincides with
the very opposite of what the law should be, as it infringes its aspiration to
universality and common wellbeing. Indeed, medieval commentators such
as Jacopo della Lana clearly recognised and discussed the legal implications
of Semiramis's story.[13] Like Minos's mock trial at the beginning of the canto
(lines 1–15, discussed in the following section), this recalling of the law
plays with such expectations and is evidently caricatural and parodic.

Semiramis is the first sinner named in Hell, and the distinctive trait
of her sins and tales is their being written about and handed down to be
read: she is the one 'of whom we read' ('di cui si legge', 58).[14] While later
in the canto reading is featured as a complex, non-linear, transforming
and transformative experience, here Semiramis's stories are introduced
in an unproblematic way: in books one reads of the shame of Semiramis.
Yet the straightforward relation between Semiramis's lawlessness and the
authority of the written text is only apparent. As with Francesca's reading of the *Lancelot* later in the canto, here too Dante points to a specific
text, Orosius's *Historia adversum paganos* I. 4, from which two bits of
semi-translation are taken: 'succedette a Nino e fu sua sposa' ('huic mortuo
Samiramis uxor successit' [upon his death, his wife Semiramis succeeded
him]) and a version of the very tongue-twister, 'libito fé licito in sua legge'
('ut cuique libitum esset liberum fieret' [that everyone would be free to do
what they wished]), in which Dante pushes the legal agenda by changing
'liberum' to 'licito' and adding 'legge'.[15] The impersonal 'si legge', however,

articulates here Semiramis's status as bride of and legal successor to Ninus, and also her territorial power. But hearsay, as well as textual authority, also apparently contributes to the account of Semiramis's imperial possessions and her extraordinary lechery. This is the amalgamated, citational view of Semiramis, widespread in the late Middle Ages, where Semiramis was a synecdoche for her city, the morally degenerate Babylon.[16]

In this compound view, evident also from the enthusiasm with which Dante's early commentators embraced her characterisation, Semiramis is presented as a character of extraordinary historical agency and, therefore, of extreme sexual transgression. The first woman to become emperor, to do 'what no other woman had done' (dress like a man, shed human blood, have absolute power, construct and legislate), displaying rare prowess in conquest and in building and walling cities, she 'must' also be sexually transgressive. She is indeed credited with every possible sexual transgression: prostitution, cross-dressing, castrating young men, committing incest, even, interestingly, bestiality. Semiramis's lust and blood-thirstiness thus merge into one, as Orosius puts it ('libidine ardens, sanguinem sitiens' [burning with lust, thirsting with blood], *Historia adversum paganos* I. 4).[17]

On the terrace of lust in *Purgatorio* XXVI, we find another powerful and sexually transgressive queen – and another confrontation between reading and the law. Dante's originality here lies not only in bringing together homosexual and heterosexual inclinations, but also in interpreting them both as 'against nature'. On each half of the cornice, the ranks of the lustful meet, exchange chaste kisses, and declare their sins:

> la nova gente: 'Soddoma e Gomorra';
> e l'altra: 'Ne la vacca entra Pasife,
> perché 'l torello a sua lussuria corra'.

> (*Purg.*, XXVI. 40–2)

> [(the new arrivals), 'Sodom! Gomorrah!' | 'Into the cow,' (the rest) 'went Pasiphae | to let the bull calf run his lust in her'.]

Later in the canto the main speaker, the poet Guido Guinizzelli, illustrates the excesses of the heterosexual lustful, emphasising the two opposite aspects of bestiality and legality:

> 'Nostro peccato fu ermafrodito
> ma perché non servammo umana legge,
> seguendo come bestie l'appetito

> in obbrobrio di noi, per noi si legge,
> quando partinci, il nome di colei
> che s'imbestiò ne le 'mbestiate schegge'.

(*Purg.*, XXVI. 82–7)

['Our sin, by contrast, was hermaphrodite. | And since we paid no heed to human law – | choosing to follow bestial appetites – | ourselves we read out our opprobrium, | speaking, on leaving here, the name of one | who made herself a beast in beastlike planks'.]

In this passage Dante rephrases the notions of 'ragione' [reason] and 'talento' [desire] from *Inferno* V into their amplifications: 'human law' and 'bestiality'. By having Guido Guinizzelli illustrate the powerful example of Pasiphae, Dante draws the reader's attention to the ultimate similarity *sub specie aeternitatis* between two extreme manifestations of what in *Inferno* V is referred to, ambiguously, as 'love': on the material/bodily side, the extreme sexual choice of 'species crossing'; on the intellectual/spiritual side, the extreme rarefaction of courtly love poetry.

The expression 'umana legge' [human law] is often glossed as 'reason' in light of the submission of reason to desire of *Inf.*, V. 39, and of a passage in *Convivio* where Dante states 'chi dalla ragione si parte e usa pure la parte sensitiva, non vive uomo ma vive bestia' [he who departs from his reason and uses merely his sensitive part lives not as a man but as a beast] (*Cvo*, II. vii. 4). The excerpt from *Convivio* points to the fact that being or becoming 'like a beast' is the consequence of sin in general and not of lust in particular, whereas in *Purgatorio* XXVI bestiality stands for only one of the subspecies of lust. According to Aquinas, bestiality was by far the worst form of lust: a sin that transgressed the bounds of humanity. Thus 'human law' might be rephrased as 'the law of nature which supervises human intercourse'; it also stands for the laws of society protecting matrimony and lineage, since Pasiphae is an adulteress to begin with and her unlawful offspring an obvious threat to Cretan society.[18]

The story of Pasiphae has many similarities with Semiramis's, thematising both the interaction between power and sexual transgression, and the 'unimaginable' character of the noblewoman's behaviour.[19] Like that of Semiramis, the tale of Pasiphae was very popular in the Middle Ages, appearing in a compound of several sources, primarily Virgilian and Ovidian.[20] Unlike the (pseudo-)historical Babylonian queen, however, her Cretan counterpart is seen as a fabulous and fictional character.[21] Bestiality had similarly 'fabulous' status in the law. As James Brundage points out, sexual practices such as Pasiphae's 'were heatedly denounced, but seldom prosecuted. Bestiality [...] hardly even appears in the records'.[22] Thus her sin appears to be more a fantasy of infringing the law than an actual transgression.

Importantly, the two passages on Semiramis and Pasiphae display the same equivocal rhyme: 'legge': 'si legge'. The purgatorial 'si legge' is traditionally interpreted as a 'si dice' voiced by the lustful, that is, 'we say, cry'. This interpretation takes into account the widespread oral, recitational and citational nature of medieval practices of reading. It evokes, again, ideas of reciting a script or the connection to practices of reading aloud, such as the *lectura evangelii*. An interesting switch occurs between the two passages. In *Inferno* the expression 'of whom we read' recalls a collection of written texts or a compound text, on which the historical agency and sexual transgression of Semiramis is constructed. Yet in *Purgatorio* the expression 'per noi si legge' adds a further layer with this 'new', oral version of Pasiphae belatedly embraced in the terrace of purgatory by the otherwise tepidly lustful poets of courtly love (who were 'lustful in words', a rather minor offence).

There is, however, a further quite striking way of reading these lines, one that also calls the reader of the *Commedia* into question: through us, through our example ('per noi') *you the reader* read ('si legge') the name of Pasiphae – which indeed appears and is read in the text at line 41. In other words, while the purging souls recite their script, the extra-diegetic reader re-reads both the old and the new story. While Dante had constructed the extra-diegetic reader in a subtle manner in the story of Francesca, with the mirror image of lovers who are reading about lovers who are reading about lovers ..., here we, the readers, fall under the spotlight – caught in the very moment of the transforming and transformative act of reading.

In both *Inferno* V and *Purgatorio* XXVI, the rhyme 'legge': 'si legge' and the transformative ways in which Semiramis and Pasiphae are read evoke a further set of questions. This in turn brings us back to Francesca. Two extreme and 'fictional' examples of lust – the extreme sexual transgression of Semiramis and Pasiphae and the rarefaction of courtly poetry – are both tied to the consistency of written texts. They contain and illustrate a median: the unprecedented, not-yet-recounted, poetry-laden testimony of Francesca da Rimini, whose crime, it seems, is to have transgressed the seemingly imperceptible line that separates a longed-for smile from a mere mouth. What about Francesca, then? What about her story, halfway between history and fiction, 'di cui' 'per noi' 'si legge'? What does her story have to say about the relations between reading, lust and the law in the canti of lust? And, most importantly, why is Francesca the first character to tell us her story in the *Commedia*?

Francesca (and Cunizza) as witness

Inferno V is one of the most heavily discussed cantos of the *Commedia*. However, one aspect is seldom mentioned: its engagement with the practice of the law, present in several important ways in *Inferno* V. The canto begins with the figure of Minos, the infernal judge, who is portrayed as recording the confessions of recently deceased souls and sentencing them to the circle most appropriate to their sins.[23] Although Minos stands as a grotesque parody of justice, the phrases 'essamina le colpe', 'giudica e manda' [technically: investigates the wrongs, judges and sentences] (*Inf.*, V. 5–6), 'si confessa' [confesses] (8), 'conoscitor de le peccata' [investigating judge of sins] (9), and 'atto', 'offizio' [act, office] (18) are all carefully employed in their technical juridical sense or with legal overtones.[24] It is no surprise, then, that this part of the canto caught the attention of legal professionals in Dante's time. Some excerpts from it were used as filler in the 'Memoriali bolognesi', the criminal registers compiled in Bologna, in 1317.[25] For a notary dealing with justice records, the canto's allusions to trial proceedings were noteworthy and especially memorable.

The technical terms of medieval justice form one of the subtexts tying the beginning of *Inferno* V to the second half of the canto. Here Francesca gives a first-hand account of the events of her adulterous love for her brother-in-law and of how they were killed by one of their kin. Here we find other traces of the legal language encountered with Minos and in Semiramis's punning 'libito', 'licito' and 'legge' (56). Francesca's use of the word 'pace' [peace] (92, 99), for instance, as well as recalling the warlike background of the canto,[26] may allude to the technical term for the officially sanctioned forgiveness of the crime by the victim.[27] Moreover, the verb and adjective 'offende' (102) and 'offense' (109), are used as technical terms for the victim of a crime ('*offensus*') in all the extant statutes of thirteenth- to fifteenth-century Florence.

It is the context of such hints at the law and its practices that encourages us to think of Francesca's direct speech as performing an act of testimony. The story of Francesca, a 'weak', unstable, inadmissible witness, embroiled in issues of lust, faces the reader with fundamental questions regarding the role and scope of testimony *before* we can delve into matters of morality, theology and poetics arising from this woman's speech. These fundamental questions – What qualifies as testimony, and what determines its value? Who gets to bear witness, and about what? How are we readers to take testimony? – are important not only in the context of Francesca, but throughout the entire *Commedia*.

In stark contrast with the historical and fictional fame of the queens and princesses that precede her, there is 'no completely independent documentation of Francesca's story' before the *Commedia*.[28] However, if history is virtually silent on Francesca, Francesca herself is not: her first-person account of the events that led to her damnation in Dante's text form the basis of all subsequent versions of her story. Early commentators thought it necessary to add details regarding Francesca and her tale. On the one hand they invented for her a 'romance' of love and death patterned on several classical and medieval archetypes – including, notably, the tale of Tristan and Iseult;[29] on the other they initiated a critical tradition of explaining her account and actions in light of her supposed character, often taken from these very archetypes.

For instance when, as early as the 1320s, Guido da Pisa analysed Francesca's speech as a collection of *sententiae* (the short and memorable maxims used to summarise a concept or a norm in Scholastic teaching and Roman law),[30] commentators hotly debated throughout the Renaissance whether these *sententiae* were true or false, considering them in reference to the moral character of the person who uttered them.[31] Benvenuto da Imola's commentary is emblematic when he warns that *sententiae* can be misleading and should always be contextualised by considering the manner, aim and situation in which they are uttered.[32] Early commentators and many later ones abided by this advice. On the one hand, they sought to give some background to Francesca's account, attempting to fill in the gaps between history and her story; on the other, they scrutinised Francesca's words so as to bring out connections between her language and her lustful character.[33] In doing so commentators replicated, wittingly or unwittingly, the practices of medieval justice – whose primary task, when gathering evidence for an inquisitorial trial, was to establish the *fama*, or reputation, of the witnesses and to assess the *fides*, or credibility, of their testimony. And indeed Francesca's *fama* and *fides* are the greatest problems with her testimony.

Justin Steinberg has written about medieval notions of *fama* and *infamia* in relation to Dante. He explains how these originally societal terms, referring to a person's reputation within a community, had special legal repercussions, damaging 'a culprit's legal capacity' and 'disqualifying him or her from specific rights. Above all, [they] targeted one's juridical credibility'.[34] As somebody who, in Dante's fiction, had already been found guilty of lust in Minos's mock trial, let alone in the divine system of punishment, Francesca would be seen as falling squarely in the category of *infame 'per sententiam'* [by sentence], her conviction effectively invalidating her moral character. Even before that, a number of details of her story brought up by commentators would put the nail in the coffin of her legal credibility *'ipso iure'* [by law]. As Steinberg writes, 'scandalous acts violating the sexual and moral norms of the community, such as adultery and sodomy, automatically defamed by law'.[35]

In establishing her *fama*, early commentators responded to this practice; they even expanded on it by showing how Francesca's story presents all the main aggravating circumstances of adulterous lust. Firstly, Francesca was a married woman, and therefore her adultery threatened the legitimacy of the offspring[36] – duly reflected in the fact that over the course of the fourteenth century 'penalties for the married woman guilty of engaging in extra-marital sex became increasingly severe'.[37] Secondly, Francesca's adultery was incestuous. Sexual relationships between two siblings-in-law ('due cognati', *Inf.*, VI. 2) fell into the category of incest, and most early commentators (Jacopo della Lana, L'Ottimo, Giovanni da Serravalle) did not fail to stress this fact.[38] Thirdly, distrusting Francesca's account of her role in the affair, commentators generally took for granted that her adultery was consensual, or at any rate not the result of violence – even though this remains one of the possible readings of the line '"il modo ancor m'offende"' ['The harm of how still rankles me'], which Lino Pertile has suggested may imply the aggressive nature of Paolo's passion.[39] The woman's consent was an aggravating circumstance which invalidated any attempt to ask for compensation on the part of the adulteress's family.[40] Lastly, a further aggravating circumstance attended the adultery if it took place in the husband or father's home.[41] The text is not explicit on such details, but early commentators seemed to agree that Francesca's husband Gianciotto caught the lovers in his own home (L'Ottimo even states 'sì come nel testo appare' [as shown clearly in the text]), and some modern scholars follow suit.[42]

It is particularly noteworthy that the 'great raconteur' Boccaccio, in his creative and expansive retelling of Francesca and Paolo's story, picks up and expands on all the aggravating circumstances in their tale. Although Boccaccio states that the marriage between Francesca and Gianciotto was a marriage of convenience, he specifies that it had been consummated and was thus legally binding; he emphasises three times Paolo and Gianciotto's relation of kin; he underlines the consensual nature of the adulterous relationship between the two lovers – and even embellishes this allegation, contradicting Dante's own account, by stating that the lady fell in love first. Finally, Boccaccio locates the adultery in the 'camera di madonna Francesca'. Even the most open-minded and 'romantic' of Francesca's readers, then, was inclined to emphasise the aggravating circumstances of adulterous lust that in a medieval trial would have made the woman an emblematic *infame* and thus irreparably compromised the *fides* of her testimony.

The manifestly unstable reputation and credibility of Francesca is of great consequence in Dante's choice of this woman as the first witness in the *Commedia*. As a quintessentially challenging case, Francesca is extraordinarily well-suited to problematise the nature of testimony: the seven-century-old reception of the poem can be taken as evidence of the ways in which readers of *Inferno* V continue to engage with the question of the credibility and truth-value of her words, as fundamental to legal proceedings as they are to reading fiction. Francesca is the first of many testing cases, which are by no means limited to *Inferno*. Indeed, as far into Dante's journey as *Paradiso* IX, we find a counterpart to Francesca's story in the scandalous salvation of the *spirito amante* Cunizza da Romano, whose story, from both the legal and the moral point of view, is not dissimilar to that of Francesca. Crucially, Cunizza is shown to be perfectly aware of the apparent outlandishness of her testimony, and the ways in which it might be received by the living, when she states that her scandalous story as well as improbable salvation '"parria forse forte al vostro vulgo"' ['will, to humdrum minds of yours, seem hard'] (*Par.*, IX. 36).

Speaking in the first person: Francesca's *dirò*

Although *Inferno* V is emblematic of Dante's own concerns with his authority and that of his *Commedia*, Dante spotlights such issues, more specifically, through the story of a woman whose fame, in the fiction of the poem, does not depend on previous myth, history, literature (as in the case of Semiramis and Pasiphae), but on her own direct speech. Francesca's words, very much alive to the historical circumstances of a woman of her times, thus become part of a new text which distinguishes itself from that literary tradition and demands a different mode of reading. Rather than focusing on the significance of her speech *qua* performance, scholars have tended to focus on its suggestions of lust, moral import, rhetorical construction and literary allusions. They have thus variously demonstrated how Francesca's words belong to a cultural or ethical context before belonging to her, thus making her a truly ventriloquised character. In particular, the ways in which Francesca favours 'constructions in which Love is subject and she is the passive object' have been interpreted morally, as 'reflect[ing] her sinful refusal of moral agency, her refusal to fashion herself as a Christian agent'.[43]

And yet, for all the attention Francesca's refusal of moral agency has received, nothing has been made of the fact that the only verb of which the woman is the singular and active subject in the canto is the keyword of the *Commedia*'s greatest tales: the verb '"dirò"' ['I will say'] (126). First used in the *Commedia* by Dante himself in this form (*Inf.*, I. 9), the verb is taken up by such illustrious men as Virgil (*Inf.*, II. 50), Ugolino (*Inf.*, XXXIII. 15), Buonconte (*Purg.*, V. 103), Thomas Aquinas (*Par.*, XI. 40) and Cacciaguida (*Par.*, XVI. 86, 124).[44] Francesca's 'dirò' stands out for a number of reasons. It is the only feminine voice among these masculine utterances, and the only direct speech among the silent queens 'di cui si legge' [of whom one reads] (58). Further, while the plurals '"noi udiremo e parleremo"' ['we, as we hear, we, as we speak, assent'] (95) and 'queste parole da lor ci fur porte' [these words, borne on to us from them, were theirs] (108) initially draw attention to Paolo's presence, Dante's address '"Francesca, i tuoi martìri"' ['Francesca [...] your suffering'] (116) and the woman's 'dirò' subtly focus our perception of who is, and who is not, doing the talking.

Francesca's verb is all the more exceptional in the context of medieval testimony. The requirement that a witness be of *bona fide*, in fact, was ubiquitous in the statutes of thirteenth- and fourteenth-century Florence; the *Statuta* of 1415 even stated explicitly that women could only give testimony 'per procuratorem', by proxy,[45] as was customary in a time when 'women's honour was a matter that concerned men'.[46] This practice is all too evident from criminal registers of the time, in which women are routinely identified as the daughters, wives, widows and even lovers of a given man.[47] In light of this historical and intratextual context, it seems extraordinarily significant that Dante decided to represent Francesca – a woman condemned for lust in the form of aggravated adultery, the most notoriously defaming of sins for a woman – as the first of the damned proper to speak out for herself. Significantly, she is never actively interrupted by any authoritative male voice, be it the pilgrim's, the narrator's or, importantly, her lover's, who is silently present at the scene of the testimony.[48]

Most strikingly, Francesca takes care to help Dante on his own journey by encouraging him to become a witness in turn. With an incidental remark in the line '"che, *come vedi*, ancor non m'abbandona"' ['that, as you see, he does not leave me yet'] (105), the lady entreats him to bear witness to her testimony. In this role, the pilgrim listens to her first speech in its entirety, pauses (109–11), then appeals to her respectfully, calling her by name (116). At the end of her second speech, his fainting ends the canto not only on a note of emotional involvement, as has been recognised, but also, inevitably, of suspended judgement (139–42). Paolo, though present, remains silent all the way through the episode, making the contrast with Francesca's storytelling all the more powerful. Through the first of many gender reversals in the *Commedia*, Francesca takes up the role of main witness while the men in the canto learn to listen.

Francesca's speech works on multiple levels. Although the content and form of Francesca's words have attracted morally conservative readers through the ages, the performance of her speech is radically progressive; it allows her on the one hand to testify to a historical legal norm and practice that considered female testimony valueless, and on the other to rebel against such norms through the speech-act, 'dirò' (126). In *Inferno* V, Francesca is portrayed as having her say, as having borne witness to her story in a metaphorical court, and thus as placing her direct speech at the origins of the history of her reception. Here we are, 'reading her' and discussing her lustfulness, her moral failures and her provincial taste in literature. But as we are busy discussing such questions history vindicates this character's greatest achievement – even as, or precisely because, we take it for granted. Francesca is represented as telling us her story in the first person, eschewing on the one hand anonymity and on the other hand other people's appropriations of her story. She is the first witness of the *Commedia* and she is a woman.

Conclusion

In conclusion, the depiction of lust in the three *cantiche* displays four women characters, Semiramis, Francesca, Pasiphae and Cunizza, surrounded by courtly poetry/poets and encircled by issues of reading, witnessing and judging. In creating stark contrasts and keen alliances between sexual transgression and the legal norm, bestiality and courtly poetry, and by nuancing, problematising and gendering the question of legal witnessing, Dante brings to light both the instability and the productivity of the concept of truth telling. Importantly, Francesca's mock trial and her witnessing, with all its *chiaroscuro*, function as a model for Dante's own witnessing and swearing by his poem: a weak, improbable, vernacular witnessing, yet performative not of its own truth, but of the nuances of writing and reading. In so doing such witnessing points out that the poetic performativity of truthfulness is a slippery concept that has little to do with moral or theological truth, and that it is fully in the hands of a rather unstable judge: the reader.

Notes

1. On Dante's realism and truth-claims, and the episode of Geryon specifically, see Teodolinda Barolini, *The Undivine Comedy: Detheologizing Dante* (Princeton: Princeton University Press, 1992), 48–73. Translations of Dante's poem are from *The Divine Comedy*, trans. and ed. Robin Kirkpatrick, 3 vols (London: Penguin, 2006–7).

2. 'Le droit savant insiste bien sur l'importance du serment que prête le témoin: *"dictum testis sine iuramento nullius est momenti"'* [Learned law firmly insisted on the importance of the oath sworn by the witness: "the words of the witness carry no weight unless sworn by oath"] (Jean-Philippe Lévy, 'Le Problème de la preuve dans les droits savants du Moyen Age', in *Recueils de la Société Jean Bodin pour l'histoire comparative des institutions. La Preuve* 2, 38 vols (Bruxelles: Éditions de la Librairie encyclopédique, 1964), XVII, 137–67 (147).

3. The practice of swearing by a book was common in liturgical, juridical and political contexts; the book in question was invariably the 'sacred text' of the Gospels. Even when undertaken in strictly regulated environments this practice was not uncontroversial among theologians and medieval canon lawyers. See Lisania Giordano, 'Iuramentum sive sacramentum: prassi giuridico-sacrale in Gregorio Magno', *Annali della Facoltà di Scienze della Formazione* 2 (2003): 99–108; Jonathan Michael Gray, *Oaths in the English Reformation* (Cambridge: Cambridge University Press, 2012), 17–50; Eyal Poleg, *Approaching the Bible in Medieval England* (Manchester: Manchester University Press, 2013), 59–107.

4. The legal nature of this passage is outlined by the *Ottimo Commento, ad loc*. All references to commentaries of the *Commedia* are taken from the 'Dartmouth Dante Project' (DDP), available online at: https://dante.dartmouth.edu.

5. Interestingly, in *Par.* XXV, the lines 'il poema sacro | al quale ha posto mano e cielo e terra' [this sacred work, | to which both Earth and Heaven have set their hands] (1–2) may also allude to the two fundamental elements of medieval oath-taking, the sacred text and its touching, also highlighted by some legal records: 'their sacrality asserted by the adjective "sacrosanct" (*seintz/sacrosanctis*); they further emphasise the physical (*corporaliter/corporament*) touch with the book' (Poleg, 77).

6. For the layers of reading and interpretation in *Inferno* V, see Elena Lombardi, *The Wings of the Doves: Love and Desire in Dante and Medieval Culture* (Montreal: McGill-Queen's University Press, 2012).

7. For a broader discussion of these themes in *Inferno* V see Elena Lombardi, '"Che libito fe' licito in sua legge." Lust and Law, Reason and Passion in Dante', in *Dantean Dialogues. Engaging with the Legacy of Amilcare Iannucci*, ed. Maggie Kilgour and Elena Lombardi (Toronto: University of Toronto Press, 2013), 125–54. For traces of the poetic love discourse, see Teodolinda Barolini, 'Dante and Cavalcanti (On Making Distinctions in Matters of Love): *Inferno* V in its Lyric Context', *Dante Studies* 116 (1998): 31–63 (42); for the *Song of Songs* see Lombardi, *Wings of the Doves*, 197–200.

8. For lust in the Middle Ages see Carla Casagrande and Silvana Vecchio, *I sette vizi capitali. Storia dei peccati nel medioevo* (Turin: Einuadi, 2000), 149–72; Bonnie Kent, 'On the Track of Lust: *Luxuria*, Ockham, and the Scientists', in *In the Garden of Evil: The Vices and Culture in the Middle Ages*, ed. Richard Newhauser (Toronto: Pontifical Institute of Medieval Studies, 2005), 349–70; Pierre J. Payer, *The Bridling of Desire: Views of Sex in the Late Middle Ages* (Toronto: University of Toronto Press, 1993); Simon Blackburn, *Lust* (Oxford: Oxford University Press, 2004). For medical aspects of lust, see Danielle Jacquard and Claude Alexandre Thomasset, *Sexuality and Medicine in the Middle Ages* (Princeton: Princeton University Press, 1988), 116–38; Massimo Ciavolella, *La malattia d'amore dall'antichità al Medioevo* (Rome: Bulzoni, 1976), and 'L'amore e la medicina medievale', in *Guido Cavalcanti tra i suoi lettori*, ed. Maria Luisa Ardizzone (Florence: Cadmo, 2003), 93–102; and Natascia Tonelli, *Fisiologia della passione. Poesia d'amore e medicina da Cavalcanti a Boccaccio* (Florence: Galluzzo, 2015). For the legal aspect of lust, see James A. Brundage, *Law, Sex and Christian Society in the Middle Ages* (Aldershot: Variorum, 1993).

9. Brundage, 374–77.

10. Teodolinda Barolini, 'Dante's Sympathy for the Other', *Critica del Testo* 14.1 (2011): 177–204.

11. Teodolinda Barolini, 'Dante and Francesca da Rimini: Realpolitik, Romance, Gender', in *Dante and the Origins of Italian Literary Culture* (New York: Fordham University Press, 2006), 304–32; Amilcare Iannucci, 'Forbidden Love: Metaphor and History (*Inferno* V)', in *Dante: Contemporary Perspectives*, ed. Amilcare Iannucci (Toronto: University of Toronto Press, 1997), 94–112.

12. The variant 'libito' or 'libido' in this line (see DDP) is an interesting case of a variant that is not a variant. In this context 'libito' (one's whim) is indeed libidinous ('libido').

13. See Jacopo della Lana, DDP, *ad loc.*

14. For Semiramis in Dante and in the Middle Ages, see Irene Samuel, 'Semiramis in the Middle Age: The History of a Legend', *Medievalia et Humanistica* 2 (1944): 32–44; Marianne Shapiro, 'Semiramis in *Inferno* V', *Romance Notes* 16 (1975): 455–6; Iannucci, 'Forbidden Love'; Andrew Scheil, *Babylon Under Western Eyes. A Study of Allusion and Myth* (Toronto: University of Toronto Press, 2016); Alyson Beringer, *The Sight of Semiramis: Medieval and Early Modern Narratives of the Babylonian Queen* (Tempe: Arizona Center for Medieval and Renaissance Studies, 2016).

15. Paulus Orosius, *Historiarum adversum paganos libri VII* (Turnhout: Brepols, 2010), in *The Library of Latin Texts. Series B*: http://clt.brepolis.net/LLTA/pages/TextSearch.aspx?key=POROS0571 (accessed 25 March 2019); translation ours.

16. Scheil, 23–6 and 126–31.

17. See the early commentaries on DDP, *ad loc.*, on Semiramis's extraordinary power and multifaceted lust. On the relation between her power and her lust, see especially the *Ottimo commento*.

18. On Pasiphae as adultress, see, for instance, Francesco da Buti (DDP, *ad loc.*). Dante recalls the story of Pasiphae also in *Inferno* XII, where the Minotaur is described as 'l'infamïa di Creti […] | che fu concetta ne la falsa vacca' [the infamy of Crete, | spawned in the womb of Pasiphae's fake heifer] (12–13). Significantly, *infamia* is the most common legal result of sexual (and other) offences – often leading to the moral disavowal of a witness. See Brundage, 207.

19. Benvenuto da Imola, *ad loc.*, notes the connection with Semiramis.

20. Renate Blumenfeld-Kosinski, 'The Scandal of Pasiphae: Narration and Interpretation in the *Ovide moralisé*', *Modern Philology* 93 (1996): 307–26; and Maria Maurer, 'The Trouble with Pasiphaë: Engendering a Myth at the Gonzaga Court', in *Receptions of Antiquity: Constructions of Gender in European Art, 1300–1600*, ed. Alison Poe and Marice Rose (Leiden: Brill, 2015), 199–229. For Pasiphae in Dante and her Ovidian intertexts, see Manuele Gragnolati, '*Inferno* V', in *Lectura Dantis Bononiensis*, ed. Emilio Pasquini and Carlo Galli, 7 vols (Bologna: Bononia University Press, 2012), II, 7–22 (17–19).

21. Indeed Servius uses Pasiphae as an example of the difference between *historia* and *fabula*, *fabula* being, like Pasiphae's story, 'against nature' (Servius, *Ad Aen.* 1.235).

22. Brundage, 473.

23. On Minos's parodic function: Lanfranco Caretti, 'Eros e castigo (*Inferno* V)' [1951], in *Antichi e moderni: Studi di letteratura italiana* (Turin: Einaudi, 1976), 7–30 (7); Gragnolati, 7–12.

24. L'Ottimo, 3rd edn, *ad Inf.*, V. 5–6 sees these lines as indicating 'tre atti judiciarii: examinatione, judicio, executione': investigation, the trial itself and the sentence. P. G. Berthier, *ad Inf.*, V. 9–12, demonstrates the juridical connotations of the expression 'conoscitor de le peccata' and relates it to Dante, *Monarchia*, I. x. 3: '*cum alter de altero* cognoscere *non possit*' [And since neither can judge the other]. The juridical terminology has been variously highlighted by the following commentators: Gregorio di Siena; Tommaso Casini and S. A. Barbi; Natalino Sapegno; Daniele Mattalia; Siro Chimenz; Anna Maria Chiavacci Leonardi, DDP, *ad loc.*; as well as by Teodolinda Barolini, 'Minos's Tail: The Labor of Devising Hell (*Aeneid* 6.431 and *Inferno* 5.1–24)', now in *Dante and the Origins of Italian Literary Culture* (New York: Fordham University Press, 2006), 132–50 (139).

25. Giovanni Livi, *Dante: suoi primi cultori, sua gente in Bologna* (Bologna: Licinio Cappelli, 1918), 26–7.

26. For the warlike background of *Inferno* V see Elena Lombardi, '"Per aver pace coi seguaci sui": Civil, Religious and Erotic Peace in *Inferno* V', in *War and Peace in Dante*, ed. John C. Barnes and Daragh O'Connell (Dublin: Four Courts Press, 2015), 173–93.

27. As in *Statuto del Podestà* [1325], found in *Statuti della Repubblica Fiorentina*, ed. Romolo Caggese, rev. G. Pinto, F. Salvestrini, A. Zorzi, 2 vols (Florence: Olschki, 1999), vol.2, III, xlv, 190.

28. Teodolinda Barolini, 'Dante and Francesca da Rimini', 304.

29. Iannucci, 'Forbidden Love'.

30. A little overzealously, Guido identifies five such *sententiae* in Francesca's speech ('*Autor in istis VIIII rithimis V sententias ponit*'), among them the famous one-liners 'Amor ch'al cor gentil ratto s'apprende' [Love, who so fast brings flame to generous hearts] (100) and 'Amor ch'a nullo amato amar perdona' [Love, who no loved one pardons love's requite] (103) (Guido da Pisa, 1327–8, *ad Inf.*, V. 100–8). At lines 121–3 Guido finds a sixth *sententia*: the Virgilian allusion

'Nessun maggior dolore | che ricordarsi del tempo felice | ne la miseria' [There is no sorrow greater | than, in times of misery, to hold at heart | the memory of happiness].

31. In addition to Guido da Pisa, see Benvenuto da Imola, *ad Inf.*, V. 103–5; Cristoforo Landino, *ad Inf.*, V. 100–6; Trifon Gabriele, *ad Inf.*, V. 100; Bernardo Daniello, *ad Inf.*, V. 100.

32. Benvenuto da Imola, *ad Inf.*, V. 103–5. See Patrick Boyde, *Perception and Passion in Dante's 'Comedy'* (Cambridge: Cambridge University Press, 1993), 298.

33. Barolini reflects on this practice in 'Dante and Francesca da Rimini', 312–13.

34. Justin Steinberg, *Dante and the Limits of the Law* (Chicago: University of Chicago Press, 2013), 17.

35. Steinberg, 17.

36. Anna Esposito, 'Adulterio, concubinato, bigamia: testimonianze dalla normativa statutaria dello Stato pontificio (secoli XIII–XVI)', in *Trasgressioni: Seduzione, concubinato, adulterio, bigamia (XIV–XVIII secolo)*, ed. by Silvana Seidel Menchi and Diego Quaglioni (Bologna: il Mulino, 2004), 21–42 (26–7).

37. Trevor Dean, *Crime and Justice in Late Medieval Italy* (Cambridge: Cambridge University Press, 2007), 138.

38. Jacopo della Lana, *ad Inf.*, V. 115–20; L'Ottimo, *ad Inf.*, V. 70–1; Johannis de Serravalle, *ad Inf.*, V. 91–3. In the scale of sexual offences, generally quite fluid, incest was often considered more serious than adultery and only one step removed from sodomy. Guido da Pisa and L'Ottimo make explicit reference to this categorisation (Guido da Pisa, *ad Inf.*, V. 37 and L'Ottimo, initial note to *Inf.* V). See also Vern L. Bullough, 'Medieval Concepts of Adultery', *Arthuriana*, 7.4 (1997): 5–15 (11–12).

39. Lino Pertile, 'Mal d'amore', in *La punta del disio. Semantica del desiderio nella Commedia* (Florence: Cadmo, 2005), 39–58.

40. Maria Serena Mazzi, 'Cronache di periferia dello Stato fiorentino: Reati contro la morale nel primo Quattrocento', *Studi storici* 27 (1986): 609–35 (614).

41. Esposito, 28. See also Riccardo Comba, '"Apetitus libidinis coherceatur". Strutture demografiche, reati sessuali e disciplina dei comportamenti nel Piemonte tardomedievale', *Studi storici*, 27 (1986): 529–76 (552) and Ignazio Baldelli, *Dante e Francesca* (Florence: Olschki, 1999), 36–7.

42. L'Ottimo, *ad Inf.*, V. 70–1. Almost all fourteenth-century commentators unequivocally place the adultery in Francesca's bedroom (*camera*). See also Baldelli, 36–8; and Pier Angelo Perotti, 'Caina attende', *L'Alighieri* n.s. 1–2 (1993): 129–34 (129).

43. Barolini, 'Dante and Cavalcanti', 32–3, and 'Dante and Francesca', 313.

44. On the role of the future tense in the *Commedia*, see Nicolò Crisafi, *Dante's Masterplot and the Alternative Narrative Models in the 'Commedia'* (Unpublished DPhil thesis, University of Oxford, 2018), chapter 3.

45. *Statuta Populi et Communis Florentiae, publica auctoritate collecta, castigata et praeposita, anno Salutis MCCCCXV*, 3 vols (Florence [Freiburg]: Michaelem Kluch, 1778), I, III, ix, 118: 'Quod nulla mulier debeat per se, sed per procuratorem agere in causa civili' [That no woman may represent herself in a civil case, but by proxy]. This requirement effectively excluded any woman who lived by herself, was foreign or resorted to prostitution.

46. Guido Ruggiero, '"Più che la vita caro": Onore, matrimonio, e reputazione femminile nel tardo Rinascimento', *Quaderni storici* 66 (1987): 753–75.

47. Comba, 541.

48. On the question of Paolo's voice, see Guglielmo Gorni, 'Francesca e Paolo. La voce di lui', *Intersezioni* 16 (1996): 383–9.

5

More than an Eye for an Eye: Dante's Sovereign Justice

Justin Steinberg

The manner in which the souls are punished in the *Commedia* seems to indicate a symbolic relationship between transgression and punishment.[1] More often than not, the punishment assumes the form of a brutal literalisation of the respective sin, so that the damned are tormented by manifestations of their own externalised psychological states. In life, the adulterous Paolo and Francesca were figuratively blown to and fro by the 'storm' of their uncontrolled passions; in Hell, a literal storm now blows them round without end.

It has become a commonplace in the field of Dante Studies to describe this 'alignment' of punishment and sin as the *contrapasso* – a neologism in Italian and the final word of *Inferno* XXVIII.[2] Yet critics' deployment of the term *contrapasso* as a descriptive category is of relatively recent vintage. When early commentators gloss this rare Latinism, a *hapax legomenon* in Dante's text, they do not extend its purview beyond canto XXVIII.[3] For example, Guido da Pisa limits the function of *contrapasso* (defined as 'sicut fecit, ita recepit' [as the person did, so he or she receives]) to Bertran de Born's punishment, since dividing persons joined through the bonds of friendship or family was by law a capital offence ('capite puniendus' [punishable by execution]).[4] For Guido this correspondence between punishment and crime was part of the text's literal meaning. Similarly, Pietro Alighieri distinguishes the 'fittingness' of the punishments in *Inferno* XXVIII – the fact that the 'pena sit conformis delicto' [the punishment conforms with the wrongdoing] – from other infernal punishments, which he interprets 'per allegoriam' [allegorically].[5]

We have to wait until the nineteenth century for commentators gradually to universalise this instance of the term *contrapasso* into a general 'law' of the poem by applying it to all the punishments of *Inferno* (and eventually to those of *Purgatorio* as well). Yet in recent decades scholars have begun to re-examine the one-size-fits-all model of the *contrapasso*, critiquing the 'allegorismo a oltranza' [extreme allegorism] necessary to make Dante's poetics of punishment conform to any given scheme.[6] Several critics have even called into question the identification of the *contrapasso* with Dante's conception of justice or with divine justice *tout court*. These scholars demonstrate that the *contrapasso* was commonly associated in contemporary scholastic thought with the *lex talionis* and the 'eye-for-an-eye' justice of the Old Testament.[7] As a consequence, they argue, Dante intends readers to interpret the *contrapasso* critically. It reflects the fallen, 'rigida giustizia' [rigid justice] (*Inf.*, XXX. 70) of the infernal city of Dis, a legalistic dystopia utterly lacking in mercy.

I would like to add my voice to this swell of critical reappraisals of the *contrapasso*, but with an important distinction. While previous scholarship has contrasted infernal punishment with divine mercy, I will focus on the tensions that arise in *Inferno* XXVIII between public and private conceptions of justice. As I hope to make clear, the problem for Dante is not that the *contrapasso* is too harsh but that, for the most extreme crimes, it is not harsh enough. Its tit-for-tat justice fails to take into account the sacrilege committed against God's public majesty. For transgressing the divine sovereign's commandments – irrespective of the damages owed private individuals – the damned must pay back more than measure for measure.

In this essay I will argue that we should be wary of referring a-critically to Dante's art of justice as the *contrapasso* for the following reasons: 1) In Dante's sources, the *contrapassum* always denotes a limited, overly narrow conception of justice; it is the imperfect justice of the Other (the justice of the Pythagoreans for Aristotle, the justice of the Jews for Albertus Magnus and Thomas Aquinas). 2) The limits of justice based on simple 'reciprocation' reside in its inherently private nature; the *contrapassum* fails to encompass public crimes, crimes against the sovereign and the body politic. 3) Consequently, when Bertran describes his punishment as a 'contrapasso', he fails to recognise the public nature of his sin and those of the other sowers of discord. 4) The *contrapasso* should not be considered the 'law' of Dante's justice since he evokes it precisely to demonstrate its limits.

I do not want to deny, of course, that some mechanism of poetic justice operates throughout the *Inferno*. Clearly, it does. I simply want to reconsider the prevailing belief that Dante waits until *Inferno* XXVIII to reveal that 'the punishment should fit the crime' – especially since he has already provided readers with ample illustrations of this principle earlier in the poem. Rather than merely offering a definition, Dante introduces the *contrapasso* at this point in order to probe the elusive nature of the 'fittingness' involved in his poetics of punishment. Above all, Dante makes a case here for a savvy and judicious deployment of discretion rather than the application of a prescribed rule. The sowers of discord are crucial to his case – not because they are exemplars of the *contrapasso*, but because they demonstrate the need to go beyond it.

The exceptional punishment of Dante's sowers of discord

Inferno XXVIII describes the punishments of the eighth sub-circle or *bolgia* of Malebolge, the eighth circle of Hell in which the sins of fraud are punished. The damned in this particular valley of Malebolge are condemned as 'sowers of scandal and schism' (*Inf.*, XXVIII. 35) for their instigation of civil and religious strife. In one of the most violent episodes of the poem, a sword-wielding demon ritually mutilates these naked sinners, making a series of purposeful and geometric cuts each time they pass by. Just as they split the corporate bodies of church and state, so their own bodies are now cleaved.

While in the other circles of Hell Dante often leaves the correspondence between sin and punishment to the reader's imagination, in this circle he explains it twice. First, at the beginning of the canto, a horribly mutilated Mohammed pronounces the general rule: "'E tutti li altri che tu vedi qui, | seminator di scandolo e di scisma | fuor vivi, e però son fessi così'" ['and all the others you see here were sowers of scandal and schism while they were alive, and therefore are they cloven in this way'] (*Inf.*, XXVIII. 34–6). Then, at the end of the canto, the troubadour poet Bertran de Born presents his punishment as an exemplary case. For having divided the young prince from his father, Henry II of England – the *head* of the kingdom – Bertran is condemned to carry his own severed head in his hands. Bertran's trunk raises his head up toward Dante and Virgil, concluding the canto with an epigraphic description of his infernal sentence:

> 'Perch' io parti' così giunte persone,
> partito porto il mio cerebro, lasso!
> dal suo principio ch'è in questo troncone.
>   Così s'osserva in me lo contrapasso'.

(*Inf.*, XXVIII. 140–2)

['Because I divided persons so joined, I carry my brain divided, alas, from its origin which is in this trunk. | Thus you observe in me the counter-suffering'.]

The relationship between the sin and punishments in this canto is thus expressed with perfect clarity. It is underlined logically by the causal conjunctions 'però' and 'perché' and grammatically by the correspondence between the passive 'partito' to the active 'parti'.

Dante thus appears to have chosen the clearest possible examples to illustrate the *contrapasso*. Indeed, although readers have long admired Dante's artistry in creating real, fleshed-out characters, the sowers of discord are almost pure personifications, animated emblems. Marched before the eyes of readers, these sinners beckon for their punishments to be read; the constant refrain of the canto is 'vedi' [behold]. When Bertran closes the canto with 'Così s'osserva in me lo contrapasso', the use of the impersonal passive construction 's'osserva' underscores the idea that legibility is the defining characteristic of the countersuffering.

Yet at the very moment that Dante-the-poet appears to define his art of poetic justice, an interpretive breakdown occurs between his character and the desecrated bodies that are paraded before him. Instead of 'reading' the sins as they are literalised on the sinners' bodies, he merely gapes at their wounds, stupefied by the novelty of God's justice. His eyes become 'drunk' with the vision of violence in the canto (*Inf.*, XXIX. 2), and Virgil reprimands him as he continues to stare at the mutilated bodies: '"Che pur guate?"' (*Inf.*, XXIX. 4–6). Dante is literally blocked ('impedito', *Inf.*, XXIX. 28) by the imagery of the sowers of discord, just as the damned are momentarily frozen in awe when they discover that he is still alive.

The punishments of canto XXVIII are in some way exceptional. Dante's character struggles to fit them into the system he has experienced so far, and Virgil notes that Dante has not been mesmerised in this manner by any of the other punishments. Most of all, Bertran himself notes that his case is unprecedented: '"Or vedi,"' he says, '"vedi s'alcuna è grande come questa"' ['now see, […] see if any is as great as this'] (*Inf.*, XXVIII. 130–2). Ironically echoing the personification of weeping Jerusalem in Lamentations, he insists that the punishment is without parallel for its magnitude. It is enormous, literally outside of the norm.

Further, at the beginning of the canto Dante claims that the violent imagery we are about to witness has never been represented before in literature. Drawing on a long tradition of epic violence, he asks readers to perform a gruesome thought experiment: to imagine all the maimed and perforated bodies ever strewn across the battlefield in Apulian territory, from the time of the Trojan colonisers to more recent battles between the forces representing church and empire. If these perforated and maimed bodies, gathered together, were all to display their wounds simultaneously, the surreal montage would not equal, 'aequar', the manner of this sub-circle of Inferno (*Inf.*, XXVIII. 20, 21). In this failed ekphrasis, Dante signals that what he is about to encounter as a character, and represent as a poet, is entirely new.

Why does Dante insist on the singularity of imagery in this canto if it is meant to illustrate the poetics of the poem as a whole? Why choose the unprecedented case of Bertran de Born to exemplify the 'law' of the *contrapasso*? These contradictions are difficult to resolve if we insist on identifying the countersuffering with God's justice. But what if Bertran were wrong about, or at least not aware of, the full significance of his punishment? What if he were using the wrong word?

The *contrapasso* in the thirteenth-century Aristotelian tradition

It is unlikely that we would have extended the *contrapasso* to include all the punishments of *Inferno* if critics had considered its original context in Aristotle's *Nicomachean Ethics* more diligently. Dante's coinage of the *contrapasso* derives from the Latin *contrapassum*, a term that would have been familiar to him from the Latin translation of Aristotle's *Nicomachean Ethics*, where the *contrapassum* denotes a reciprocal suffering or 'passion' that responds to any illicit action: 'If a man should suffer that which he did, right justice would be done.'[8]

Bertran's formula for the *contrapasso* is strikingly similar to this sentence, supposedly uttered by the mythic judge Rhadamanthus. Yet it is almost never mentioned in the secondary literature that Aristotle himself disparages the primitiveness of countersuffering justice; instead he ascribes it to others (namely, the Pythagoreans) and distinguishes it from his more encompassing and flexible conception of rectificatory justice:

> Some think that the *contrapassum* is without qualification just, as the Pythagoreans said; for they defined justice without qualification as *contrapassum*. Now *contrapassum* fits neither distributive nor rectificatory justice – yet people want even the justice of Rhadamanthus to mean this: 'If a man should suffer that which he did, right justice would be done'. For in many cases *contrapassum* and rectificatory justice are not in accord. For example, if a man who holds sovereign power has struck someone, he should not be struck back; and if someone has struck the sovereign, he should not only be struck back but also punished. Moreover, there is quite a difference between voluntary and involuntary actions.[9]

Aristotle specifies here two crucial instances where the *contrapassum* falls short. First, it does not take into consideration what would happen if one of the parties involved in a dispute were a public official. Second, it does not distinguish between voluntary and involuntary actions. These brief remarks on retaliatory justice serve as a transition between the more fleshed-out discussions of distributive and rectificatory justice, and the ensuing section on economic justice.

In distributive justice (*iustitia distributiva*), common goods (such as honour and wealth) are allotted by a central authority to recipients as rewards for their service. Distributive justice is calculated proportionately, according to a ratio guaranteeing that greater service receives greater reward. In rectificatory justice – sometimes also called corrective or directive justice (*iustitia directiva*) – a judge restores the former equality between two parties before it was upset by force or fraud. To 'correct' or 'rectify' the situation, the amount of damages owed is calculated arithmetically, rather than proportionately, and this sum is subtracted from the offending party and added to the injured one. Rather than negotiating the aftermath of a transgression, economic or reciprocal justice deals instead with commodity exchange (equalising goods, not people). Economic justice determines, for example, how many shoes a shoemaker must give a builder in exchange for one house. In an economic context, *contrapassum* – understood now as proportionate reciprocation rather than arithmetic retaliation – plays a critical role in consolidating the social ties among citizens.

In contrast to the extended discussion of the proportionate application of the *contrapassum* in economic exchanges,[10] Aristotle's treatment of the retributive aspects of the countersuffering is little more than an aside. Modern commentators' tendency to pass over it is thus understandable. Medieval commentators, on the other hand, greatly expanded upon the Greek philosopher's brief remarks – no doubt in large part because they finally touch upon questions of intentionality, guilt and public order otherwise absent from his discussion of particular justice. Aristotle's critique of *contrapassum* justice was crucial for these scholars (and subsequently, I will argue, for Dante), because in a treatise dedicated almost entirely to private forms of reparation – the justice of lawsuits and compensation – it is the only place where Aristotle hints at the necessity of a public penal order, the only place he speaks of *punishing* a subject rather than of *rectifying* a situation.

In his first commentary on the *Nicomachean Ethics*, Albertus Magnus's concise gloss on the discussion of the *contrapassum* introduces several issues that will remain fundamental for all future interpretations of Aristotle's text. First, he categorically denies the notion that the *contrapassum* is synonymous with justice without qualification.[11] Second, he associates the *contrapassum* with the 'eye for an eye' justice of the Old Testament as expressed in Exodus. Most importantly for our purposes, Albertus claims that, in the case of the citizen striking the sovereign, damage is done not only to the ruler as a private individual, but also to the impersonal political authority that he embodies:

> If the sovereign (*princeps*) strikes someone, it is not necessary for justice that he be struck back, because the striking of one and the other is not of equal weight. For in the case of the sovereign, it derogates his authority, which he holds over the state (*rem publicam*). Similarly, if someone strikes the sovereign, it is not right that he is only struck back, but he must additionally be punished by death.[12]

Although Albertus might seem to be simply paraphrasing the original text at this point, Aristotle never explicitly invokes the state's authority, nor does he make any mention of the death penalty.

In his second, more expansive commentary on the *Ethics*, Albertus uses his discussion of countersuffering to provide a primer on legitimate and illegitimate violence. Because a ruler possesses the general legal authority to use violence against his subjects, he may strike without being struck back. Moreover, regardless of the legality of his actions, if he were to be punished in kind it would do great damage to the common good as it would 'enervate' his authority, an authority that malefactors need to fear if it is to be an effective deterrent.[13]

In the case where a citizen strikes the sovereign, Albertus appeals directly to the Roman law of treason, the *crimen laesae majestatis*.

> Moreover, if the sovereign should be struck, one incurs the crime of *laesae majestatis* on account of the harm caused to the common good, which the legislator meant to protect more than [to protect] the sovereign himself. If, therefore, whoever has struck the sovereign receives a countersuffering (*contrapatiatur*) of the same kind and quality that he inflicted on the sovereign, the crime of *laesae majestatis* is not compensated, only that against a private person. And this is not just.[14]

Striking the sovereign violates the majesty of his 'second', sublime body, and it is for this offence against the public good that the culprit must be punished 'forte multo plus' [much more strongly] than the mere 'tantum quantum' of the private countersuffering. Albertus further specifies that that those who have violated the corporate body of the state should be decapitated and dismembered ('capitis vel membri detruncatione') – the very punishment inflicted on the schismatics in *Inferno* XXVIII.

In his commentary on the *Nicomachean Ethics*, Aquinas for the most part follows the arguments of his teacher and joins him in refuting the 'false' and 'erroneous' opinion that the *contrapassum* equates to justice in all cases.[15] However, in anticipating a potential objection to Aristotle's text, he introduces a crucial distinction between property damage and personal injury. Aquinas asks how are we to reconcile Aristotle's treatment of the magistrate striking the private citizen, and vice versa, with his earlier statement that, in matters of corrective justice, all are equal before the law? Why does the Philosopher reintroduce personal status into his discussion at this point? Aquinas explains that the question of rank remains relevant only in assessing the objective amount of damage incurred. With regard to external things, such as money, the status of the parties does not matter. But clearly worse damage is done and greater compensation needs to be paid when someone strikes the ruler, since 'that injury is done not only to the person of the ruler, but also to the whole commonweal (*totam rempublicam*)'.[16]

In Aquinas's oft-cited (and oft-misunderstood) discussion of the *contrapassum* in *Summa Theologiae*, he further elaborates on the potential limitations of countersuffering justice, if narrowly conceived (i.e., arithmetically rather than proportionately).[17] As in his previous discussions of personal injury, he correlates the *contrapassum* with the *lex talionis*, citing Exodus 21. 23–4, 'He shall render life for life, eye for eye'. He also argues, as before, that whoever strikes a ruler needs to be punished much more severely ('multo gravius') than when the victim is an ordinary citizen.[18]

But then Aquinas revises his earlier comments about property damages, claiming that the *contrapassum* is an inadequate measure for assessing these as well. If a thief is punished according to reciprocal justice and pays back exactly what he took, the state will not receive its due as co-victim:

> In like manner when a man despoils another of his property against the latter's will, the action surpasses the passion if he be merely deprived of that thing, because the man who caused another's loss himself would lose nothing, and so he is punished by making restitution many times over (*multiplicius restituat*) because not only did he injure a private person, but also the common weal, the security of whose protection he has infringed (*quia etiam non solum damnificavit personam privatam, sed rempublicam, eius tutelae securitatem infringendo*).[19]

The strict reversal of passion for action fails to account for the damage done to the common good; a residual needs to be paid for the transgression itself. This supplementary punishment is owed in extreme crimes which directly target the state's symbolic power, such as when someone strikes the sovereign. Even in lesser crimes such as theft, the *res publica* possesses a claim that it may extract in the form of punishment 'many times over'. In this final formulation, Aquinas echoes the jurists of his time, who were beginning to recognise that even interpersonal crimes threatened the state's authority.

Bertran de Born's mistake: the *contrapasso* as limited justice

As I hope now should be clear, the sowers of discord are punished for exactly the type of crime that the *contrapassum* fails to encompass. They have harmed not only private individuals but the public good – namely the sanctified bodies of church, republic, city and kingdom. For such acts of sacrilege, their punishment exceeds the tit-for-tat justice of the *lex talionis* and they pay an extra 'debt' owed to the state in the currency of their body parts. In short, the sinners in this canto need to lose *more* than an eye for an eye.

Since the public crimes of the schismatics so clearly exemplify the type of case for which the countersuffering was insufficient, why then does Dante have Bertran classify his punishment as a *contrapasso*? One response might be that the definition is ironic: that Bertran remains unaware of the full implications of his sin even in the afterlife. He takes responsibility for pitting Henry II against the young prince as private 'persone' (*Inf.*, XXVIII. 139), but not for the damage this feud caused the body politic.

In fact, the sowers of discord engage in a *realpolitik* that belies their scepticism about abstract corporations. They do not believe any reality lies behind the metaphor of the body politic. Only brute actions have a head: 'Capo ha cosa fatta' (*Inf.*, XXVIII. 107). As an ironic punishment for such nominalism, the demon cuts their bodies into parts which remain nevertheless formally whole (and thus capable of perpetually healing and being reinjured). Indeed, what is uncanny about Bertran's punishment is not so much that he has lost his head, but that his detached parts still function as an organic unit.

Of course, when Aristotle and the scholastics criticise the limits of the countersuffering, they are talking about human justice, not divine justice. Bertran is punished in canto XXVIII because he broke not human laws, but God's commandments. He did not merely harm the Crown; he disobeyed the Divine Sovereign. It is only by analogy that we can compare Bertran's mortal sin against God's order to a public crime against the state's majesty. That said, the analogy possesses an ancient theological pedigree and was often evoked to justify the everlasting torments of the damned.[20]

In the *City of God*, for example, Augustine responds to the apparent excessiveness of eternal damnation by evoking the analogous earthly punishments of slavery, exile and capital punishment. In contrast with lesser penalties, these punishments last a lifetime (the earthly equivalent of eternity) because they definitively sever the culprit from the human community:

> As for the criminal who suffers capital punishment for some grave offence, do the laws estimate his punishment according to the time that it takes to kill him, which is very short, and ignore the fact that he is removed forever from the company of the living? Thus the removal of men from this mortal community by the punishment of the first death corresponds to the removal from the Immortal City by punishment of the second death. For just as the laws of the former city have no power to recall to that community one who has been put to death, so, when a man has been condemned to the second death, the laws of that other City cannot call him back to life eternal.[21]

In the *Summa Contra Gentiles*, Aquinas similarly compares the eternal exile of the damned with the physical and social deaths incurred for treasonous crimes against the state:

> Natural equity seems to demand that each person be deprived of the good against which he acts, for by this action he renders himself unworthy of such a good. So it is that, according to civil justice, he who offends against the state is deprived completely of association with the state, either by death or by perpetual exile. Nor is any attention paid to the extent of time involved in his wrongdoing, but only to what he sinned against.[22]

For both Augustine and Aquinas, crimes that threaten the very foundation of the secular order must be punished extraordinarily. This form of discretionary punishment reserved for the *crimen exceptum* serves as a model, in turn, for comprehending divine justice against the damned: whoever violates the immensity of divine majesty earns a punishment that is similarly beyond measure.

In this respect it is not only Bertran who deserves to be punished in excess of the *contrapasso*, but all of the sinners in Hell. Bertran's case is nevertheless especially illustrative. Since he simultaneously betrayed both the earthly and divine monarch, his endlessly repeated capital punishment exemplifies the sovereign justice that rules the entire otherworld. This must be what Guido da Pisa and Pietro Alighieri mean when they categorise the punishments of the schismatics as 'literal' in contrast to the 'allegorical' punishments of the other cantos. The capital punishment of Bertran for his capital crime serves as a focal case for the discretionary punishments that all the damned – as traitors to the divine state – incur.

In conclusion, when we describe the manner in which punishments fit sins in the *Commedia* indiscriminately as a *contrapasso*, we reproduce Bertran's mistake. For Dante and his contemporaries, countersuffering justice was always limited justice – a form of justice particularly ill-equipped to respond to the enormous crime of violating God's majesty.[23] In this light, Dante evokes the *contrapasso* perhaps less to describe the relationship between sin and punishment and more to warn against an overly mechanistic interpretation of this dynamic. That is, critics are right to identify *Inferno* XXVIII as a highly self-reflexive moment in the poem, just not one in which Dante announces the 'law' of his imagined otherworld. On the contrary, Dante makes a case in this valley of Hell for the indispensability of *judgement* when challenged with the unforeseen. Unlike the robotic bureaucrat Minos, both judge and artist must be willing to use their discretion.

Dante realises, of course, that this freedom can easily exceed ethical bounds, just as the Pilgrim's fascination with injured bodies spills over into the next canto. Viewed in the darkest light, the broken bodies of the schismatics display the effects of a kind of judicial activism. In exercising his right to go beyond the limits of the *contrapasso*, Dante thus daringly associates his innovative art with the art of discretionary punishments.[24] For more than we perhaps care to admit, the poet's celebrated originality owes an unspoken debt to the boundless 'creativity' of the modern penal order.

Notes

1. The introduction to this essay is borrowed from my earlier discussion of the *contrapasso* in 'Dante's Justice? A reappraisal of the *contrapasso*', *L'Alighieri* 44 (2014): 59–74.
2. Text and translations from the *Commedia* are based on *The Divine Comedy of Dante Alighieri*, ed. and trans. Robert Durling (New York–Oxford: Oxford University Press, 1996–2011).
3. For a survey of the commentators' glosses on *contrapasso*, see Peter Armour, 'Dante's *Contrapasso*: Contexts and Texts', *Italian Studies* 55.1 (2000): 1–20, and Victoria Kirkham, '*Contrapasso*: The Long Wait to *Inferno* 28', *Modern Language Notes* 127.1 (2012): S1–S12.
4. 'Qui separat alios, seu amicitia seu parentela coniunctos, caput a corpore portat divisum, quia secundum leges talis est capite puniendus. Et sic observatur in eo contrapassus, quia debet recipere id quod fecit' [He who separates others who are joined by either friendship or kinship

carries his head divided from his body, because according to the law such a crime is punishable by execution. And thus the *contrapasso* is observed here, for as the person did, so he or she receives]: Guido da Pisa, *Expositiones et Glose: Declaratio super Comediam Dantis*, from 'Dartmouth Dante Project' (DDP), at: https://dante.dartmouth.edu/.

5. 'Post hec auctor intelligendus est loqui de dictis vulnerationibus harum animarum potius per hanc rationem, quod pena sit conformis delicto, quam per allegoriam' [Hence the author is understood to be speaking about these souls' aforementioned wounds for this reason – that the punishment conforms with the wrongdoing – rather than allegorically]: Pietro Alighieri, *Commentarium* (second redaction), *ad Inf.*, XXVIII. 139–42 (DDP).

6. See Valerio Lucchesi, 'Giustizia divina e linguaggio umano. Metafore e polisemie del contrapasso dantesco', *Studi danteschi* 63 (1991): 53–126, in particular 55. For a variety of perspectives, but in a similarly critical vein, see also Richard Abrams, 'Against the *Contrapasso*: Dante's Heretics, Schismatics and Others', *Italian Quarterly* 27 (1986): 5–19; Peter Armour, 'Dante's *Contrapasso*'; Davide Bolognesi, 'Il contrapasso come chiasma. Appunti su *Inferno* XXVIII', *L'Alighieri* 36 (2010): 5–20; and Kenneth Gross, 'Infernal Metamorphoses: An Interpretation of Dante's "Counterpass"', *Modern Language Notes* 100 (1985): 42–69.

7. See especially Anthony Kimber Cassell, *Dante's Fearful Art of Justice* (Toronto: University of Toronto Press, 1984); Daniela Castelli, 'L'errore rigorista e la "fisica dell'anima" in una *Commedia senza lex talionis*', *Studi danteschi* 78 (2013): 154–95; Giuseppe Mazzotta, 'Metaphor and Justice (*Inferno* XXVIII)', in *Dante's Vision and the Circle of Knowledge* (Princeton: Princeton University Press, 1993), 75–95; and Lino Pertile, 'Canto XXIX: Such Outlandish Wounds', in *Lectura Dantis: 'Inferno'*, ed. Allen Mandelbaum et al. (Berkeley: University of California Press, 1998), 387–91.

8. This is rendered in Latin as 'Si paciatur qui fecit, vindicta recte fit', in Aristotle, 'Ethica Nicomachea: Translatio Roberti Grosseteste Lincolniensis sive "Liber Ethicorum" B. Recensio Recognita', in *Aristoteles Latinus*, vol.XXVI, parts 1–3, fasc.4, ed. R. A. Gauthier (Leiden: Brill; Brussels: Desclée de Brouwer, 1972–4), 462.

9. '*Videbitur* autem aliquibus et *contrapassum* esse simpliciter iustum, ut Pythagorici dixerunt. Determinabant enim simpliciter iustum *contrapassum* alii. Contrapassum autem non congruit, neque in distributivum iustum, neque in directivum, quamvis *voluerit* hoc dicere. Et Radamantis iustum. Si paciatur que fecit, vindicta *recte* fit. Multis enim in locis dissonat; puta si in principatum habens percussit, non oportet repercuti; et si principem percussit, non percuti solum oportet, set et puniri. Adhuc involuntarium et voluntarium differt multum': Aristotle, 'Ethica Nicomachea', 462.

10. Both Armour and Bolognesi make much of Aristotle's economic discussion. Although these treatments are suggestive in their own right, I ultimately feel their emphasis on economic exchange is misplaced given the clearly punitive aspects of the canto. As Aquinas makes clear in *Summa Theologiae*, IIa–IIae, q. 61, a. 4 co., the *contrapassum* most properly applies to personal injury and in a secondary, analogous sense to property damages. Only thirdly is its meaning transferred to voluntary economic exchanges (commutations).

11. '[E]rgo cum ipsi voluerunt, quod iustum universaliter sit contrapassum, sententia eorum falsa fuit': Albertus Magnus, 'Super Ethica Commentum et Quaestiones', V, l; VII, 402, ed. Wilhelm Kübel, in *Opera Omnia*, XIV. I (Münster: Aschendorff, 1968–72), 343.

12. 'Si princeps aliquem percutit, non oportet per iustitiam, ut repercutiatur, quia percussio huius et illius non sunt aequi ponderis, quia in illo derogatur auctoritati, quam princeps habet super rem publicam; et ideo etiam, si aliquis percutiat principem, non oportet, quod tantum percutiatur, sed insuper plectitur capite': Albertus Magnus, 'Super Ethica', p.342.

13. 'Princeps enim percutiens ex auctoritate habet quod percutit: peccat autem in hoc quod non secundum legem percutit: et ideo non tota percussio injusta est: propter quod ad tantum et tale non contrapatitur. Adhuc autem auctoritas est in principe, quam oportet timori esse propter malos quia aliter commune bonum non salvatur enervata auctoritate continentis. In magnum ergo damnum cederet urbanitatis, si princeps contrapateretur': Albert the Great, *Ethica*, V, tr. II, 8, in *Opera Omnia*, ed. Auguste Borgnet, 38 vols (Paris: Vives, 1891), VII, 354b.

14. 'Adhuc si princeps percutiatur, crimen laesae majestatis incurritur: quod fit ex laesione communis boni, quod magis intendit salvare legislator quam proprium. Si ergo qui percussit principem, non nisi tantum e tale contrapatiatur, quale et quantum intulit principi, crimen laesae majestatis non corrigitur, sed tantum privatae personae injuria: hoc autem justum non est': Albert the Great, *Ethica*, 354b–355a.

15. For the 'falsam sententiam' and 'sententiam erroneam' that the *contrapassum* should be un-
qualifiedly equated with justice, see Thomas Aquinas, 'Sententia libri Ethicorum', in *Opera
Omnia*, vol.XLVII (Rome: Editio Leonina, 1882), 5.8.1.1. See also Aquinas's gloss on Aristotle's
example of the magistrate striking and being struck by a private person: 'Circa quarum primam
dicit quod in multis locis talis vindicta invenitur dissonare verae iustitiae, ut si aliquis in prin-
cipatu constitutus percusserit aliquam privatam personam, non requirit hoc iustitia quod princeps repercutiatur, et similiter, si aliquis percutiat principem, oportet quod non solum percutiatur, sed quod etiam gravius puniatur' [With regard to the first reason, he says that in many
situations such vengeance is found to be at odds with true justice, so that if the appointed ruler
strikes a private person, justice does not require that the ruler be struck in return; and similarly, if anyone strikes the ruler, it is necessary that such a person not only be struck but also
punished more severely] : Aquinas, 'Sententia Ethic.', 5.1.8.4, 290a–b.
16. 'Videtur autem hoc esse contra id quod philosophus supra dixerat, quod in iustitia commutativa non attenditur diversa conditio personarum, sed lex utitur omnibus quasi aequalibus.
Sed attendendum est quod ibidem philosophus dixit quod in commutativa iustitia lex attendit
solum ad differentiam nocumenti. Manifestum est autem quod quando nocumentum attenditur circa subtractionem rei exterioris, puta pecuniae, non variatur quantitas nocumenti secundum diversam conditionem personae, sed quando est nocumentum personale, tunc necesse
est quod quantitas nocumenti diversificetur secundum conditionem personae. Manifestum est
enim quod maius est nocumentum cum aliquis percutit principem, per quod non solum personam ipsius sed totam rempublicam laedit, quam cum percutit aliquam privatam personam.
Et ideo non competit iustitiae in talibus simpliciter contrapassum' [However, this seems to contradict what the Philosopher said earlier, that in commutative justice the differing rank of individuals is not taken into account; instead the law treats all as if equals. But it should be noted
that what the Philosopher said there was that in commutative justice, the law considers only
the nature of the damage. It is obvious, though, that when one considers damage resulting
from the taking of property, such as money, the amount of damage does not differ according to
a person's rank, but when the injury is personal, then it is inevitable that the amount of injury
differs according to a person's rank. For it is obvious that there is greater injury when someone
strikes a ruler, than when someone strikes a private person, for the reason that injury is done
not only to the person of the ruler, but also to the whole commonweal. Therefore *contrapassum*
alone is not adequate for justice in such matters]: Aquinas, 'Sententia Ethic.', 5.1.8.5, 290b.
17. Although Dante may not have been familiar with Aquinas's discussion of the *contrapassum* in
the *Summa Theologiae*, I have included it here because it provides the most lucid contemporary
treatment of the distinction between compensatory and punitive damages, which I am arguing
is at the heart of Dante's depiction of the punishments in *Inferno* XXVIII. In addition, it has
become standard practice to cite these passages in modern commentaries on canto XXVIII,
often out of context and without consideration as to whether Aquinas is proposing a solution
or merely raising an objection.
18. 'Et ideo ille qui percutit principem non solum repercutitur, sed multo gravius punitur.' Latin
and English texts from Thomas Aquinas, *The Summa Theologiae of Saint Thomas Aquinas: Latin-English*, trans. the Fathers of the English Dominican Province (Scotts Valley: NovAntiqua,
2010), II.II, q. 61, a. 4, co.
19. 'Similiter etiam cum quis aliquem involuntarium in re sua damnificat, maior est actio quam esset passio si sibi sola res illa auferretur, quia ipse qui damnificavit alium, in re sua nihil damni-
ficaretur. Et ideo punitur in hoc quod multiplicius restituat, quia etiam non solum damnificavit
personam privatam, sed rempublicam, eius tutelae securitatem infringendo.' Aquinas, *Summa
Theologiae*, II.II, q. 61, a. 4, co.
20. In the other direction, justifying harsh treatment for suspects of heresy and treason as rebels
against God's order, see Jacques Chiffoleau, *La Chiesa, il segreto e l'obbedienza* (Bologna: Mulino, 2010), 127–48.
21. Augustine, *City of God*, trans. Henry Bettenson, ed. Gillian R. Evans (London: Penguin, 2003),
XXI.11.2.
22. 'Naturalis aequitas hoc habere videtur, quod unusquisque privetur bono contra quod agit: ex
hoc enim reddit se tali bono indignum. Et inde est quod secundum civilem iustitiam, qui contra
rempublicam peccat, societate republicae privatur omnino, vel per mortem vel per exilium
perpetuum: nec attenditur quanta fuerit mora temporis in peccando, sed quid sit contra quod
peccavit': Thomas Aquinas, *Summa Contra Gentiles* (Rome: Editio Leonina Manualis, 1934),
3.144.4, 402b.

23. See Julien Théry, '"Atrocitas/enormitas". Per una storia della categoria di "crimen enorme" nel basso Medioevo (XII–XV secolo)', trans. Benedetto Borello *Quaderni storici* 44, 131.2 (2009): 329–75. See also these general studies: Jacques Chiffoleau, 'Le crime de majesté, la politique et l'extraordinaire. Note sur les collections érudites de procès de lèse majesté du XVIIè siècle et leurs exemples médiévaux', in *Le procès politique (XIVè-XVIIè siècles): Actes du colloque de Rome (20-22 janvier 2003)*, ed. Yves-Marie Bercé (Rome: Collection de l' École française de Rome, 2007), 577–662; and Edward Peters, '*Crimen exceptum*: The History of an Idea', in *Proceedings of the Tenth International Congress of Medieval Canon Law: Syracuse, New York, 13–18 August 1996*, ed. Kenneth Pennington, Stanley Chodorow and Keith H. Kendal (Vatican City: Biblioteca Apostolica Vaticana, 2001), 137–94.
24. For a more extended discussion of the connection between judicial discretion and poetic licence, see Justin Steinberg, *Dante and the Limits of the Law* (Chicago: University of Chicago Press, 2013), 40–52.

6

'Ritornerò profeta': The *Epistle* of St James and the Crowning of Dante's Patience*

Filippo Gianferrari

a Zyg, *With never-ending gratitude(e nove anni di ritardo)*

Paradiso XXV opens with some of the boldest claims of the whole *Commedia*. Not only does Dante present his poem as a 'sacred work' – in the making of which God too has a role – but he also grants himself the title of *poeta* – a title, it should be noted, that up to this point in the poem had been reserved for the great poets of antiquity. In these lines, moreover, the author expresses the apparent hope of a possible return to Florence. There, by his own authority and with an unspecified *cappello*, he will crown himself in the place of his christening – St John's Baptistery:

> Se mai continga che 'l poema sacro
> al quale ha posto mano e cielo e terra,
> sì che m'ha fatto per molti anni macro,
>   vinca la crudeltà che fuor mi serra
> del bello ovile ov' io dormi' agnello,
> nimico ai lupi che li danno guerra;
>   con altra voce omai, con altro vello
> ritornerò poeta, e in sul fonte
> del mio battesmo prenderò 'l cappello;
>   però che ne la fede, che fa conte
> l'anime a Dio, quivi intra' io, e poi
> Pietro per lei sì mi girò la fronte.

(*Par.*, XXV. 1–12)

[If it ever happen that the sacred poem, to which both Heaven and earth have set their hand, so that for many years it has made me lean, | vanquish the cruelty that locks me out of the lovely sheepfold where I slept as a lamb, an enemy of the wolves that make war on it, | with other voice by then, with other fleece I shall return as poet, and at the font of my baptism I shall accept the wreath: | for there I entered the faith that makes souls known to God, and later Peter so circled my brow because of it.]

Much scholarly effort has focused on how best to interpret the poet's longing for this improbable return to Florence. Recent studies tend to read the poet's hope as sardonic, or as referring to an altogether different dimension outside the realm of human history, whether theological or poetic.[1] However, the meaning of the peculiar crowning indicated by the poet, and of the relationship between poetic glory and the theological virtue of hope, remains a fascinating subject for further enquiry.

Few interpret these problematic lines in light of the biblical subtext suggested by the author himself – the *Epistle* of St James (James from now on), which appears to be the catalyst for this astonishing declaration. The pilgrim's meeting with the Apostle, and their *disputatio* on the theological virtue of hope, occupy the centre of this *canto*, yet James's actual authority appears almost peripheral to it. Although the pilgrim claims to have derived his hope mostly from reading James (*Par.*, XXV. 76–7), he quotes instead other authorities to define this virtue (Peter Lombard's *Sententiae* III. 26. 1; David's Psalms 9. 11; and Isaiah 61. 7). Furthermore, at line 100, St John takes up the last portion of what should be 'St James's canto'. Why, then, St James, and why here?[2]

To shed some light on the subject, this brief essay focuses on the following question: why does Dante call himself a 'poeta' – for the first and only time in the *Commedia* – only a few lines before meeting St James? After examining the reception of James, I turn to the intertextual correspondences whereby Dante weaves some of James's principal teachings into his self-legitimisation as a divinely inspired poet. Unfortunately, limitations of space prevent me from dealing here with the fascinating question of the influence that the medieval pan-European veneration of St James the Greater may have exerted on Dante.[3] The aim of the present work is to explore the relevance of James for the poet's theorisation of his own poetics and ethical justification of his divinely inspired message.[4]

Reframing the Epistle of St James

Dante's familiarity with James is beyond doubt.[5] It should be noted, however, that the poet's first two direct quotations from James occur in *Convivio* IV and that, from then on, references surface with a certain regularity in his other works. This fact suggests that Dante's meditation on this text became ever more urgent, beginning at the time of *Convivio* IV. To grasp the depth and extension of such a meditation, an understanding of James and its medieval reception is in order.

The actual authorship of James and its dating raises more questions than answers, as does the history of its reception in the West.[6] James the Greater, son of Zebedee, was certainly not the author of this letter, which has traditionally been attributed to another apostle, James the Lesser, son of Alpheus.[7] James acquired full Scriptural status in the Roman Church thanks to Augustine's authority and, by Dante's time, had become one of the canonical epistles of the New Testament. Its memorable aphorisms, helpful for moral exhortation, played a considerable role in the development of Christian piety.[8]

James's rather heterogeneous text touches on various moral issues and delivers messages that may at times seem contradictory. In the first paragraph, the Apostle exhorts the faithful to be patient and endure any tribulations in order to become perfect in their faith (1. 2). He then invites his readers to turn in hope towards Heaven in order to obtain wisdom, because 'every best gift, and every perfect gift, is from above, coming down from the Father of lights' (1. 17). Humility and patience, therefore, are necessary for every righteous work of faith. The ultimate test of sincere faith is the works that it produces, as faith without works is dead (2. 26). No-one, however, should presume to make oneself a master for others, as any good works come from God alone and not from human intelligence or eloquence (3. 1). Self-proclaimed masters have only wicked intentions in their hearts and do not possess the true wisdom that comes from above. Instead, their wisdom is 'earthly, sensual, devilish' (3. 15).

In the third paragraph, the Apostle develops his condemnation of vicious masters into a vehement attack against the misuse of the tongue to deceive others and exalt oneself. To discipline the tongue – James maintains – means to be perfect. The tongue is for the whole body like the bit for the horse and the rudder for the ship: no matter how small, it controls the whole person, 'the tongue is indeed a little member, and boasteth great things' (3. 5). The tongue also resembles a tiny, uncontrollable spark: 'behold how small a fire kindleth a great wood. And the tongue is a fire, a world of iniquity' (3. 5–6). James's epistle, therefore, which was traditionally identified with the theological virtue of hope, shows an almost absolute pessimism with regard to the nature of the tongue and the possibility of taming it: 'but the tongue no man can tame, an unquiet evil, full of deadly poison' (3. 8).

James's vision of the tongue, as naturally inclined to evil, exerted a pervasive influence on medieval culture; it became a primary biblical source for most twelfth- and thirteenth-century ethical treatises on the sins of the tongue.[9] Moreover, James played a crucial role in the semiotic representation of the sin of the tongue, as it established a notable variation on the biblical motif of the tongue of fire, by stressing how small a spark the tongue really is – 'Ecce quantus ignis' – and yet how great the blaze it can ignite – 'quam magnam silvam incendit'. This imagery recalls another *sententia* that was overwhelmingly popular from antiquity to the Middle Ages: 'parva saepe scintilla magnum excitavit incendium' [a small spark often kindles a great fire].[10] As several studies have shown, James's imagery and its medieval reception strongly influenced Dante's representation of the *contrapasso* of the eighth *bolgia* – in which Ulysses, Diomedes and Guido da Montefeltro are enclosed by tongues of fire, in punishment for their sinful misuse of eloquence.[11] But this is really only one side of the *Epistle*'s notable influence on Dante's poetics.

Taken at face value, James 3 represented a serious hindrance for anyone who presumed to speak for God, such as preachers, or in God's place, such as prophets. The canonical exegesis of James – i.e., the one later collected in the *Glossa Ordinaria* on the Bible – also authorised an opposite and rather edifying reading of the Apostle's treatment of the tongue. Such reading was sanctioned by the conclusion of James's third paragraph, which offers a positive alternative model: 'But the wisdom, that is from above, first indeed is chaste, then peaceable, modest, easy to be persuaded, consenting to the good, full of mercy and good fruits, without judging, without dissimulation. And the fruit of justice is sown in peace, to them that make peace' (James 3. 17–18). Unlike vicious, self-proclaimed masters, those who are truly virtuous receive wisdom from above; like patient farmers, they sow the fruit of justice.

To solve the apparent contradiction between the pessimistic condemnation of the tongue and the hopeful conclusion in James 3, Augustine argues that James does not mean to chastise the tongue *tout court*, but maintains that whereas no man can tame the tongue, God can.[12] James's intention, therefore, would be to invite his readers to ask God's grace in taming the tongue. Bede developed Augustine's view in his *Super divi Jacobi Epistolam* – the only extant, complete commentary on James, and later incorporated into the *Glossa Ordinaria* on the Bible (1080–1130).[13] Bede argues that since James describes the tongue as the 'rudder' and the 'horse bit' of the whole body, this organ may and must be tamed for good use. Elsewhere, Bede's transformative exegesis surfaces more clearly when he interprets James's imagery of the tongue as a dangerous spark of fire. Despite James's negative evaluation of the tongue's power, Bede glosses the Apostle's statement that 'the tongue is indeed a little member, and boasteth great things' (3. 5):

> Certainly it exalts great rewards if the action of the mind at the helm directs it well [...] but if [the mind directs the tongue] badly on the other hand, it exalts great evils of destruction for itself and its connections [...]. It exalts life, therefore, if it teaches the church well, death on the contrary if it behaves perversely, for it is opposed to those who, destitute of both life and knowledge, presumed to teach and thereby did greater harm to the church. (*Comm. on James*, 3. 5)[14]

Bede emphasises the importance of the *intentio cordis* [the intention of the heart] in order for the tongue to be put to good use so that it might bring great rewards. Furthermore, Bede opposes to the malicious and destructive fire of the tongue the image of the Pentecostal fire that purifies and enlightens the heart and mind. He claims that good masters, those who ask and receive Wisdom from above, burn with this spiritual fire: 'Holy teachers are set on fire by it [the saving fire] both that they themselves may burn with loving and that by preaching they may set others on fire with fiery tongues, as it were'(*Comm. on James*, 3. 6). Bede's commentary, therefore, helped to turn the perception of James's apparent condemnation of all pastoral teaching into a prescription on how to pursue preaching that was ethical and divinely sanctioned. The effectiveness of Bede's reading can be gauged from the *Glossa ordinaria*, which introduces the *Epistle* as an instructional text 'de mandatione magistrorum' [on the mandate of the teachers] (*Prologus Ieronimi*); reinterprets James's exhortation to speak rarely and listen always as an indication to the teacher 'ne ante tempus presumat docere' [lest he presume to teach before being ready] (1. 19); and, finally, translates James's whole discourse into a warning against those who are not legitimate teachers, 'hos ergo ab officio verbi removet, ne impediant veros predicatores' [these, therefore, he removes from the office of the word, lest they hinder true preachers] (3. 1).[15]

Sower of peace: *Epistle* V

Dante's references to James indicate that he was not impervious to this canonical exegesis. In his commentary on his *canzone, Le dolci rime d'amor ch'i' solia*, he translates James 5. 7, arguing for the importance of time as the agent that brings all human works to fulfilment:

> Onde dice santo Iacopo apostolo nella sua Pistola: 'Ecco lo agricola aspetta lo prezioso frutto della terra, pazientemente sostenendo infino che riceva lo temporaneo e lo serotino'. E tutte le nostre brighe, se bene venimo a cercare li loro principii, procedono quasi dal non conoscere l'uso del tempo.

> (*Cvo*, IV. ii. 10)

> [Hence St. James the Apostle says in his Epistle: 'Behold, the husbandman waits for the precious fruit of the earth, patiently abiding until he receives the early and the late'. All our troubles, if we carefully seek out their source, derive in some way from not knowing how to make a proper use of time.]

Words must be uttered with especially great discretion, when both sender and receiver are in the right disposition to communicate properly. Several chapters later (*Cvo*, IV. xx. 6), Dante translates James again to prove that nobility is a wholly divine gift, as both the recipient's natural predisposition to nobility and the gift of nobility itself are freely bestowed by God: 'secondo la parola dell'Apostolo: "Ogni ottimo dato e ogni dono perfetto di suso viene, discendendo dal Padre de' lumi"' [According to the words of the Apostle: 'Every good gift, and every perfect gift comes from above, descending from the Father of lights'].

James surfaces again in Dante's *Epistola* V – not as a direct quotation this time but as a series of clear echoes. Scholars have noted that Dante's references to the fruit of justice, 'fructum iustitie', rendered by the *agricolae* at the right time, 'in tempore messis' (*Ep.*, V. ii. 6), and to the fruit of true peace, 'viride [...] fructiferum vere pacis' (V. v. 16), may echo James 3. 18, 'Fructus autem justitiae, in pace seminatur, facientibus pacem' [And the fruit of justice is sown in peace, to them that make peace].[16] The significance of these references to James may easily go undetected in the wealth of biblical echoes that punctuate Dante's *Epistola* V.

A consideration of the particular historical context and message of this *Epistola*, however, suggests that James may well have played a distinctive role in Dante's prophetic self-legitimation here.[17] This letter is the first of three that Dante devotes to the Emperor's journey to Italy, where he was due to be crowned, in Rome, by Pope Clement V (*Ep.* V–VII). The opening of the letter overflows with the poet's joy at the imminent restoration of political order in Italy, through the re-establishment of imperial rule, whose 'signa [...] consolationis et pacis' [signs [...] of consolation and peace] are already approaching (*Ep.*, V. i. 2). In the letter's dedication, Dante presents himself as a messenger of peace, unjustly exiled, 'exul inmeritus orat pacem' (V. i. 1). Therefore the letter opens by emphasising the author's role as peacemaker as well as his unjust suffering. The latter is reiterated in the first paragraph by the mention of his long and faithful watch in the desert: 'qui diu pernoctavimus in deserto' (V. i. 3). Here already, but increasingly so in later passages, the author singles out a specific group of readers among the letter's generic audience – the whole of the Italian people – and identifies them as those who have suffered with him. To them in particular Dante promises the fruits of the peace to come, and to them he addresses his invitation to forgive and make peace: 'Parcite, parcite iam ex nunc, o carissimi, qui mecum iniuriam passi estis' [Forbear, forbear, from henceforth, well-beloved, who with me have suffered wrong] (V. v. 17).

Reading Dante's epistle alongside James's, we can appreciate several striking parallels. First, James addresses his letter to the twelve tribes of Israel that are scattered and far from Jerusalem, hence identifying an audience that is exiled outside its own city, 'James the servant of God, and of our Lord Jesus Christ, to the twelve tribes which are scattered abroad [*sunt in dispersione*], greeting' (1. 1). The *Glossa Ordinaria* explains that: 'Qui tamen omnes in dispersione fuerunt variis casibus a patria profugi et in numeris caedibus mortibusque et aerumnis ubicumque erant ab hostibus oppressi' [They, however, were all dispersed, refugees from their homeland for different reasons, and everywhere they were oppressed by mass slaughter, death, tribulations and enemies] (James 1. 1). The condition of diaspora and continuous harassment that distinguishes James's addressees is the same as that which Dante shares with his most cherished readers. Second, the opening of James's letter invites the faithful to endure all sorts of tribulations and persecutions: 'My brethren, count it all joy, when you shall fall into divers temptations; knowing that the trying of your faith worketh patience. And patience hath a perfect work; that you may be perfect and entire, failing in nothing' (1. 2–4). As already noted, both Dante and his readers find legitimation in their own patient endurance, as stressed by the author's illuminating word choice: 'qui mecum iniuriam *passi estis*' (the Latin noun *patientia* expresses the capacity of suffering and derives from the verb *patior*). Third, but most important, toward the conclusion of his *Epistle*, James invites his readers to make peace and not begrudge one another because the Lord is soon to come:

> Be patient therefore, brethren, until the coming of the Lord. Behold, the husbandman waiteth for the precious fruit of the earth: patiently bearing till he receive the early and latter rain. Be you therefore also patient, and strengthen your hearts: for the coming of the Lord is at hand. Grudge not, brethren, one against another, that you may not be judged. Behold the judge standeth before the door. (5. 7–9)

This is also Dante's exhortation to his own readers as they prepare for the Emperor's advent. How relevant James 5. 7–9 was for the poet is revealed by its quotation at *Convivio*, IV. ii. 9–10. There Dante quotes James to support his claim that time alone brings desire to its fulfilment, granting its gifts to those who are patient, and also to argue that virtually all our quarrels ('brighe') originate from impatience, 'dal non conoscere l'uso del tempo' (*Cvo*, IV. ii. 10).

In *Epistola* V, precisely by reworking the Apostle's imagery of the providential rain, which he had already quoted in *Convivio* IV, Dante points out that the time to make peace is finally at hand. Between the two references to James's 'fructum iustitie' and 'fructiferum vere pacis' – in *Epistola* V. ii and v respectively – Dante exhorts his readers to become husbandmen and help him sow peace, lest the heavenly rain fall on the unsown field: 'Assumite rastrum bone humilitatis, atque glebis exuste animositatis occatis, agellum sternite mentis vestre, ne forte celestis imber, sementem vestram ante iactum preveniens, in vacuum de altissimo cadat' [Take the mattock of true humility, and break up the parched clods of your pride, making smooth the field of your minds, lest perchance the rain from heaven, coming before the seed has been sown, fall in vain from on high] (*Ep.*, V. v. 15). James 5. 7 maintains that the good *agricola* waits readily and patiently to receive the 'temporaneum et serotinum', i.e. the early and the later rain. Accordingly, in his *Epistola* V, Dante warns his readers to become such industrious ploughmen, who do not let the providential rain fall in vain.

Dante's extensive appropriation of James's imagery in his *Epistola* V attests to the relevance of this biblical model in the poets's legitimation of his own message and authority. The particular line from James that Dante chooses to echo twice, 'Fructus autem justitiae, in pace seminatur, facientibus pacem', marks the end of James 3, where the Apostle condemns the misuse of the tongue and invites everyone to ask for God's wisdom instead. Dante endorses the Apostle's invitation and represents himself and his ideal readers as the good *agricolae*. Through these references to James, Dante also endorses another model of patience put forward by the Apostle: 'Take, my brethren, for an example of suffering evil, of labour and patience, *the prophets*, who spoke in the name of the Lord' (James 5. 10, emphasis mine). In *Epistola* V, in the wake of a new imperial hope, Dante finds in James a fitting theorisation of his own prophetic voice, namely that of an actual political peacemaker. Acting as the prophet of the providential Empire, Dante presents himself as a sower of peace who prepares the field for the coming of the Emperor and the ripening of the fruit of justice.

Perhaps not coincidentally, at the end of *Epistola* V, there appears the image of the small spark that kindles a great fire, 'prima scintillula huius ignis' (V. viii. 24). Whereas James applies this image to the tongue's pernicious power (James 3. 5–6), Dante deploys it instead to express the idea that God can operate his wondrous work through human instruments. Chief evidence of this fact is found in the history of the Roman Empire: 'Nam si *a prima scintillula huius ignis* revolvamus preterita [...] nonnulla eorum videbimus humane virtutis omnino culmina transcendisse, et Deum per homines, tanquam per celos novos, aliquid operatum fuisse' [For if we survey the past, from the first tiny spark of this fire [...] we shall see that certain of them [the events of Roman history] have altogether transcended the highest pitch of human effort, and that God at times has wrought through man as though through new heavens] (*Ep.*, V. viii. 24, emphasis mine).

Furthermore, Dante explains that sometimes we operate merely as instruments of God's work: 'Non etenim semper nos agimus, quin interdum *utensilia Dei* sumus; ac voluntates humane, quibus inest ex natura libertas, etiam inferioris affectus inmunes quandoque aguntur, et obnoxie voluntati eterne sepe illi ancillantur ignare' [For it is not always we who act, but sometimes we are the instruments of God; and the human will, in which liberty is by nature inherent, at times receives direction untrammelled by earthly affections, and subject to the Eternal Will oft-times unconsciously becomes the minister thereof] (*Ep.*, V. viii. 25, emphasis mine). Dante articulates this theory with regard to the providential role of the Roman Empire in *Convivio* IV. iv. 12. There the author explains that Rome's military power was 'cagione instrumentale' [instrumental cause], whereas God was the 'cagione movente' [moving cause]: 'sì come sono li colpi del martello cagione [instrumentale] del coltello, e l'anima del fabro è cagione efficiente e movente; e così non forza, ma ragione, [e ragione] ancora divina, [conviene] essere stata principio dello romano imperio' [as the blows of a hammer are the cause of a knife, while the mind of the smith is the efficient and moving cause; and thus not force but reason, and more-over divine reason, must have been the origin of the Roman Empire]. In *Epistola* V, Dante's argument about the providential nature of the Roman Empire culminates with a vigorous invitation to his readers: God Himself established the institution of the Empire and provides Italy with a new Emperor: 'videte quoniam regem nobis celi et terre Dominus ordinavit' [behold how the Lord of heaven and of earth hath appointed us a king] (*Ep.*, V. x. 29). The ultimate legitimation of Dante's prophetic authority, therefore, springs forth from the evidence that the content of his prophetic message, namely the coming of the Emperor, is the work of divine wisdom.

Apostolic investiture: *Paradiso* XXIII–XXVII

Suggestively, the same imagery from James found in *Epistola* V also appears in *Paradiso* XXIV–XXV, immediately before Dante the pilgrim meets the Apostle. At the end of *Paradiso* XXIV, facing St Peter, Dante concludes his *Credo* by stating that the primary tenets of his faith have 'rained' down upon him and have been 'kindled' in him by the Old and New Testament respectively:

> 'anche la verità che quinci *piove*
>   per Möisè, per profeti e per salmi,
> per l'Evangelio e per voi che scriveste
> poi che l'ardente Spirto vi fé almi;
>   [...]
>   De la profonda condizion divina
> ch'io tocco mo, la mente mi sigilla
> più volte l'evangelica dottrina.
>   Quest'è 'l principio, quest'è la *favilla*
> *che si dilata in fiamma* poi vivace,
> e come stella in cielo in me scintilla'.

(*Par.*, XXIV. 135–8, 142–7)

['by the truth that rains down from here | through Moses, through prophets, and through psalms, through the Gospel and through all of you, who wrote when the burning Spirit made you nourishers. | [...] About the profound nature of God on which I touch now, my mind is sealed numerous times by the teachings of the Gospels. |

This is the origin, this is the spark that expands then into a lively flame and like a star in the sky flashes within me.']

This key imagery – highly redolent of James – represents the transfer of divine wisdom from the Gospel to the poet, and then from him to his readers.[18] Not by chance, this symbolic *translatio* of authority comes after Dante's claim that the ultimate proofs undergirding his faith are the miracles that God performed through the Apostles. Like humble ploughmen, they planted the good vine of the Gospel:

> 'sanza miracoli, quest'uno
> è tal, che li altri non sono il centesmo:
>   ché tu intrasti povero e digiuno
> in campo, a seminar la buona pianta
> che fu già vite e ora è fatta pruno'.

(*Par.*, XXIV. 107–11)

['without miracles, this one miracle is such that the others are not a hundredth of it: | for you came into the field poor and hungry to sow the good plant, formerly a vine but now become a thornbush.']

Dante's representation of the Apostles here echoes James's own example of the good *agricolae*, already used by the poet in *Epistola* V, to represent the husbandmen who would receive the Emperor's 'vineam' and harvest the fruit of justice (*Ep.*, V. ii. 6). Through their evangelical sowing, the Apostles became 'utensilia' [utensils] of God's miracles – to use Dante's term from *Epistola* V. viii.25. As in the *Epistola*, moreover, so too in *Paradiso* XXIV this idea is accompanied by the image of the spark and the flame. The calculated repetition suggests the technical precision with which Dante deploys this imagery, which he had used to represent the relationship between 'cagione movente' and 'instrumentale' in the divinely willed triumph of the Roman Empire (*Cvo*, IV. iv. 12). In the *Commedia* the poet draws on the same image to represent God's providential interventions by means of human authors, such as the apostles and, by extension, himself.

At *Paradiso* XXIV, one might say, Dante even employs James against James by proposing a compelling alternative to the epistle's stigmatisation of the tongue as the deadliest spark. Thus he represents himself as someone whose wisdom comes from above, like rain and fire, and who speaks as a mere conduit of such fire – like the holy teachers who, according to Bede's commentary on James, 'are set on fire' by the saving fire that purifies their hearts. Moreover, as St Peter declares, it was grace that opened Dante's mouth, thereby legitimising the poet's words as coming from God: "'la Grazia, che donnea | con la tua mente, la bocca t'aperse | infino a qui come aprir si dovea'" ['The grace that woos your mind has | opened your mouth until now as it should be opened'] (*Par.*, XXIV. 118–20).

The opening of the following canto further sanctions Dante's divinely inspired voice. As we noted earlier, the author of the *Commedia* claims that the poem is 'sacro' [sacred] and authored by 'e cielo e terra' [both Heaven and earth] (*Par.*, XXV. 1–2). Scholars have wondered whether Dante here refers to the subject matter or to the authorship of his poem.[19] Recently academic consensus has increasingly tended toward the second interpretation – namely, that the phrase 'e cielo e terra' refers to the *Commedia*'s double authorship, both divine and human. I should like to suggest, however, that the meaning of the periphrasis is more radical than has been generally assumed.[20] If we consider that at the end of the preceding canto Dante deploys the spark and fire imagery in order to present himself as one of the divine *utensilia*, it seems reasonable to interpret the reference to 'e cielo e terra' as the definitive claim that the actual author – 'cagione efficiente e movente' – of the *Commedia* is really God Himself.

This interpretation derives from a simple consideration: Dante generally deploys the periphrasis 'Heaven and earth' to indicate God as maker. At the end of *Epistola* V, where Dante asserts the divine election of the Emperor, he presents God as Lord of Heaven and Earth: 'regem nobis *celi et terre* Dominus ordinavit' (*Ep.*, V. x. 29, emphasis mine). Again, he uses the same periphrasis to identify Christ in *Paradiso* XXIII, where the *Commedia* is defined as 'sacrato poema' for the first time (*Par.*, XXIII. 62). Here the poet calls Christ the wisdom and power that reunited Heaven and Earth: "'quivi è la sapïenza e la possanza | ch'aprì le strade tra 'l cielo e la terra'" (*Par.*, XXIII. 37–8, emphasis mine). Finally, Dante refers once more to God as the maker of Heaven and Earth precisely in *Paradiso* XXV, when he first meets James. Summoned to raise his eyes and gaze on the Apostle, Dante quotes *Psalm* 120. 1: 'ond' io levëi li occhi a' monti' (38). Medieval readers would have certainly been able to recall the next few lines of the Psalm, which read as follows: 'Levavi oculos meos in montes, unde veniet auxilium mihi. Auxilium meum a Domino, *qui fecit caelum et terram*' [I have lifted up my eyes to the mountains, from whence help shall come to me. My help is from the Lord, *who made heaven and earth*] (emphasis mine). The author himself, therefore, through David's authority, offers the key that unlocks the meaning of the enigmatic words 'e cielo e terra', which is really just a periphrasis for God as maker. Like David, Dante places his trust in the poem's success in the Author of Heaven and

Earth. God is the 'fabro' who shaped the *Commedia*, whereas Dante is His 'martello', or 'cagione instrumentale', like Roman military power and the Apostles.[21]

I would argue, moreover, that it is not by chance that Dante lays such a claim in anticipation of his meeting with James. The poet is simply following the advice of the Apostle who, at the opening of his epistle, recommends that 'if any of you want wisdom, let him ask of God, who giveth to all men abundantly, and upbraideth not; and it shall be given him' (1. 5). Furthermore, in light of James, Dante reminds the reader of all the tribulations – chiefly the exile – that he had patiently endured to God's ends in the making of this sacred text: 'sì che m' ha fatto per molti anni macro, | vinca la crudeltà che fuor mi serra | del bello ovile ov'io dormi' agnello, | nimico ai lupi che li danno guerra' [so that for many years it has made me lean, | vanquish the cruelty that locks me out of the lovely sheepfold where I slept as a lamb, an enemy of the wolves that make war on it] (*Par.*, XXV. 3–6). Dante, therefore, opens James's canto in *Paradiso* by following closely the Apostle's guidelines on how to become a patient husbandman and prophet of God: first asking for wisdom from above and then testifying to his own patient endurance.

Between the end of *Paradiso* XXIV and the beginning of XXV, Dante returns to stake the claims already rehearsed in *Epistola* V for reframing his own prophetic voice once more, in light of James.[22] This time, however, Dante's prophetic message has significantly changed.[23] Consistently throughout the five cantos of the Fixed Stars (*Paradiso* XXIII–XXVII), we find the image of Apostolic sowing.[24] At *Paradiso* XXIII, Dante defines the Church Militant as 'quelle arche ricchissime che fuoro | *a seminar* qua giù buone bobolce!' [rich arks that were such good ploughmen for the sowing down here!] (131–2), which echoes James's invitation to cleanse oneself from all impurity and malice – 'immunditiam' and 'abundantiam malitiae' – in order to receive the word that has been sown in us, 'suscipite *insitum* verbum' (1. 21, emphasis mine).[25] At *Paradiso* XXIV. 109–11, as already mentioned, Peter is presented as the humble husbandman who goes to sow the field – which is preceded by the image of the 'larga ploia' [the plentiful rain] of the Holy Spirit (91). At *Paradiso* XXV. 84, James's martyrdom is described as leaving the field, '"l'uscir del campo"' ['my retirement from the field'], and his epistle instils hope in the poet like rain (78). Finally, at *Paradiso* XXVI. 64–5, Dante declares that he loves all God's creatures, using the agricultural metaphor again and identifying God as the supreme gardener: '"le fronde ove s'infronda tutto l'orto | de l'ortolano etterno ... "' ['the leaves wherewith all the orchard of the eternal Gardener flourishes ...'].

Dante's insistence on this particular imagery throughout the cantos of the Fixed Stars cannot be accidental, given the fact that the pilgrim's meeting with James lies squarely at their centre.[26] Upon meeting St James in *Paradiso*, Dante echoes James to represent himself as the Apostolic husbandman. The poet too precedes the Lord – not the Emperor this time – renewing his readers' theological hope and sowing the spiritual peace that derives from God's charity.[27] In a sense, therefore, Dante returns to James's *Epistle* to shift his self-representation from Imperial to Apostolic sower and prophet.

'Ritornerò *profeta*': James's Crown

It is time to return to the question that opened this essay and explore the relationship between Dante's self-crowning as 'poeta' and James's authority. As the proposed interpretation suggests, in *Paradiso* XXIII–XXV, Dante identifies his work and his authority with that of the Apostles through a consistent use of imagery strongly reminiscent of James's *Epistle*. In so doing, the poet presents himself as God's instrument, while attributing to Him, who is the maker of Heaven and Earth, the authorship of the *Commedia*.

I would argue that by calling himself a 'poeta' in such a context, Dante reconfigures the term according to James's models: the *agricola* and the *propheta*. In so doing Dante conflates poetic and prophetic glories, constructing his certain hope of the future poetic crowning on the same premises that make him a prophet: '"uno attender certo | de la gloria futura, il qual produce | grazia divina e precedente merto"' ['a sure expectation of the future glory, produced by God's grace and preceding merit'] (*Par.*, XXV. 67–9). In observance of James's two pivotal rules, the poet's certainty of poetic glory lies in God's grace, which authored the *Commedia*, and in his own merits – the suffering he patiently endured to be God's instrument as scribe of the poem and sower of peace. The enigmatic lines that open *Paradiso* XXV, therefore, fulfil primarily a rhetorical purpose: they are not merely autobiographical, but provide the two ethical proofs of Dante's divinely inspired authority according to James.[28]

The meaning of the 'altra voce' and the 'altro vello' [with other voice by then, with other fleece] (7), with which the poet hopes to make his return to Florence, also becomes more apparent. Dante's different voice and humble garment, made of animal fleece, are those given by God to his prophets.[29] Furthermore, the enigmatic image of the 'cappello' [wreath] (9) that Dante will wear over his baptismal font may be read in light of James. In the first paragraph of his *Epistle*, James promises that all those who patiently suffer will receive the crown of eternal life: 'Blessed is the man that endureth temptation; for when he hath been proved, he shall receive the crown of life, which God hath promised to them that love him' (James 1.12). The 'cappello' that Dante will receive is that of the *poeta-profeta*, who has suffered in faith and in hope of God's coming. The fact, moreover, that he shall receive it in the place of his christening is an acknowledgement that such crowning can be won by all Christians, if they remain faithful to the grace they received at the time of their baptism and accept martyrdom and persecutions in Jesus's name. Tellingly, the other mention of Florence's baptistery in *Paradiso* is made by Dante's ancestor, Cacciaguida, who died fighting as a crusader and is celebrated in Heaven as a martyr (*Par.*, XV. 134–5).

In *Monarchia* I. i. 6 Dante quotes James 1. 5 again, to argue that the hope of successfully completing his treatise lies not in his own strength but in God's superabundant grace: 'Arduum quidem opus et ultra vires aggredior, non tam de propria virtute confidens, quam de lumine Largitoris illius "qui dat omnibus affluenter et non improperat"' [It is indeed an arduous task, and one beyond my strength, that I embark on, trusting not so much in my own powers as in the light of that Giver who 'giveth to all men liberally, and upbraideth not']. In the lines preceding this quotation, moreover, Dante expresses his desire for authorial success in terms that remind us of the pilgrim's encounter with St James in *Paradiso* XXV: 'tum etiam ut *palmam* tanti bravii primus in meam gloriam adipiscar' [so that I may be the first to win for my own glory the honour of so great a prize] (*Mon.*, I. i. 5, emphasis mine). The trophy that Dante wishes to win for himself, as *auctor*, is the very *palma* that St James received as a prize for his martyrdom, after leaving the field where he worked as God's husbandman: '"l'amore ond'ïo avvampo | ancor ver' la virtù che mi seguette | infin la *palma* e a l'uscir del campo"' ['the love with which I am still aflame toward the virtue that followed me to my palm and my retirement from the field'] (*Par.*, XXV. 82–4, emphasis mine). Dante's conflation of prophetic, apostolic, and poetic glory could not be more definite, and points consistently to James as its pivotal model.

I would like to end by noting that on one point at least Dante seems to take no notice of James's advice. Towards the end of his *Epistle*, James warns that 'above all things, my brethren, swear not, neither by heaven, nor by the earth' [*neque per caelum, neque per terram*] (5. 12, emphasis mine), to which the *Glossa* adds the attenuating clause: 'nisi necessitas cogat' [unless it is necessary]. We cannot help but conclude that at *Paradiso* XXV. 2, only a few lines before recounting his meeting with St James, Dante found it fitting and necessary to contradict the Apostle and 'swear' on 'cielo e terra' that he 'ritornerà poeta'.

Notes

*   I wish to thank John Ahern, Zygmunt G. Barański, Erik Ellis, Simone Marchesi, and Rebecca West for their invaluable comments on previous drafts of this work. I also thank Pietro Delcorno for his helpful clarifications on the history of the *Glossa ordinaria*. All commentaries on the *Commedia* referred to here have been consulted via the Dartmouth Dante Project, https://dante.dartmouth.edu (last accessed 2 April 2019). Translations from Dante's *Convivio* are by Richard Lansing, consulted via the Princeton Dante Project, http://etcweb.princeton.edu/dante/pdp/convivio (last accessed 2 April 2019). Translations of the *Glossa Ordinaria* are mine.

1. See for instance the essays collected in *Se Mai Continga ... Exile, Politics and Theology in Dante*, ed. Claire E. Honess and Matthew Treherne (Ravenna: Longo, 2013).

2. Dante's choice might have been forced by the traditional identification of Peter, James and John with the three theological virtues. See the commentary by Anna Maria Chiavacci Leonardi, *ad Par.*, XXV. 32–3. On the intriguing question about the connection between Dante's reading of the *Epistle* and the theological virtue of hope, see now the study by Sandra Carapezza, '"Grazia divina e precedente merto". L'Epistola di Giacomo come fonte della speranza', *L'Alighieri* 58 (2017): 93–105. Unfortunately, this essay came to my attention only after completing this essay.

3. In *VN*, 29. 6–7 [Barbi XL. 6–7] and in *Cvo*, II. xiv. 1, Dante discusses the traditional associations of the Apostle's name with one of the most famous pilgrimage routes – to Santiago de Compostela – and with the Galaxy – named the 'Via di Sa' Jacopo'. For a preliminary study on the subject, see Gian Luca Pierotti, 'La "legenda sancti Jacobi" nei canti del cielo stellato', *Rivista di Letteratura Italiana* 28.3 (2010): 9–20. On James's medieval cult and legends, see at least Karl D. Uitti, 'The Codex Calixtinus and the European St. James the Major: Some Contextual Issues', in *'De Sens Rassis': Essays in Honor of Rupert T. Pickens*, ed. Keith Busby et al. (Amsterdam: Rodopi, 2005), 645–66.

4. For sake of brevity, I have limited bibliographical references in this essay to the essential. For more bibliography on the subject, see my forthcoming essay, '"Poca favilla gran fiamma seconda" (*Par.*, I. 34). Riscrivere un proverbio tra Cino, San Giacomo, e San Girolamo' (forthcoming, *Le Tre Corone* 7, 2020).

5. Dante quotes directly from the *Epistle* at least three times: in *Cvo*, IV. ii. 9–10 (James 5. 7); IV. xx. 6 (1. 17); *Mon.* I. i. 6 (1. 5); and almost certainly he echoes James 3. 18 in *Ep.*, V. 3, 5. Some have suggested that other echoes may be found in *Cvo*, IV. xii. 8; *Rime*, 38b. 14; *VN*, 1. 18 [Barbi III. 7]; *Par.*, I. 34; XXV. 77; *Ep.*, I. 2. See Giorgio Brugnoli, 'Epistula Catholica Beati Jacobi Apostoli', in Giorgio Brugnoli, *Studi danteschi*, 3 vols (Pisa: ETS, 1998), III, 19–24.

6. David B. Gowler, *James Through the Centuries* (Hoboken: Wiley, 2014), 7.

7. Dante's misattribution of the *Epistle* to James Major, in *Paradiso* XXV. 77, may reflect precisely such a mistaken assumption. See Gian Roberto Sarolli, 'Giacomo (Iacopo) Maggiore', in the *Enciclopedia Dantesca (ED)*, 6 vols (Rome: Istituto dell'Enciclopedia Italiana, 1970–8), III (1971), 147–8.

8. Gowler, 5.

9. See Carla Casagrande and Silvana Vecchio, *I peccati della lingua: disciplina ed etica della parola nella cultura medievale* (Rome: Istituto della Enciclopedia Italiana, 1987), 6.

10. To get a sense of how proverbial this image was in the Middle Ages, see Hans Walther and Paul Gerhard Schmidt, *Proverbia Sententiaeque Latinitatis Medii Ac Recentioris Aevi: Nova Series/ Lateinische Sprichwörter und Sentenzen des Mittelalters und der frühen Neuzeit in alphabetischer Anordnung* , 3 vols (Göttingen: Vandenhoek & Ruprecht, 1982–6), 39397–39402c.

11. See at least Richard Bates and Thomas Rendall, 'Dante's Ulysses and the *Epistle* of James', *Dante Studies* 107 (1989–1990): 33–44; Alison Cornish, 'The *Epistle* of James in *Inferno* 26', *Traditio* 45 (1989): 367–79; Giacomo Gambale, 'Dante, *l'Epistula Iacobi* e il *De Peccato Linguae*. Per una lettura filosofica di *Inferno XXVI*', *Studi danteschi* 74 (2009): 179–98, then revised and extended in Giacomo Gambale, *La lingua di fuoco: Dante e la filosofia del linguaggio* (Rome: Città nuova, 2012), 102–11; Gabriella I. Baika, 'Tongues of Fire and Fraud in Bolgia Eight', *Quaderni d'italianistica* 32.2 (2011): 5–26. On *contrapasso*, see also Justin Steinberg's essay in this volume.

12. Augustine, *Liber de natura et gratia contra Pelagium* 1.15. Consulted at http://www.augustinus.it/latino/natura_grazia/index.htm (last accessed 13 May 2018).

13. The manuscripts, however, date between 1140–70. See Beryl Smalley, 'Glossa Ordinaria', in *Theologische Realenzyklopädie*, 36 vols (Berlin: De Gruyter, 1984), III, 452–7.

14. *The Commentary on the Seven Catholic Epistles of Bede the Venerable*, ed. and trans. David Hurst, O.S.B. (Kalamazoo: Cistercian Publications, 1985), 39.

15. *Biblia Latina cum glossa ordinaria: Facsimile reprint of the editio Princeps Adolph Rusch of Strassburg 1480/81*, ed. Karlfried Froehlich and Margaret T. Gibson (Brepols: Turnhout, 1992), *ad loc.* This edition provides a helpful indication of the principle exegetical trends that were already present in the most popular glosses circulating at Dante's time, and were later assembled in this *editio princeps*.

16. The second echo has been noted by Elisa Brilli, 'Reminiscenze scritturali (e non) nelle epistole politiche dantesche', *La Cultura* 3 (2007): 439–55 (445).

17. Studies have generally noted the importance of St Paul and Isaiah as main models for Dante's prophetic self-representation in *Ep.* V. See at least Paola Rigo, 'Tempo liturgico nell'epistola ai Principi e ai popoli d'Italia', *Lettere Italiane* 32 (1980): 222–31, then in Paola Rigo, *Memoria classica e memoria biblica in Dante* (Florence: Olschki,1994), 33–44; and Giuseppe Ledda, 'Modelli biblici e identità profetica nelle *Epistole* di Dante', *Lettere Italiane* 60.1 (2008): 18–42 (23–6).

18. Dante's use of the imagery of the spark that kindles a great fire in the *Commedia* is complex and symbolically charged. I discuss the question at length in my forthcoming essay '"Poca favilla gran fiamma seconda"'.

19. For a summary of this discussion, see Robert Hollander's commentary, *ad Par.*, XXV. 2.

20. Hollander, *ad Par.*, XXV. 2.

21. My reading touches on a complex issue that I cannot examine further in this essay, but to which I plan to return elsewhere. For now, I wish to note that, while proposing a slight variation on the reading of *Par.*, XXV. 1–2 proposed by Zygmunt G. Barański ('Dante Alighieri: Experimentation and (Self-)Exegesis', in *The Cambridge History of Literary Criticism*, ed. Alastair J. Minnis and Ian Johnson (Cambridge: Cambridge University Press, 2005), 559–82, esp. 578–9), my interpretation in no way diverts from the theory of double-authorship of sacred texts that characterised thirteenth- and fourteenth-century Scriptural exegesis and informed Dante's theory of authorship. *Accessus* to the Bible regularly divide the Aristotelian 'efficient cause' further into a primary efficient cause, namely God, and an instrumental efficient cause, namely the poet; this is the distinction that Dante also seems to imply with the image of the blacksmith at *Cvo*, IV. iv. 12. See Alastair J. Minnis, *Medieval Theory of Authorship* (London: Scolar Press, 1984), 73–159, esp. 102. I believe that with the periphrasis 'e cielo e terra' at *Par.*, XXV. 2, Dante may identify God as the primary (or moving) efficient cause of the poem, thereby implying his own role as instrumental (or moved) efficient cause.

22. There are numerous parallel themes, images and intertextual references that indicate the special bond between Dante's *Epistola* V and *Paradiso* XXV: the theme of exile and homecoming; the references to the *Exodus*, Isaiah and James; the imagery of sowing and rain; and the reference to God as maker of Heaven and Earth.

23. On Dante's recantation at *Par.*, XXV of his position in *Ep.*, V–VII, see Claire E. Honess, '"Ritornerò Poeta …": Florence, Exile, and Hope', in *Se mai continga …*, 84–103.

24. James is, of course, only one of the possible sources for the image of Apostolic sowing. However, it is certainly a crucial one, given that the subtext of the *Epistle* surfaces in the cantos of the Fixed Stars and particularly in *Paradiso* XXV. On the sources of this imagery, see Pierotti, 17–18.

25. 'Bobolce' has been interpreted either as 'ploughmen' who sow the good seed or as the ploughed and fertile fields ready to receive the seed. The latter reading allows a more fitting echo of James's passage.

26. Hope, according to Chiavacci Leonardi, is the 'motivo guida di tutta la sequenza del cielo Stellato' [the driving motif of the whole sequence of cantos of the Heaven of the Fixed Stars] (Note to *Par.*, XXV, trans. mine).

27. Giuseppe Ledda has suggested that Dante presents himself as a prophet whose particular mission is to reawaken the theological virtue of hope: 'Dante e la tradizione delle visioni medievali', *Letture Classensi* 37 (2008): 119–42 (142).

28. On the interpretation of these lines in light of Dante's rhetorical self-representation, see, at least, Giuseppe Ledda, *La guerra della lingua: ineffabilità, retorica e narrativa nella 'Commedia' di Dante* (Ravenna: Longo, 2002), 103–15, and 289–90.

29. For a compelling reading of 'voce' and 'vello' as references to St John the Baptist, see Stefano Prandi, 'Canto XXV. "Ritornerò Poeta"', in *Lectura Dantis Romana. Cento Canti per Cento Anni. Paradiso. Vol. III. 2. Canti XVIII–XXXIII*, ed. Enrico Malato and Andrea Mazzucchi (Rome: Salerno, 2015), 723–46 (730–31).

7

Ethical Distance and Political Resonance in the *Eclogues* of Dante

Sabrina Ferrara

When he received Giovanni del Virgilio's epistolary poem – either during the second half of 1319, at the end of that year or else at the beginning of 1320[1] – Dante was already in Ravenna, writing the last part of the *Paradiso*.[2] Everything suggests he had finally discovered the *locus amoenus* which would allow him to work on his verses (*Ecl.*, IV. 70–3), surrounded by a group of admirers with the same inclinations and tastes (*Ecl.*, IV. 57–62) and honoured by the Lord of the city (*Ecl.*, III. 80), himself a lover of poetry. The reception of Del Virgilio's verse epistle, and the exchange that followed, interrupted, at least for a time, the composition of Dante's epic poem. Invited to answer the Bolognese writer's challenge, he did so in his own terms and according to his own agenda, giving birth to his only work of Latin poetry.[3] In studying this correspondence, scholarship has mainly focused on the relationship between Italian and Latin; questions concerning style;[4] the latent tension between Dante, Albertino Mussato and the emerging new culture of the time; and, consequently, on the theme of poetic coronation.[5]

It is worth pointing out that in this correspondence, and especially in the opening epistle, Giovanni del Virgilio does not suggest he wanted Dante to 'rewrite' his *Commedia* in Latin, nor to abandon his project.[6] His intention was rather to urge him to compose poetry in Latin addressed to scholars,[7] who could then have honoured him with the poet's laurel crown – Mussato had received it in 1315, and the unspoken shadow of this particular coronation hangs over this correspondence.[8] Additionally, Del Virgilio considers that the poet should have chosen a topic from contemporary history (*Ecl.*, I. 26–9).

The focus of my critical attention in the present essay, now that Del Virgilio's objectives have been clarified, will be to establish the poetical and ethical role played by Dante in the cultural landscape of the mid-fourteenth century – a period characterised by a singular *querelle* between the ancients and the moderns.[9] In addition, I will review the interaction between the Latin verse correspondence with Giovanni del Virgilio, with selected passages from the *Commedia*, to show how Dante extends and refines his reflections on the contemporary political scene within the bucolic exchange. The essay reveals that Dante's establishment of an ethical distance between himself and his Bolognese university interlocutor combines long-meditated political reflection with an innovative poetic programme – one that looks far beyond matters of language and style in his discussion of what kind of poetry truly merits a laurel crown.

Dante and Giovanni del Virgilio: ethical distance and poetic authority

To begin with the exchange's opening poem, Giovanni del Virgilio's *Eclogue* I, the invitation from the Bolognese professor indicates that some contemporary scholars at least did not really recognise or accept Dante's undermining of the rhetorical divisions between literary genres/styles, with the related choices concerning readership and public, which had been codified in the medieval *Artes*, following classical models.[10] This is clearly indicated in Dante's answering verses, when he bursts into a rhetorical dialogue which vehemently reasserts the existence of an erudite class writing in the vernacular. Del Virgilio's definitive response expresses his disagreement with this: 'Clerks scorn the | vernaculars' (17–18).[11] In reality, the *questione della lingua* conceals a deeper concern: what should be the qualities of the modern poet? Not only do both poets' positions appear irreconcilable in the manner in which they are expressed, but they also reveal a reciprocal misunderstanding between the profoundly innovative nature of Dante's poetry on the one hand and the new poetics of the *preumanesimo padovano* – of which Del Virgilio is clearly the representative – on the other.[12]

Moreover, the grammarian's position is rather ambiguous. Though he is aware of the originality of Dante's verses,[13] this awareness seems limited to the most superficial, linguistic and stylistic aspects; he argues that these innovations would prevent the learned from appreciating the whole complex ideological framework of Dante's epic poem. At the same time this conception of the *Commedia* as an all-embracing work, in human, spiritual and poetic terms, is precisely what limits Dante, in turn, in his understanding of the innovative elements present on the Paduan scene; he therefore fails to grasp what this circle has to offer.

Conscious of the gap between them, Del Virgilio takes an initiative whose aim seems to be the reduction, if not the abolition, of this distance. He uses poetic/linguistic arguments which reveal, however, that he misrepresents Dante's position. The reasons put forward by Giovanni del Virgilio, 'in temerity the goose', to try to convince the Florentine poet, 'the clear-toned | swan' (56–7),[14] recall the main points of Dante's *nuova poetica*, but in a negative way. According to Del Virgilio, the underlying ideology of the *Commedia* is too elevated for readers of the vernacular. These cannot and do not understand it – the proof being that his verses are the object of trivial popularisation[15] – and this simply because Italian is not the language of knowledge, but merely that of the common people.[16] In addition, the classical poets did not write in the vernacular,[17] and Dante himself had never addressed any verses to 'pale scholars'.[18] An even more personal touch via the use of flattery, a call to glory and the prospect of a possible poetic coronation – themes to which Dante was certainly sensitive – are placed in such a context that they fail to resonate with the Florentine poet.[19]

It is thus obvious that the Bolognese professor's epistolary poem shows no understanding of Dante's poetic/authorial and ethical/redemptive itinerary, thus reducing his initiative to a mere linguistic/stylistic choice.[20] Dante responds positively to Del Virgilio's invitation to write verses in Latin by adopting the classical language himself; however, his choice of the Virgilian bucolic model – as opposed to the genre classified as 'epic', 'tragic' or 'historical' – illustrates his refusal of a *milieu* and a cultural project which Del Virgilio was trying to impose on him.[21] What may appear as linguistic and stylistic distancing on Dante's part assumes a new significance when he is seen to be motivated by a proud authorial claim. In effect he is asserting a new poetics based on a common language and a humble style, or *polistile,* answering the multifaceted requirements of a conception of poetry which aims to be ethical, knowledgeable and generally all-encompassing, whether it be in the vernacular or in Latin. Dante thus adopts a clear stance, contributing to the most heated poetic debate of the time, in replying to Giovanni's/Mopsus's contempt – '"Hast thou not marked the scorn wherewith he greets | The speech of Comedy which women's chat | Stales on the lip, which the Castalian sisters | Blush to receive?"' (76–9).[22] The latter can do nothing but accept it.[23]

For Del Virgilio, poetry is a purely aristocratic form. For Dante it remains what he had expressed in the *Convivio*: a 'vivanda' [courses] (to be accompanied with 'barley bread')[24] offered to those who do not constitute a learned class 'by profession'. This is at least the case in the *Inferno* and the *Purgatorio*, and thanks to the polysemy characteristic of the *Commedia*. It is well known that the *Paradiso* is a different matter, as only those able to taste the 'pane delli angeli' [bread of angels] (*Cvo*, I. i. 7) are able to understand this part of the work. In any case, what remains fundamental is the concept of an aesthetic union in which the 'parola ornata' [ornamented speech] (*Inf.*, II. 67) reminiscent of Virgil carries meaning. Poetic discourse, however steeped in rhetoric,[25] has the role of transmitting content, truth and knowledge – thus assuming a social, moral and spiritual function through the figure of the poet, who is a vessel of the word of God, *scriba Dei*. This is the only way of bridging the gap between eloquence and ethics. These considerations shed light on Dante's reservations concerning those authors he saw as limited to a purely aesthetic approach, reusing classical genres without improving them. In his eyes, these writers tend to be reduced to mere imitators who adapt ancient forms to contemporary subjects, probably purely on the basis of circumstance and with no ethical depth.

This position, added to the strong element of provocation contained in Del Virgilio's verses, is the cause of the explicit attack on the contemporary absence of poetry made by Dante under the bucolic guise of Tityrus, in *Ecl.*, II. 50–2: '"O Melibœus, [...] scarce | One vigil-keeping Mopsus hath the muse | Known to maintain"'.[26] The lines originate from the ignorance declared by Meliboeus (usually identified as Dino Perini, a young Florentine resident in Ravenna), a situation which is useful to Dante's discourse. The young shepherd's lack of skill, which obliges him to ask Tityrus/Dante to take him under his wing, gives Tityrus the opportunity to answer, highlighting the demanding training required to become a true poet. The latter is here symbolised by Mopsus (Del Virgilio), who is congratulated for the long nights spent studying with the Muses – '"Mopsus still | Year in year out himself hath dedicate | To the Aonian mountains"' (36–8)[27] – and also for his pallor, characteristic of the learned.[28]

Although he uses the same terms in his reply, Dante does not consider himself equal to the scholars to whom Del Virgilio alludes – Del Virgilio himself, certainly, but also those who would have crowned Dante if he had followed their recommendations. By contrast, Dante's reply clearly underlines his difference. If the eulogy to Mopsus/Del Virgilio can be seen, at least in part, as a rhetorical prerequisite, it does not escape the reader that the peculiarities that define Mopsus as a poet – sleepless nights and weariness – are the same as those which Dante, with some very minor variations, attributes to himself in the *Commedia*.[29]

So far, it would seem that a form of 'poetic' assimilation between Mopsus/Del Virgilio and Tityrus/Dante can be found. Yet, in reality, this system of references constitutes a subtle antiphrasis. I believe the evidence for this is to be found, precisely, in lines 35–6: '"others vie | To master lore litigious"'.[30] These words, which may appear almost casual in the eulogy of Mopsus/Giovanni, in fact constitute, on the contrary, the very foundation of Dante's thought. In the *Convivio*, in a direct assault on the contemporary *literati* (the learned, specifically those educated in Latin culture), the poet had clearly asserted that 'they do not deserve to be called educated, since they do not acquire education for its own sake, but only as a means to gain money and status'; their characteristic craving for money and honours 'removes every trace of nobility of mind, which is the deepest source of man's desire for this food'.[31] In the third book of the treatise, his reference to 'lawyers, doctors and almost all religious, who study not in order to become wise but in order to acquire money or rank' illustrates the coherence of Dante's thinking as reasserted in the bucolic verses.[32] Sociologically, these non-*literati* correspond to the legal and medical faculties of the secular medieval universities, while the mention of a religious public clearly refers to the professors of the *Studia* run by the mendicant orders.[33]

Dante's blame is thus aimed, at least partially, at the scholars associated with both secular and religious institutions, taken as the chief representatives of official culture. Clearly Del Virgilio himself was a product of these institutions. And yet, as a possible result of the sincere admiration he expresses towards the Florentine poet, he is excluded from Dante's fierce criticism.[34] However, this is not the case for the scholars Del Virgilio considers as his models. It is thus quite possible to recognise in the statement '"others vie | To master lore litigious"' (35–6) the judge Lovati and probably also the notary Mussato, both of whom were implicitly presented by the Bolognese professor as paradigms of the erudite poet. Thus a disagreement which appears on one level to be merely stylistic and literary in nature is in fact related to a far more profound ethical issue present in all of Dante's work: his attack on all those learned people who, while boasting of their poetry, spend far more of their time in the pursuit of profitable activities, particularly in the field of law.[35] It is precisely this view that allows Dante to invert Del Virgilio's reference to the 'pallor' of those he admires, using the same term to contest the validity of the Bolognese writer's reference to these people as 'real' poets.

Dante thus appropriates the figure of Tityrus/Virgil, and identifies himself with the ancient Roman poet in his *Commedia* – a new *Aeneid* – and in his eclogues – an innovative and audacious imitation. In so doing, he asserts his difference and distances himself from the 'neo-Latin' world of Bologna and Padua. The latter, in his eyes, is interested only in stylistic imitation of the ancients. What Dante has to offer instead is a form of poetry, or maybe of 'humanism', which, while making the most of knowledge of the classics, is also able to appropriate them and give them a new meaning, in contrast to the learned humanism *di scuola* championed by Del Virgilio.

In this sense, the *Commedia* is an *imitatio* of the *Aeneid* in the most authentic sense of the word: it gives new life to its values and adapts the Latin model to a new context, both Christian and vernacular. The profound and reciprocal misunderstanding between Dante and Del Virgilio is confirmed by their exchange. The Bolognese master never fully grasps Dante's linguistic choices nor, more importantly, the originality of his poetry.[36] In effect, he remains blind to the extraordinary innovation of Dante's verses,[37] especially those of the *Paradiso*, which distance this work not only from any known rhetorical structure, but also from any of the traditional genres that his Florentine interlocutor, clearly, did not wish to follow.[38]

This incomprehension is reflected in Del Virgilio's reluctance to place Dante in the canon of learned poets – a distinction for which the Florentine poet yearned (as he reveals in *Inf.*, IV. 101–2).[39] Though the Bolognese professor is a very attentive reader of the *Commedia*, the fact remains that he does not appreciate the profound meaning of Dante's self-classification as sixth among the poets of antiquity in *Inferno* IV, but especially as first among his contemporaries, on the basis of the elevated nature of his poetry. It is this independence, gained through 'long study' (*Inf.*, I. 83) and creative polysemic assimilation, which is acknowledged by Virgil – the greatest of the ancient poets mentioned in the *Commedia*. Such independence serves to distinguish Dante from all the poets of his own time.

In Dante's view, as already mentioned, the new literary movement of the day – as represented, for example, by the Paduan initiative[40] – consisted of nothing more than a sterile reproduction of old forms or models. By contrast, Dante's effort to gain knowledge of, and appropriate, the classics, particularly Virgil, led him to a form of authorial reinvention which can be seen in the *Commedia*. In his eyes, his own difference from the modern cultural project then developing could not be greater: while Del Virgilio is trying to come closer to the neo-Latinists, Dante is moving in the opposite direction. Del Virgilio then joins the lyric game with a bucolic answer containing his proposal for Dante's coronation. However, this still shows his lack of understanding. In his poem he makes a repeated call to Tityrus/ Dante to come and visit Mopsus: "Hither | come!"' (68–9, 73),[41] and issues a threat to turn to Mussato, explicitly opposing the latter to Dante.

Faced with Tityrus/Dante's refusal, Mopsus/Giovanni will now turn to the Paduan, metaphorically represented by 'Phrygian | Muso' (91–2),[42] in order to quench his thirst.

Del Virgilio and Dante thus seem engaged in a real *querelle des anciens et des modernes ante litteram*, at least a century before the dispute between the rigorous humanists and the defenders of the vernacular.[43] Yet this anachronistic comparison is misleading, in the sense that both parties to the *Eclogues* are convinced that they are the true representatives of modernity. This is certainly true in Dante's case – not only as regards the astonishing inventiveness of his *Commedia*, but also, less consciously, for his scrupulous revival of the bucolic genre, a real 'classical innovation' of the Middle Ages.[44] His insistent claim for the *Commedia*'s originality in terms of language and ethical underpinning does not prevent him from also bringing a breath of fresh air to literature in Latin, with his return to the bucolic genre.[45] Undoubtedly, Dante was also conscious of the stylistic originality of his reply to Del Virgilio; equally undoubtedly, he shapes it so as to defend his own poetic contribution in the vernacular. As for Del Virgilio, he is so immersed in the new, 'neo-Latin' offerings that he considers them the *spiritus novus* of his time.

The *Eclogues*'s political dimension: past echoes and contemporary concerns

Believing his first answer had already exhausted the topic, Dante does not respond to Del Virgilio's provocation. In the following epistle (*Ecl.* IV), which constitutes the final text in their correspondence, he changes register. Taking inspiration from Del Virgilio's verses,[46] he shifts the reasons for his refusal to the political situation – a matter already alluded to in his previous reply (*Ecl.* II).[47]

In 1319, the year in which Del Virgilio most likely sent his first verse epistle (*Ecl.* I), Dante was 54 years old. He had abandoned the active political stage a few years before, following the last 'political' epistle he addressed to the Cardinals, who were meeting in conclave in Carpentras following Clement V's death on 20 April 1314. Dante seems to have found in Ravenna 'l'ultimo rifugio', a peaceful place of refuge conducive to his composition of the *Paradiso*.[48] Del Virgilio's invitation inspired in him a real *ars poetica in factis*, and gave him an opportunity to clarify his position in relation to the cultural context of the time. Moreover, the invitation incited him to look at the political situation once again. On the one hand, this modified his supposed lack of interest in politics during the last years of his life. On the other, it brought back to him distant echoes of a past that had remained dormant without being completely forgotten.

In the first part of his exchange with Del Virgilio (that is, in *Egloga* II), the reference to the inhospitality of Guelf Bologna – expressed in classical terms by the absence of the divinity in the city (*Ecl.*, II. 41) – is in effect a clear allusion to the capital sentence hanging over the poet's head, and consequently to the danger that the place represented for him. That Bologna constituted a real danger for Dante, and that he perceived it as such, is clearly apparent in the allusion he makes to the local context in this first poetic reply. This can probably be explained by his personal and political situation. A few years before he had finally settled in peaceful Ravenna, finding calm there until the moment in 1319 when Del Virgilio's epistle suddenly reached him, powerfully stirring up the past. These two distinct moments,[49] the contemporary reality and the remembrance of the past, are highlighted by Mopsus/ Del Virgilio himself – both when he reassures Tityrus/Dante concerning the potential dangers of Bologna[50] and when he mentions the probable reluctance of Iolaus/Guido da Polenta to allow the poet to leave Ravenna.[51]

Tityrus/Dante firmly shifts the conversation onto political matters. In his next verse letter he focuses on the figure of Polyphemus, putting his words into the mouth of his bucolic *alter ego,* Alphesiboeus. Among the numerous conjectures made in the attempt to find a historical iden- tification for the Cyclops, the most likely person would now appear to be Fulcieri da Calboli. He served as *capitano del popolo* in Bologna in the years 1299–1300 and then again from June to December 1321, and had already been appointed in March of that year.[52] This identification seems plausible precisely because of the alarm it provoked in the mind of the exiled poet. In general the political climate in Bologna was dominated at the time by a rigorous Black Guelfism, no matter which specific indi- vidual was in charge. In consequence, the city would naturally have been hostile to a White exile.[53] More specifically, however, Fulcieri was a man with strong links to Florence; he had been *podestà* there in 1303, distin- guishing himself for his Guelf intransigence and ruthlessness against the Whites. Consequently, Fulcieri must have crossed Dante's path, if only indirectly, during the first years of his exile.

In autumn 1302 the *Universitas partis Alborum* [Association of the Party of the Whites], together with the poet, left Arezzo to settle in Forlì. Here it was hosted by Scarpetta degli Ordelaffi, the city's Ghibelline lord. Scarpetta became *capitano* of the exiled Whites after the death of

Alessandro dei Guidi di Romena; he was also a political enemy of the Guelfs' De' Calboli, who had been exiled from Forlì in 1294. It was in Forlì that the expedition was organised against the castle of Pulicciano near Borgo San Lorenzo, possession of which meant control of the Mugello valley. Scarpetta led the White exiles, while the *podestà* Fulcieri headed the Florentines from 'within the city', the *intrinseci*.

Their conflict thus turned into a sort of civil war between the two most powerful families of Forlì.[54] The Florentines led by Fulcieri were the victors in March 1303, and Fulcieri's cruelty to the losers gained him a place in history.[55] This is precisely how Dante chose to present him in *Purg., XIV.* 58–64, through Guido del Duca's discourse. Indeed, the reprisals against the Whites who had remained in Florence after the victory of the Mugello are described in this passage with such violence and darkness that they clash with the elegiac tone of the *Purgatorio*. Yet it is this very contrast that makes the comments ring true.[56]

As with many episodes from this earlier period, these events must have marked the poet deeply. In 1321, after more than 15 years, he finds himself facing newly awakened memories of these months, probably channelled into the figure of the horrendous Polyphemus, devourer of Acis. In the depiction of the Dantean Cyclops, the *Egloghe*'s editors identify the influence of two episodes from Ovid's *Metamorphoses* involving Polyphemus as protagonist: the story of Acis and Galatea and the story of Achaemenides.[57] It might be useful to note here, as Gabriella Albanese has done, that linguistic clues also link Ovid's descriptions to the verses of *Purgatorio* dedicated to Fulcieri.[58] For instance, the image of the bodies of the Florentine Whites being sold alive to Forlì's *podestà* ('Vende la carne loro essendo viva', 61) seems to echo *Met., XIII.* 865 and *Met., XIV.* 192–6, 208–9,[59] yet one may also recognise in them *Aeneid, III.* 626–7.[60] Indeed, Fulcieri's entire description – which focuses on the loss of humanity that transforms him into an 'antica belva' [old cattle] (62), 'sanguinoso' [all bloodied] (64) and living in a 'trista selva' [wicked wood] (64) – goes beyond Ovid's descriptions. It rather recalls the savagery of Virgil's Cyclops, a creature more beast than man (*Aeneid, III.* 588–654).[61] If Fulcieri is not presented as a cannibal in the *Commedia*, in contrast to the bucolic Polyphemus,[62] he still appears as a bloodthirsty monster.

Although it is difficult objectively to establish a direct link between the purgatorial canto and *Egloga IV*, it is possible in the light of these comparisons to imagine, over and above the bucolic metaphor, that at the time of writing of the *Purgatorio* Dante had in mind Ovid and

Virgil's descriptions of Polyphemus and adapted them to describe Fulcieri. Years later, when he revived the bucolic genre with reference to the particular political situation of a Bologna dominated by the figure of the infamous Fulcieri, Dante remembered the character he had created in his vernacular poem; he thus gave birth to a new, revived Polyphemus.

From this perspective, I am convinced by Petoletti's hypothesis that 'l'idea di introdurre Polifemo possa avere contribuito a far spostare la scena bucolica in Sicilia' [the idea of introducing Polyphemus may have contributed to the relocation of the bucolic setting to Sicily].[63] Similarly it seems likely that Fulcieri's nomination as *capitano del popolo* in Bologna, precisely at the time of this correspondence, had rekindled Dante's already vivid memory of the man and his deeds. Though this gives shape to the successful composition of his bucolic verses, it might also have reinforced his refusal of Del Virgilio's proposal, inciting him to reaffirm his choice of the 'dewy fields of Pelorus' (i.e. Ravenna) as a *locus amoenus*. The literary distance Dante reaffirms at the beginning of the correspondence concerning the linguistic, poetic and ethical conception of the *Commedia* finds itself transferred and confirmed, this time in relation to the political sphere.

This is also seen in his second answer, which, thematically, follows the order of the historical events of the exchange. Precisely because he wanted to highlight his distance from contemporary political affairs, Dante uses the bucolic fiction he had initially introduced for purely poetic reasons and imbues it with a different meaning, relocating his fiction to Sicily. This new background gives him the opportunity to introduce the dark figure of Polyphemus, in order once more to reaffirm his detachment from the struggles taking place between the factions. It is also significant that, at the very same period, Dante was composing the triptych involving Cacciaguida (*Paradiso* XV–XVII). Here his posture of disdainful isolation is well summed up in the famous expression 'averti fatta parte per te stesso' [become a party unto yourself] (*Par.*, XVII. 69), clearly underlining Dante's own convictions.

However, apart from considerations related to danger and personal safety involved in the never-ending fight between the Guelfs and the Ghibellines – and in spite of Dante's detachment from their struggles – what clearly emerges from his bucolic verses is a fundamentally ethical distance from political involvements. To Dante these are now things of the past; an aspect to which he might also be alluding in the bucolic verses with his reference to Tityrus's great age. From now on Dante will limit his global ethical and political thought to his all-embracing epic poem, far from any passing 'city lay' ('"civile [...] carmen"', *Ecl.*, III. 27–8).

His position here is closely linked to his poetics and explains, at least in part, his silent refusal to become involved in the composition of a poem on a contemporary historical subject, especially any of those suggested by Del Virgilio. In fact, of the four topics suggested,[64] two (Henry VII's deeds and the conflicts between the Paduans and Cangrande) had already been dealt with by Mussato,[65] creating another situation of comparison between the Paduan poet laureate and the Florentine Dante. The bucolic fiction thus becomes for Dante an ideal setting in which he can reassert his own ethical position, in terms of both poetics and politics, as well as his own distance from a world that seems to him ever more remote, at a time when he is increasingly focused on reaching the 'città celeste' [heavenly city].

Notes

1. On the dating of this correspondence, see Dante Alighieri, *Epistole, Ecloge, Questio de situ et forma aque et terre*, ed. Manlio Pastore Stocchi (Rome–Padua: Antenore, 2012), 148. The editor sets the beginning of the exchange between the end of 1319 and the earlier part of 1320, and the rest of the correspondence through the rest of 1320; he suggests the last eclogue by Dante was written in 1321. Gabriella Albanese offers more precise dates, choosing the second half of 1319 for Del Virgilio's first epistle and setting Dante's answer, together with Del Virgilio's following reply, in 1321: 'Introduzione', in *Egloghe*, ed. Gabriella Albanese, in Dante Alighieri, *Opere*, ed. Marco Santagata, 2 vols (Milan: Mondadori, 2011–14), II (2014), 1595–6. The latest editor of the *Eclogues*, Marco Petoletti, follows his two predecessors, suggesting late 1319 for the first letter from Giovanni del Virgilio and leaving open the date of Dante's first answer, then dating the first *Eclogue* by Del Virgilio to spring–summer 1320 and the final, concluding answer from Dante to late spring 1321: 'Nota introduttiva', in *Egloge*, ed. Marco Petoletti, in Dante Alighieri, *Le opere. V. Epistole, Egloge, Questio de aqua et terra*, ed. Marco Baglio, Luca Azzetta, Marco Petoletti and Michele Rinaldi (Rome: Salerno Editrice, 2016), 493–500. From now on I shall indicate these texts as *Ecl.* and follow the traditional numbering. Marco Santagata agrees with a chronology occurring between the end of 1319 and the beginning of 1320: *Dante. Il romanzo della sua vita* (Milan: Mondadori, 2012), 301.

2. Dante's movements between Verona, Mantua and Ravenna during this last period of his life remain obscure; the period between 1318 and 1320, when the poet settled in Ravenna, then governed by Guido Novello, remains particularly problematic. See Eugenio Chiarini and Pier Vincenzo Mengaldo, 'Ravenna', in *Enciclopedia Dantesca (ED)*, ed. Umberto Bosco, 6 vols (Rome: Istituto dell'Enciclopedia Italiana, 1984 [1st edn 1970–8]), IV, 857–66; Giuseppe Billanovich, 'Tra Dante e Petrarca', *Italia Medioevale e Umanistica* 8 (1965): 1–44; Giuseppe Indizio, 'Le tappe venete dell'esilio di Dante', in Giuseppe Indizio, *Problemi di biografia dantesca* (Ravenna: Longo, 2013), 93–114, esp. 108–13. Santagata believes Dante arrived in Verona around the middle of 1316, and left around the middle of 1318 or in 1319: Santagata, *Dante*, 296, 300. Inglese is less definite about the chronology; however, he estimates that Dante arrived in Ravenna between 20 January 1320 and the summer of that year, when he received Del Virgilio's epistle: Inglese, *Vita di Dante. Una biografia possibile* (Rome: Carocci, 2015), 139–42. Information on Giovanni del Virgilio

is scarce: see Guido Martellotti, 'Giovanni del Virgilio', in *ED*, III, 193–4; Emilio Pasquini, 'Giovanni del Virgilio', in *Dizionario Biografico degli Italiani*, 90 vols (Rome: Istituto dell'Enciclopedia Italiana, 1960–2017), 38 (1990), 404–9; Giuseppe Indizio, 'Giovanni del Virgilio maestro e dantista minore', in Indizio, *Problemi*, 449–69.

3. For the correspondence, preserved in nine manuscripts and in particular in Boccaccio's famous 'Zibaldone Laurenziano' (Biblioteca Medicea-Laurenziana, Florence, MS Pluteo XXIX 8), see Giuseppe Billanovich, 'Giovanni Del Virgilio, Pietro da Moglio, Francesco da Fiano', *Italia Medioevale e Umanistica* 6 (1963): 203–94; Guido Martellotti, 'Egloghe', in *ED*, II, 644–6; Luciano Gargan, 'Dante e Giovanni del Virgilio: le Egloghe', in Luciano Gargan, *Dante, la sua biblioteca e lo studio di Bologna* (Rome-Padua: Antenore, 2014), 112–41; Giuliano Tanturli, 'La corrispondenza poetica di Giovanni del Virgilio e Dante fra storia della tradizione e critica del testo', *Studi Medievali* 52 (2010): 809–45; and Gabriella Albanese, 'Tradizione e ricezione del Dante bucolico nell'Umanesimo. Nuove acquisizioni sui manoscritti della corrispondenza poetica con Giovanni del Virgilio', *Nuova Rivista di Letteratura Italiana* 14 (2011): 9–80.

4. For the theory of styles and the 'cosiddetto pre-umanesimo' [so-called pre-humanism] relative to this epistolary exchange, see Claudia Villa, 'Il problema dello stile umile e il sorriso di Dante', in Claudia Villa, *La protervia di Beatrice. Studi per la biblioteca di Dante* (Florence: SISMEL-Galluzzo, 2009), 215–32 (219).

5. On poetic coronation in the *Commedia* as well as in Petrarch and Boccaccio, see Aldo Rossi, 'Dante, Boccaccio e la laurea poetica', *Paragone* n.s. 12 (1962): 3–41; Michelangelo Picone, '*L'amato alloro*: Dante fra Petrarca e Boccaccio', in Michelangelo Picone, *Scritti danteschi*, ed. Antonio Lanza (Ravenna: Longo, 2017), 649–69; and Michelangelo Picone, 'Il tema dell'incoronazione poetica in Dante, Petrarca e Boccaccio', *L'Alighieri* 25 (2005): 5–26. On the theme of the coronation and its intricacies in *Paradiso* and in the *Eclogues*, with Mussato and his Paduan circle in the background, see Corrado Bologna, 'Dante e il latte delle Muse', in *Atlante della letteratura italiana*, ed. Sergio Luzzato and Gabriele Pedullà, 2 vols (Turin: Einaudi, 2010), I, 145–55. For poetic coronations prior to Petrarch's, see Francesco Paolo Terlizzi, 'Le incoronazioni poetiche', in *Atlante della letteratura italiana*, I, 141–4. For an interesting, two-sided interpretation of Mussato's crowning as both poetic and imperial, see Gabriella Albanese, '*De gestis Henrici VII cesaris*: Mussato, Dante e il mito dell'incoronazione poetica', in *Enrico VII, Dante e Pisa a 700 anni dalla morte dell'imperatore e dalla 'Monarchia' (1313–1323). Atti del convegno internazionale (Pisa-San Miniato, 24–26 ottobre 2013)*, ed. Giuseppe Petralia and Marco Santagata (Ravenna: Longo, 2016), 161–202 (193–202). More generally see Nadia Cannata and Maddalena Signorini, '*Per trionfare o Cesare o poeta*. La corona d'alloro e le insegne del poeta moderno', in *Dai pochi ai molti. Studi in onore di Roberto Antonelli*, ed. Paolo Cannettieri and Arianna Punzi (Rome: Viella, 2014), 3–37 (10–18 on Dante).

6. Bologna argues otherwise, 149.

7. See *Ecl.*, I. 23–4, and *Ecloge* (Petoletti), 493. Dante addressed his epic poem, and his works more generally, to a varied and disparate readership: for more detailed discussion of this point see Sabrina Ferrara, *La parola dell'esilio. Autore e lettori nell'opera di Dante dopo l'esilio* (Florence: Cesati, 2016).

8. Marino Zabbia, 'Albertino Mussato', in *Dizionario Biografico degli Italiani* 67 (2012), 520–4; Ronald G. Witt, 'Un poeta laureato: Albertino Mussato', in *Atlante della letteratura italiana*, I, 134–9; Ronald G. Witt, *The Two Latin Cultures and the Foundation of Renaissance Humanism in Medieval Italy* (Cambridge: Cambridge University Press, 2012), 463–5.

9. To describe Dante's role as 'ethical' refers not only to the moral aspect of his poetry, but also to the complex system of conceptual stratification – juridical, theological, redemptive and so forth – that pervades it.

10. Most famously, for instance, via Horace's *Ars poetica*.

11. *Ecl.*, I. 15. I will not insist here on the association between vernacular writing and women readers evoked by Tityrus/Dante in the dialogue with Meliboeus in *Ecl.*, II. 52–4, as this would deserve more substantial development. The question has been partially treated by Luigi Spagnolo, 'La lingua delle *muliercule*: ideologia preumanistica e questioni di autenticità nel Dante latino', *La lingua italiana* 11 (2015): 37–65. However, the author considers the *Eclogues* a forgery by the Bolognese orator. For the English translations of the *Eclogues*, see *Dante and Giovanni del Virgilio*, trans. Philip H. Wicksteed and Edmund G. Gardner (New York: Haskell House Publishers, 1970); the line numbers of the English translation are given in brackets

when, as in this case, they do not correspond to the Latin original. Translations are sometimes slightly modified for clarity.

12. The movement is defined as 'Paduan pre-humanism' by Guido Billanovich, 'Il preumanesimo padovano', in *Storia della cultura veneta*, II. *Il Trecento*, (Vicenza: Pozza, 1976), 19–110. However, I prefer to define this phenomenon, following Inglese, with the expression 'letteratura neo-latina' [neo-Latin literature] (Inglese, *Vita di Dante*, 141).

13. Del Virgilio himself recognises, at the beginning of his epistolary poem: 'Pyeridum vox alma, *novis* qui *cantibus* orbem | mulces letifluum' (*Ecl.*, I. 1–2).

14. *Ecl.*, I. 50: 'Quos strepit arguto temerarius anser olori'.

15. *Ecl.*, I. 12–13: 'Que tamen in triviis nunquam digesta coaxat | comicomus nebulo, qui Flaccum pelleret orbe'.

16. *Ecl.*, I. 15: 'Carmine sed layco: clerus vulgaria tempnit'.

17. *Ecl.*, I. 17–19: 'Preterea nullus, quos inter es agmine sextus, | nec quem consequeris celo, sermone forensi | descripsit'.

18. *Ecl.*, I. 6–11: 'Tanta quid heu semper iactabis seria vulgo, | et nos pallentes nichil ex te vate legemus? | Ante quidem cythara pandum delphyna movebis, | Davus et ambigue Sphyngos problemata solvet, | Tartareum preceps quam gens ydiota figuret | et secreta poli vix experata Platoni' [6–12: Such weighty themes | why wilt thou still cast to the vulgar, while we pale | students shall read nought from thee as bard? Sooner | shalt thou stir the curving dolphin with the harp, and | Davus solve the riddles of equivocating Sphinx, than that | unlettered folk shall figure the precipice of Tartarus and | secrets of the pole scarce unsphered by Plato]; I. 21–2: 'Nec margharitas profliga prodigus apris, | nec preme Castalias indigna veste sorores' [24–5: Cast not in prodigality thy pearls before the swine, | nor load the Castalian sisters with a garb unworthy of them].

19. For the promised rewards: *Ecl.*, I. 23–4: 'At, precor, ore cie que te distinguere possint | carmine vatisono, sorti comunis utrique'; I. 33–4: 'Si te fama iuvat, parvo te limite septum | non contentus eris, nec vulgo iudice tolli'; I. 35–40: 'En ego iam primus, si dignum duxeris esse, | clericus Aonidum, vocalis verna Maronis, | promere gimnasiis te delectabor, ovantum | inclita Peneis redolentem tempora sertis, | ut prevectus equo sibi plaudit preco sonorus | festa trophea ducis populo pretendere leto'; and for further flattering comment, I. 45–6: 'Ni canis hec, alios ad te pendendo, poeta | omnibus ut solus dicas, indicta manebunt'.

20. If it is true, as Bellomo states, that Del Virgilio's verse epistle is the 'prima documentata reazione alla grande novità dantesca costituita dal poema' [the first documented reaction to the great novelty of the Dante's poem], his total incomprehension is no less obvious: see Saverio Bellomo, *Filologia e critica dantesca* (Brescia: La Scuola, 2008), 129.

21. Ronald G. Witt, *In the Footsteps of the Ancients. The Origins of Humanism From Lovato to Bruni* (Leiden: Brill, 2000), 81–173, observes that Lovato and the circle of the Paduan 'humanists' do not seem to differentiate between epic and tragic genres (123–4). The most important historiographic work of the time, *De gestis Henrici VII cesaris* by Albertino Mussato, combines, at least in its second part, the tones of epic tragedy with objective historical observation. See Albanese, '*De gestis Henrici VII cesaris*', 163, 192.

22. *Ecl.*, II. 52–4: '"Comica nonne vides ipsum reprehendere verba, | tum quia femineo resonant ut trita labello, | tum quia Castalias pudet acceptare sorores?"'. Mopsus's disapproval seems to be an echo of Mussato's position on the tragic style, as the only one worthy of celebrating a noble subject: see *Ep.* I, *Ad collegium artistarum*, in Enzo Cecchini, 'Le epistole metriche del Mussato sulla poesia', in *Tradizione classica e letteratura umanistica per Alessandro Perosa*, ed. Roberto Cardini et al., 2 vols (Rome: Bulzoni, 1985), I, 95–119 (102–6).

23. *Ecl.*, II. 51: '"Concedat Mopsus!"'.

24. *Cvo*, I. xiii. 12.

25. *DVE*, II. iv. 2.

26. *Ecl.*, II. 36–7: '"O Melibee, decus vatum, quoque nomen in auras | fluxit, et insomnem vix Mopsum Musa peregit"'.

27. *Ecl.*, II. 28–30: '"Montibus Aoniis Mopsus, Melibee, quot annis, | [...] | se dedit et sacri nemoris perpalluit umbra"'.

28. On learned pallor, commentators refer not only to *Purg.*, XXXI. 140–1, but also to 'nos pallentes' in *Ecl.*, I. 7, the term used by Del Virgilio to indicate the learned poets. See the notes to *Ecloge* (Pastore Stocchi), 172; *Egloghe* (Albanese), 1623–32; *Egloge* (Petoletti), 550–1.

29. In *Par.*, XXV. 3, pallor is replaced by thinness.

30. *Ecl.* II. 29: '"satagunt alii causarum iura doceri"'.

31. *Cvo*, I. ix. 3: 'non si deono chiamare litterati, però che non acquistano la lettera per lo suo uso, ma in quanto per quella guadagnano denari e dignitate'; I. ix. 2: 'da ogni nobilitate d'animo li rimuove, la quale massimamente desidera questo cibo'.

32. *Cvo*, III. xi. 10: 'li legisti, medici e quasi tutti religiosi, che non per sapere studiano ma per acquistare moneta o dignitade'.

33. See *Cvo* (Fioravanti), 467 and *La filosofia in Italia al tempo di Dante*, ed. Carla Casagrande and Gianfranco Fioravanti (Bologna: il Mulino, 2016), 11–122.

34. *Ecl.*, II. 37. Del Virgilio himself, in his reply, will assume the lonely position attributed to him by Dante (*Ecl.*, III. 6). Without participating in the controversy against those who pursue profitable activities, he mentions, however, those people who dedicate themselves to activities other than literature (*Ecl.*, III. 7). It is interesting to note that, instead of the 'technical' expression 'causarum iura doceri' ['to master lore litigious,' i.e., to focus on juristic learning] used in *Ecl.* II. 29 ('"satagunt alii causarum iura doceri"'), the Bolognese master chooses the neutral 'causis adigentibus' [summoned by their affairs] (*Ecl.*, III. 7: 'Irruerant alii causis adigentibus urbem'), which semantically brings back the substantive 'causa' to its more general meaning.

35. See the famous verses in *Par.,* IX. 133–5, XI. 4–5, and XII. 82–4. Dante's position will be taken up again, on a stronger polemical note, by Boccaccio and Petrarch. For instance, about 20 years later, Petrarch writes about Lovato in *Rerum memorandarum libri*, 61. 1: 'Lovatus patavinus fuit nuper poetarum omnium "quos nostra" vel patrum nostrorum "vidit etas" facillime princeps, nisi iuris civilis studium amplexus et novem Musis duodecim tabulas immiscuisset et animum ab eliconiis curis ad forensem strepitum deflexisset' [Lovato of Padua would obviously be the first of all the modern poets 'living in our' (that is, of our fathers) 'times', if he had not dedicated himself to the civil law, and if he had not mixed the nine muses with the twelve tables, and if he had not directed his attention away from the Heliconian arts to the noise of the courts]: see Francesco Petrarca, *Rerum memorandarum libri*, ed. Marco Petoletti (Florence: Le Lettere, 2014).

36. Dante was perfectly aware of this and, in his answer, felt the need to highlight, precisely, the implications that the 'comica verba' had had at all stylistic levels (*Ecl.*, II. 52–4).

37. Del Virgilio is aware of the modernity of Dante's poetry – after *Ecl.*, I. 1 ('novis […] cantibus') he will call his verses '"carmina […] | nova"', in *Ecl.* III. 68–9 – which deserves full admiration. However, it seems that he considers only Dante's Latin *oeuvre* worthy of being taught ('"Parrasii iuvenesque senes, et carmina leti | qui nova mirari cupiantque antiqua doceri"'). On this point see *Ecloge* (Pastore Stocchi), 192; *Egloghe* (Albanese), 1747–8; *Egloge* (Petoletti), 592.

38. *Ecl.*, II. 61: '"Nulli iuncta gregi nullis assuetaque caulis"'; but see also *Par.*, II. 1–18.

39. *Ecl.*, I. 17–19: 'Preterea nullus, quos inter es agmine sextus, | nec quem consequeris celo, sermone forensi | descripsit'. From Del Virgilio's point of view, excluding Dante from the category of learned poets is not without further autobiographical (and political) consequences. This is clear when he alludes to the poet's exile not only from his city, but also from the community of true *letterati*. Consequently his inclusion would also correspond to his social reintegration: see Bologna, 148.

40. Dante might have formed this opinion by reading Mussato's texts, of which he almost certainly knew the *Ecerinis*. See Paolo Baldan, 'Dante, Mussato e il Colle di Romano', in *Nuovi studi ezzeliniani*, ed. Giorgio Cracco (Rome: Istituto Storico Italiano per il Medioevo, 1992), 575–88. Dante does not perceive the methodological innovations of the new humanist school: its critical approach to antiquity, its searches for classical texts in libraries, its attempt to reconstruct the Latin language philologically and its opening to cultural exchanges, which will all become the basis of the new humanist era. On Dante and Mussato, see Ezio Raimondi, 'Dante e il modello ezzeliniano', in *Dante e la cultura veneta. Atti del Convegno di studi organizzato dalla Fondazione Giorgio Cini, in collaborazione con l'Istituto universitario di Venezia, l'Università di Padova, il Centro scaligero di studi danteschi e i Comuni di Venezia, Padova, Verona (30 marzo–5 aprile 1966)*, ed. Vittore Branca and Giorgio Padoan (Florence: Olschki, 1966), 51–69; Giorgio Padoan, 'Tra Dante e Mussato', *Quaderni veneti* 24 (1996): 27–45.

41. *Ecl.*, III. 67, 72: '"Huc ades"'.

42. *Ecl.*, III. 88–9: '"Frigio Musone"'. Martellotti already found Del Virgilio's assertion quite unexpected in a context of *captatio benevolentiae*: Guido Martellotti, 'Mussato, Albertino', in *ED*, III 1066–8.

43. Giacinto Margiotta, *Le Origini italiane de la Querelle des Anciens et des Modernes* (Rome: Editrice Studium, 1953); Vito R. Giustiniani, 'Gli umanisti e la *querelle des anciens et des modernes*', in *L'educazione e la formazione intellettuale nell'età dell'Umanesimo. Atti del II convegno internazionale, 1990*, ed. Luisa Rotondi Secchi Tarugi (Milan: Guerini, 1992), 63–71.

44. On the medieval tradition of the bucolic genre, see Francesco Macrì-Leone, *La bucolica latina nella letteratura italiana del XIV secolo, con una introduzione sulla bucolica latina nel Medioevo* (Turin: Loescher, 1889), 5–42; Enrico Carrara, *La poesia pastorale* (Milan: Vallardi, 1906); Guido Martellotti, 'Dalla tenzone al carme bucolico', *Italia medioevale e umanistica* 7 (1964): 325–36; Guido Martellotti, 'La riscoperta dello stile bucolico (da Dante a Boccaccio)', in *Dante e la cultura veneta*, 335–46. On Virgil's reception in the Middle Ages, it is still useful to refer to the classic study by Domenico Comparetti, *Virgilio nel Medio Evo*, ed. Giorgio Pasquali (Florence: La Nuova Italia, 1981; 1st edn, 1872).

45. The fact that Dante is very conscious of his own modernity already appears in *Purg.*, XXIV. 55–7, and *Purg.*, XXVI. 112–14. It is obvious that, for him, the concept of modernity itself is closely connected to vernacular poetry, and to the evolution of the poetry and art of his time (see *Purg.* XI), in direct contrast to the neo-Latin modernity represented by Del Virgilio and the Padua school. These brief observations are the fruit of stimulating exchanges with Johannes Bartuschat, whom I wish warmly to thank, during a conference that took place at the Centre d'Etudes Supérieures de la Renaissance de Tours, 20–22 June 2017, on *The Dynamics of the Relationship with the More Recent Past in Early Modern Europe: Between Rejection and Acknowledgement*, organised by Maria Clotilde Camboni and Chiara Lastraioli.

46. *Ecl.*, III. 72–6: '"Huc ades, et nostros timeas neque, Tityre, saltus: | namque fidem celse concusso vertice pinus | glandiferæque etiam quercusque arbusta dedere. | Non hic insidie, non hic iniuria, quantas | esse putas"'.

47. *Ecl.*, II. 41: '"Sed timeam saltus et rura ignara deorum"'.

48. The expression derives from Corrado Ricci, *L'ultimo rifugio di Dante* (Milan: Hoepli, 1921; 1st edn 1891).

49. On political temporality in the *Egloghe*, see Sabrina Ferrara, 'Il senso del tempo nelle *Egloghe* di Dante', *Italianistica* 44.2 (2015): 199–218.

50. *Ecl.*, III. 72–6.

51. *Ecl.*, III. 80–3.

52. I will not repeat the debate here, but simply refer the reader to the analysis and bibliographies contained in the most recent editions: see *Ecloge* (Pastore Stocchi), 206–7; *Egloghe* (Albanese), 1775–8; *Egloge* (Petoletti), 622–4. See also Gabriella Albanese and Paolo Pontari, 'Il notariato bolognese, le *Egloghe* e il Polifemo dantesco. Nuove testimonianze manoscritte e una nuova lettura dell'ultima *Egloga*', *Studi danteschi* 81 (2016): 13–130; Margaret Worsham Musgrove, 'Cyclopean Latin: intertextual readings in Dante's *Eclogues* and Góngora's *Polifemo y Galatea*', *Classical and Modern Literature* 18.2 (1998): 125–36.

53. Martellotti offers a more global interpretation ('La riscoperta dello stile bucolico', 335–46); also *Ecloge* (Pastore Stocchi), 207.

54. Santagata, *Dante*, 151; Inglese, *Vita di Dante*, 72–4.

55. Dino Compagni, *Cronica*, ed. Davide Cappi (Rome: Istituto Storico Italiano per il Medioevo, 2000), II. 30; Giovanni Villani, *Nuova cronica*, ed. Giuseppe Porta (Parma: Guanda, 1990–1), VIII. 59.

56. Guido Mazzoni, 'Dante e il Polifemo bolognese (*Eclogae*, II, 73 segg.)', in Guido Mazzoni, *Almae luces malae cruces. Studi danteschi* (Bologna: Zanichelli, 1941), 349–72.

57. Ovid, *Met.*, XIII. 738–897, and XIV. 154–222: see Ovid, *Metamorphoses*, II. Books IX–XV, English translation Frank J. Miller (Cambridge, MA–London: Harvard University Press, 1958). In the second episode Polyphemus is presented as the monster who eats Ulysses's companions alive after having been blinded. As for Acis, Ovid writes that he is killed by a rock thrown by the Cyclops.

58. See *Egloghe* (Albanese), 1776.

59. The Ovidian references run as follows: '"*Viscera viva traham*"' ['I'll tear his vitals out alive']; '"O si quis referat mihi casus Ulixem | aut aliquem e sociis, in quem mea saeviat ira, | viscera cuius edam, cuius viventia dextra | membra mea laniem, cuius mihi sanguis inundet | guttur et elisi trepident sub dentibus artus"' ['O that some chance would but bring Ulysses back to me, or some one of his friends, against whom my rage might vent itself, whose vitals I might devour, whose living body I might tear asunder with my hands, whose gore might flood my throat and whose mangled limbs might quiver between my teeth']; '"Visceraque et carnes cumque albis

ossa medullis | *semianimesque* artus avidam condebat in alvum"' ['he filled his greedy maw with their vitals and their flesh, their bones full of white marrow and their limbs still warm with life'].

60. Virgil, *Eclogues. Georgics. Aeneid, Books 1–6*, trans. H. Rushton Fairclough (Cambridge, MA–London: Harvard University Press, 1999): '"Vidi atro cum membra fluentia tabo | manderet, et tepidi tremerent sub dentibus artus"' ['I watched while he devoured their limbs, all dripping with black blood-clots, and the warm joints quivered beneath his teeth'].

61. Translations of *Purg.* XIV from Dante Alighieri, *The Divine Comedy*, ed. Allen Mandelbaum (Berkeley: University of California Press, 1981).

62. *Ecl.*, IV. 76–7: '"Quis Poliphemon" ait "non horreat" Alphesibeus | "assuetum rictus humano sanguine tingui"'.

63. *Ecloge* (Petoletti), 624. See also Lino Pertile, 'Le *Egloghe* di Dante e l'antro di Polifemo', in *Dante the Lyric and Ethical Poet. Dante lirico e etico*, ed. Zygmunt G. Barański and Martin McLaughlin (London: Legenda, 2010), 153–67 (157–64).

64. *Ecl.*, I. 26: 'Iovis armiger' (Henry VII's military intervention); I. 27: 'Que lilia fregit arator' (victory of Uguccione della Faggiuola over the Guelfs at Montecatini); I. 28: 'Dente molosso' (Paduan defeat by Cangrande della Scala); I. 29: 'Ligurum montes et classes Parthenopeas' (Robert of Anjou's siege of Genoa, held by Marco Visconti's Ghibellines).

65. Respectively in *De gestis Henrici VII cesaris* and, implicitly, in the *Ecerinis*.

Two Reflections on Dante's Political and Ethical Afterlives

8
Dante's *Fortuna*: An Overview of Canon Formation and National Contexts

Catherine Keen

On 23 October 1373 Giovanni Boccaccio launched a new initiative in the already flourishing tradition of reading and studying Dante: he began the first ever publicly funded and freely accessible lecture series on Dante. The series was commissioned in response to popular demand, following a petition from the Florentine public to the city's governing councils to establish a series of readings commenting on 'their' Dante – the Florentine author who, only a few decades earlier, had used accessible, Florentine vernacular to compose his *Commedia* (the poem was concluded in 1321, the year of Dante's death). Boccaccio's series was inclusive. In the surviving transcriptions we find references addressed to amateur 'uditori' [listeners], as well as the more erudite 'lettori' who might eventually read his thoughts in published form. It was also intensive; in just over three months he delivered around 60 lectures, but reached only the middle of the *Inferno* (XVII. 17) before the series ended in January 1374.[1]

The original petition piously justified the request for lectures by noting that this kind of divulgative commentary on the poem would assist its general audience better to understand the poem's moral intent, and so benefit from its lessons on the avoidance of vice and pursuit of virtue. In line with the medieval classification of most art poetry as concerned with ethics, this justification glossed over the poem's potentially controversial aspects, politically and theologically speaking, and stressed the social and moral positives of the popular passion for Dante.[2]

The Florentine public who desired one local intellectual heavyweight, Boccaccio, to introduce them to the work of another, Dante, were at the vanguard of what has proved a centuries-long tradition of public enthusiasm for Dante. Boccaccio's open lectures inaugurated that special form of literary engagement that has come to be known as *Lectura Dantis*: a public reading of Dante's poem, canto by canto, with accompanying exposition. *Lectura* series have been held from the fourteenth century onwards in Italian civic and university centres across the peninsula, gradually coming to find their place in cultural programmes from Turin to Palermo, as well as in the non-Italian world.

Such lectures form a distinctive strand within a long-standing reception of Dante so multifaceted as to defy description. Over the centuries the *Commedia* has been studied, read aloud and performed by groups popular and elite, secular and clerical, institutional and informal. It has been illustrated in painting and sculpture, and has inspired music, theatre and eventually cinema, television and online responses. Modern Italians' Dante enthusiasms no longer find expression in petitions for public lecture series, but he is still capable of providing the focus for mass engagement with questions of culture, and of social and political participation. This has recently been shown, for instance, by the huge success of Roberto Benigni's 'TuttoDante' performances. These evolved between 2002 and 2015, as both live and televised performances, in which Tuscan comic Benigni gave readings of complete canti from the *Commedia*, accompanied by satirical commentary on the present-day political and social scene.[3] Thus, although the idea of a 'national poet' has fallen somewhat out of favour over the past century, Dante's stature as an Italian cultural icon remains firm.

Outside the peninsula too, and especially from the nineteenth century onwards, Dante has become recognised as a 'global' figure and a focus for cultural interests beyond Italy's national borders – in European and North American centres and also, albeit more sporadically, in Latin America, Australia, the Middle East, Africa and Asia. Indeed, the international reception of Dante is a vast and heterogeneous phenomenon in its own right. It is represented by translation, commentary, adaptation and imitation, as well as academic and popularising study, and covers visual, theatrical and musical responses as well as textual ones.[4]

What follows here offers a brief overview of some of the varied 'afterlives' of Dante in both popular and scholarly circles, and inside and outside Italy. Dealing with a *fortuna* extended over some seven centuries, the account is necessarily partial and schematic. The aim is to survey some phases of the evolution of the national and international reputation of Dante and his *Commedia*, especially in relation to ethical and political themes, providing a broad (and necessarily incomplete) overview of the 'afterlife' of a major cultural figure. This in turn serves to complement the more focused account that follows, in Claire Honess and Matthew Treherne's reflection on a research project on Dante in twenty-first-century Britain that drew both scholarly and popular strands into its programme of study.

Making the poem accessible: lecture, commentary, controversy

To return, then, to the opening example, the *Lectura Dantis* form has since its inception always been public and performative by definition. Its basis lies in reading the *Commedia* aloud, and in providing oral commentary. Though such lectures are often designed for future publication, and these days are often sponsored within university environments, the presumption of live delivery before an audience always keeps in mind the importance of spontaneous, direct encounter with a text that Dante made deliberately open and accessible in language and form.[5] (Some iterations of Benigni's shows and readings could thus also be classified as *Lecturae Dantis*.)[6] For these reasons, the practice of *Lectura Dantis* is usually distinguished from the type of Dante criticism provided by written commentary. This ranges from highly specialist, academic analysis aimed primarily at erudite readers to more accessible, generalist approaches. One distinct sub-category, with an even longer history than the *Lectura Dantis*, is the form of commentary that annotates the entire *Commedia*, canto by canto. It too generally aims to support and explain the poem in all its literary, socio-political and spiritual complexity, with the expansiveness and erudition permitted by written delivery.

For modern Dante scholars, the online 'Dartmouth Dante Project' has become an almost indispensable 'virtual library' of such commentaries (as attested across the essays in this volume). The Project currently houses 77 commentary texts, ranging from very early production in both Italian and Latin – Boccaccio is a relative latecomer, sixteenth on a list that opens with Jacopo Alighieri, Dante's son, commenting on the *Inferno* in vernacular around 1322[7] – up to full commentaries from the last two decades; the latest in English is that of Robert Hollander, from 2000 to 2007, and in Italian that of Nicola Fosca, from 2003 to 2015. Beyond these *vade mecums* to the poem, huge numbers of scholarly monographs and articles pour out every year, from the academic communities of Italy, Europe, the Anglophone world and beyond.

The popularity of Dante's poem as an instant 'bestseller' from the moment of its completion onwards is attested also by often cited anecdotes, and by diverse types of evidence from near-contemporary sources.

For instance, the earliest recorded evidence of the *Commedia*'s circulation takes the form of a single *terzina* (*Inferno,* III. 94–6) that a Tuscan notary working for the Bologna government in 1317 transcribed inside the cover of a register of legal cases.[8] It evidently formed a familiar part of the cultural repertory of this civil servant, only a few years after complete manuscripts of the *Inferno* had become available. He saw no incompatibility in jotting poetic material from Dante into the formal, bound volume of his working records as a professional lawyer. Still in Dante's own lifetime, the Latin correspondence that the poet exchanged with Bologna professor Giovanni del Virgilio in the *Eclogues,* discussed in Sabrina Ferrara's essay in this volume, also attests to the acclaim Dante had won by his audacious, new, vernacular poem – as well as to the unease that the professional academic felt about the potential for trouble in such popularity and accessibility. Trouble for Dante, and for his enthusiastic readers, on the grounds of the poem's more controversial political and spiritual episodes, but also trouble for a traditional hierarchisation of culture in which the highest prizes, or so Del Virgilio suggests, should go to more rarefied and elitist, Latin products aimed at adept readers rather than at the crowd.[9]

This unease persisted over the next several decades. Petrarch famously expressed an anxiety not to share the fate of Dante, claiming that the too-accessible, vernacular poem was often mangled by ignorant, inner-city crowds.[10] Franco Sacchetti's *novella* about a blacksmith who recites Dante, inaccurately, while working in his forge provides another iteration of such fastidious concerns over the dangers of popularity. In Sacchetti's story, indeed, the anxieties of policing taste and culture turn inwards. The fiction makes Dante himself the one who objects to popular performance and attacks the blacksmith for his mangling of the *Commedia*'s verses.[11]

These early readers explore positions of scholarly distance, recommending withdrawal from the vulgar crowd and from certain forms of popular success. Over the centuries, inevitably, the reputation of Dante's *Commedia* has been transformed. There have been periods of relative cultural neglect of Dante, or of distaste for aspects of his aesthetic or thematic concerns, especially in the Seicento and Settecento. However, he has never disappeared from view. In the first three centuries, and again from the late eighteenth century onwards, the *Commedia* in particular has attracted consistent, if not uncontroversial, attention from both erudite and popular readerships.[12] From the sometimes unsettling, culturally unorthodox, avant-garde standing of its first circulation, the poem has gradually become a – indeed, *the* – cornerstone of the Italian peninsula's literary canon, with a perennial presence in lists of European literary masterpieces.[13]

Del Virgilio, Petrarch and Sacchetti provide snapshots of possible disturbance to what are primarily literary-aesthetic values deriving from the *Commedia*'s vernacular accessibility. On the grounds of content, too, it has historically suffered Inquisitorial censure, even outright censorship, from the Roman Catholic Church. Controversies still recur, marking the problematic potential of different episodes for various groups of readers, often themselves with markedly different sensibilities. While the Catholic Church, especially during the Counter-Reformation, objected principally to its pejorative commentary on corruption within the papal Curia, twentieth- and twenty-first-century readerships have variously found the *Commedia*'s stance on confessional difference, on race and on gender, sex and sexuality particularly unsettling.[14]

Establishing an Italian canon: Dante and the politics of national culture

Famously, works of literature, and pre-eminently the *Commedia*, have been totemic reference points in the history of nation founding and building in Italy. Long before political unity as a modern nation-state was a realistic possibility, Dante's poem was acclaimed as a kind of virtual *patria* – an instrument for drawing the peninsula's educated classes together through intimate, shared familiarity with its language and ideas. With the birth of serious nationalist movements in the early Ottocento, the poem's political passages could be pilfered for inspiring slogans and imagery. Alongside this, Dante's personal biography became romanticised as a kind of blueprint for Risorgimento patriots-in-exile. They likened the contemporary liberation movements, and the vicissitudes of would-be-nationalist intellectuals, to Dante's medieval experiences of civil war and banishment from Florence.[15]

Dante played an important role in some of the first cultural programmes for the nascent Italian state. The 600th anniversary of his birth, celebrated in May 1865, fell conveniently only months after the February transfer of the new state's capital from Turin to Florence, following the final achievement of Unification in 1861 (Rome remained capital of the resistant Papal State until 1871). A recent micro-historical study by Mahnaz Yousefzadeh dissects the political and cultural importance of the celebrations to the newly created Kingdom of Italy.[16] The 'Festa di Dante' was organised largely by the municipality of Florence, but promoted as a genuinely national event and dignified by the presence of the new king, Victor Emmanuel II. The festival saw crowds pour into the city from across the peninsula, bringing together the regions and classes of the new nation: some 50,000 are estimated to have attended in total over the three-day celebration, from regions as far apart as Sicily and Piedmont.[17] The Dantean enthusiasm that gathered workers, free-thinkers and schoolchildren into the crowds, as well as academics and aristocrats, seems somehow to echo the sentiments expressed 500 years before in the 1373 petition for a public *Lectura Dantis* in the city.

The celebrations included much erudite activity, but the aspiration to make it also an inclusive event was witnessed by the production of affordable books and pamphlets, even kitsch Dante souvenirs, to mark the occasion. Henry Clark Barlow, a British observer and official representative at the *Festa*, wrote of the 'barrowloads of brooches, pins, and buttons' with portraits of Dante on sale. Barlow sported his own improvised medal of a self-defined 'Most Noble Empyrical Order of Dante Allighieri and United Italy', combining a portrait of Dante and a tricolour rosette, having failed (he claimed) to convince the king to create a new 'Order of Saint Dante'.[18] The presence of foreign dignitaries such as Barlow gave a semi-diplomatic feeling to the celebrations and stressed their unifying, patriotic character for the new Italy. The events were also raised above the ephemeral by the decision to link the festival with a ceremony to unveil the huge statue of Dante in Piazza S. Croce, with its patriotic inscription 'A DANTE ALIGHIERI | L'ITALIA | M DCCC LXV'.[19] The statue still stands today, although its aggrandised image of Dante has been critiqued by later generations. For instance, as part of his 'TuttoDante' series, Roberto Benigni has urged his audience to reshape their image of Dante, and envision him not in the portentous form immortalised by the S. Croce statue and its ilk, but rather as a youthful, colloquial, semi-contemporary, whose poetry they could enjoy rather than endure.[20]

The same taste for co-opting visual representations of Dante as symbols of wider nationalism persisted into the twentieth century across the political spectrum: not only both the late Ottocento and early Novecento Liberal governments, but also the Fascist regime populated Italian public spaces with statues and busts of the poet.[21] The postwar period has inevitably proved more cautious in promoting nationalist symbols, with regard to Dante as with others, but he remains a familiar visual icon. As recently as 2002, for instance, with Italy's adoption of the euro, a profile portrait of Dante was adopted for Italian-issue two-euro coins, confirming his literal 'currency' as a national symbol. For philatelists, meanwhile, Dante's image has appeared on the postal service's stamps for 1865, 1921 and 1965. More playfully, a commemorative issue for the 90th anniversary of Walt Disney in 2018 included a 95-cent stamp depicting the famous Italian 'Topolino' [Mickey Mouse] images from *L'Inferno di*

Topolino. These showed Mickey as Dante and Pippo [Goofy] as Virgil, representing a culturally-specific melding of Italian and American icons, high and popular culture, from the postwar decades.[22]

Towards an *Edizione Nazionale*

The 1865 Dante celebrations were elaborate and aimed to be an inclusive, unifying experience for the whole Italian nation. Subsequent centenaries have been less effusive and more academic in emphasis. The two major twentieth-century centennials each fell not far distant from the World Wars. Recent collective experiences of violence, grief and, in the case of the Second World War, of guilt and confusion relating to the nation's experience of Fascism, would have made it difficult still to link Dante commemorations to the kind of nationalist sentiment that had been conjured in 1865.

For the 1921 sexcentenary of Dante's death, though the day again focused attention on Florence, with processions and speeches at S. Croce,[23] priority was given to creating scholarly and philological monuments to Dante – notably in the form of the *Edizione Nazionale*, which published carefully edited texts of Dante's complete *oeuvre* in a single, standard edition.[24] This was the fruit of a project for producing critically edited, philologically accurate reference texts for the whole of Dante's *oeuvre*, to which the scholarly community had been committed for some time. The project had matured over a long period. It was first projected for 1865 and then taken in hand more seriously with the foundation of the *Società Dantesca Italiana* (SDI) in 1888, as the national association for academic Dante studies. The project fitted the nineteenth-century universities' emphasis on philology, and was intended to 'repatriate' an important strand of Dante scholarship, following the production of significant modern reference editions by German and British textual critics: Karl Witte's editions of the *Commedia, Monarchia* and *Vita nuova*, and Edward Moore's *Tutte le opere*.[25]

These philological ambitions having been disrupted by the First World War, the 1921 edition in the end presented scholarly but not yet fully critical editions as reference texts for the *opera completa*. Work proceeded during the interwar years, but with financial, professional and political conditions all under stress during the Fascist *Ventennio*, and with a definitive disruption of the endeavour at the outbreak of the Second World War, only the *Vita Nuova* went to press between the wars in the official *Edizione Nazionale*. This was the 1932 reissue of Michele Barbi's *Vita Nuova*, in similar though expanded form to his pre-existing 1907 and 1921 versions.

Since the end of the Second World War, the national edition's remaining volumes have appeared at quite long intervals, reflecting the daunting complexity of the editorial tasks involved. Giorgio Petrocchi's edition of *La Commedia secondo l'antica vulgata* was prepared for the sept-centenary of Dante's birth in 1965 (the four volumes appeared between 1966 and 1967), as was Pier Giorgio Ricci's *Monarchia*. As the remaining works appeared between the 1980s and 2000s, updated editions were already being commissioned for works produced earlier in the series. For instance, Prue Shaw's new *Monarchia* appeared in 2009, the first volume in the project to be curated by a non-Italian.[26] The revival of the *Edizione Nazionale* project at the start of the twenty-first century reflects the need to take account of new discoveries and new methodologies on the strictly philological side. It also reveals a desire to provide new tools for the academic community's interrogation of Dante's works as a collective, international endeavour – at the end of a century in which visions of a unifying Italian national culture were placed under strain in ways that the celebrants of 1865 would have found hard to conceive.

The *Commedia* between totalitarianism and resistance

During the Fascist *Ventennio*, the 'official' Italian reception of Dante via national education at school and university level naturally fell under the regime's authority. If Dante had already been politicised as the unifying, national poet of the Risorgimento and Liberal Italy, the nationalist cultural programmes of Mussolini's government sought to co-opt him still more closely, dressing him – in Stefano Albertini's expressive phrase – in a black shirt. At the most extreme, Dante's interests in Roman antiquity, and his dreams of universal peace and justice under the governance of an ideal Roman emperor, were ruthlessly and anachronistically claimed as *avant la lettre* prognoses of the Fascist Party's imperialist ambitions.[27] Selective Dantean quotes adorned the regime's cultural and educational directives, and in textbooks and manuals the political commentaries and prophetic passages of the *Commedia* were often discussed with a strong ideological emphasis. One notable example, Domenico Venturini's tellingly titled *Dante Alighieri e Benito Mussolini*, works its way systematically through analyses of these passages, alongside chapters with titles such as 'Il sistema politico di Dante e il sistema politico del Duce Magnifico della nuova Italia. Unità di commando, continuità di governo, direttiva di un Capo supremo' [The political system of Dante and the political system of the Great *Duce* of the new Italy. Unity of command, continuity of government, direction by a supreme Leader].[28] Assimilation of Dante to Mussolini's vision of revived, fascist *romanitas* and a triumphalist new Italian culture also informed the project for a physical Dante monument to be built in Rome: the *Danteum* by Giuseppe Terragni. Designed to stand on the via dei Fori Imperiali (at the time known significantly as the via dell'Impero), in the ideological heart of the city as shaped by Mussolini's archaeological programmes, the monument was intended to combine the functions of a museum – or, in Terragni's terminology, a 'temple' dedicated to Dante – with a library and research space, thus serving both general and specialist readers.[29] However, the outbreak of war almost immediately after its commissioning in 1938 left the project unrealised.

In academic and research circles, Dante studies were markedly less affected by regime politics. The academies saw some clashes between ethical and political philosophies and systems of literary interpretation, but overtly politicised readings were generally avoided in scholarly circles.[30] Benedetto Croce (personally increasingly critical of the regime) remained a strong influence, with his 'aesthetic' rather than philological-historicist approach to the poem. However, Giovanni Gentile, the regime's favoured philosopher and Minister for Education between 1922 and 1924, developed in his own writings on Dante an interest in exploring Dante's theories of state that evolved towards more politicised ends.[31] The specialist production of textual and literary critics engaged in research on Dante thus tended not to receive direct interference from the Fascist government, except insofar as it controlled the entire university system. Requirements for academics to follow national educational policies necessarily affected the classroom. An oath of loyalty to the regime was imposed for university teachers (1931) and finally the notorious Racial Laws of 1938 excluded Jewish staff and students from the universities. Under these laws Dante critics of the stature of Mario Fubini and Attilio Momigliano, to name only two, lost their posts.

Beyond Italy too, across Europe, a steady stream of intellectuals had been on the move through the interwar decades, under the pressures of repressive or totalitarian politics in Italy, Germany and elsewhere. A well-known case is Erich Auerbach's: he lost his post at the University of Marburg under Nazi Germany's Nuremberg Race Laws in 1935 and moved to a position at the University of Istanbul; here he completed the work on *Mimesis* that includes the famous chapter on Farinata and Cavalcante, from *Inferno* X.[32] Antonio Gramsci addressed the same canto in particular in the fragmentary but penetrating reflections on Dante composed during his imprisonment under Mussolini's regime.[33]

Another important but painful strand of Dantean responses in the upheavals of the Second World War itself can be traced among writings produced by Resistance members, or by survivors of Nazi occupation or deportation. These often take the form simply of brief notes, quotations or allusions, recalling how a turn to literary and intellectual reflection provided a distraction or a refuge from the consequences of war. Those partisans who chose 'Dante' or 'Alighieri' as their *noms de guerre* expressed, in that choice alone, a desire to reclaim the poet as a symbol of Italian identity in opposition to that of the Fascist regime.[34] Dante could also be reclaimed from within the concentration camps, where in some cases copies of Dante circulated clandestinely, or where recitations of or conversations on Dante could draw prisoners together. Primo Levi's chapter on 'Il canto di Ulisse' in *Se questo è un uomo* [*If This is a Man*] has become the emblematic example of how an educated Italian could turn to Dante's poetry to resist the inhumanity of war and the *Lager* system, and to express a determination to survive.[35]

Yet another powerful response to Dante, emerging from an environment in which literary culture represented a means of resistance to totalitarianism, is Osip Mandelstam's 'Conversation about Dante', written in Stalin's USSR.[36] Dante has also been a point of reference in North American civil rights movements, as documented in Dennis Looney's study of African-American 'Freedom Readers'; their engagement with Dante has fed into literary, artistic, musical and cinematic production, from the late nineteenth century up to the present day.[37] In all of these very varied circumstances, across different places and periods, Dante's readers have responded strongly to the reflections on justice, community and freedom expressed in the *Commedia*, finding that his works struck a chord with their own conditions. For many, too, there was also biographical identification with the image of a poet in exile.

Contemporary Dante: afterlife and future prospects

Mandelstam, Auerbach and Primo Levi are names that stress how broad the reach of Dante has become over the past century, confirming the expansion of his reputation from Trecento Florence and the Italian regions outward across Europe and finally around the globe. Like Dante himself, both Dante scholarship and non-academic responses to Dante are plurilingual or plurivocal: not only are they expressed in the many different national languages of an international readership, but also, within and between the nations, they are expressed across diverse registers and media.

At the academic level Dante remains a focus for study, at home in Italy and abroad, and Dante scholarship is published in multiple languages, though dominated by Italian and Anglophone (especially North American) publications. There is increasingly frequent academic interchange between Italian- and English-speaking circles, fostered by reciprocal translations of major monographs and the willingness of specialist journals to accept publications in different languages. Some component of formal study of Dante remains obligatory in the modern Italian school system. In addition, he is an author taught in universities around the world, whether on the focused 'monographic' courses of specialised degrees in Italian culture or medieval studies or on 'great books' courses in comparative and translated literature. The Società Dantesca Italiana has its counterparts in scores of national and local associations for Dante studies across the Old and New Worlds. This gives opportunities for fostering collaborations between experts who dedicate their careers to studying Dante's *oeuvre*, as well as for encouraging lectures, workshops, readings and other activities designed to draw non-specialists too into the conversation.

I have said little in this chapter about Dante's *fortuna* in the visual arts or music – areas beyond my immediate expertise – or even about re-workings and responses in literary form. The list of titles alone would be enormous. To take just a pair of offerings each from Italian and English, and from the twentieth century, how can one deal adequately with a Dante reception that embraces both Primo Levi's testimony to the Shoah and the chirpy Topolino cartoon-strip? Both T. S. Eliot's modernist experimentation in *The Waste Land* and Dan Brown's pulp thriller, *Inferno*?[38] With the further expansion of communication systems via digital and new media resources, Dante's afterlife continues to thrive. Even jokey or superficial references to Dante confirm that his image tends to be associated consistently with questions concerning justice and morality.[39]

More prolonged engagement – by contemporary artists, writers, scholars and wider audiences – show that his poetry continues to generate strongly felt political and ethical responses. The image of Dante, or of scenes from his great poem, are used, for instance, by contemporary activists to speak about compelling problems of social justice. The past decade's crises of migration and political exclusion have seen passionate appeals to the figure of Dante as exile, or to the 'inferno' of the refugee condition, by advocates and politicians.[40] Significant contemporary philosophers and public intellectuals such as Giorgio Agamben, Alisdair MacIntyre or Martha Nussbaum have turned to Dante in exploring modern theories of ethics and justice.[41] The *Commedia*'s combined *gravitas* of moral and intellectual endeavour, with its boldness of poetic imagination, continues to spark responses in readers of all kinds. Modern audiences, like those of seven centuries ago, often feel the need for guidance in their approach to Dante. Yet the intimate, vernacular appeal of his poetry remains open to new audiences and new ways of reading as another centennial approaches, in 2021.

Notes

1. Current knowledge of the lectures depends, of course, on their written preservation, as presumably intended for eventual manuscript publication. On Boccaccio's *Esposizioni*, see Aldo Vallone, 'Lectura Dantis', in *Enciclopedia Dantesca (ED)*, 6 vols (Rome: Istituto dell'Enciclopedia Italiana, 1984; 1st edn 1970–8), III (1971), 606–9; Stephen Botterill, 'Reading, Writing and Speech in the Fourteenth- and Fifteenth-Century Commentaries on Dante's *Comedy*', in *Interpreting Dante: Essays on the Traditions of Dante Commentary*, ed. Paola Nasti and Claudia Rossignoli (Notre Dame: University of Notre Dame Press, 2013), 17–29 (20–1); Simon Gilson, 'Modes of Reading in Boccaccio's *Esposizioni sopra la Comedia*', in *Interpreting Dante*, 250–82 (253–4); Guyda Armstrong, 'Boccaccio and Dante', in *The Cambridge Companion to Boccaccio*, ed. Guyda Armstrong, Rhiannon Daniels, Stephen J. Milner (Cambridge: Cambridge University Press, 2015), 121–38 (130–1). The lectures are available as Giovanni Boccaccio, *Esposizioni sopra la Comedia,* ed. Giorgio Padoan (Milan: Mondadori, 1965); online, via the 'Dartmouth Dante Project' (DDP) (https://dante.dartmouth.edu/).
2. Gilson, 255, 264–70. On literature and ethics, see A. J. Minnis, *Medieval Theory of Authorship: Scholastic Literary Attitudes in the Later Middle Ages* (London: Scolar, 1984); and the essays in the collection *'Libri poetarum in quattuor species dividuntur': Essays on Dante and 'Genre'*, ed. Zygmunt G. Barański, supplement to *The Italianist* 15 (1995).
3. Ronald de Rooy, 'Dante all'insegna dell'Unità,' *Incontri* 26.2 (2011): 64–72 (69–71); Brendan Hennessey, Laurence E. Hooper and Charles L. Leavitt IV, 'Realisms and Idealisms in Italian Culture, 1300–2017', *The Italianist* 37.3 (2017): 281–8 (285).
4. Among numerous studies of Dante's international *fortuna*, representative samples are discussed by contributors to the edited volume *Dante nel mondo*, ed. Vittore Branca (Florence: Olschki, 1965), covering European countries from Finland to Greece, as well as the Arabic-speaking world, Brazil, Japan, the USA and the USSR. More recently, *Dante in the Long Nineteenth Century: Nationality, Identity, and Appropriation*, ed. Aida Audeh and Nick Havely (Oxford: Oxford University Press, 2012) covers Bengali and Turkish as well as European and North American responses. The volume *L'opera di Dante nel mondo: edizioni e traduzioni nel Novecento*, ed. Enzo Esposito (Ravenna: Longo, 1992), covers similar languages and adds Hebrew, Farsi and Mandarin to the picture, as well as translations into Latin and into Italian dialects. Dante also recurs consistently across the centuries in *Storia della letteratura italiana. 12: La letteratura italiana fuori d'Italia*, ed. Luciano Formisano (Rome: Salerno, 2005).
5. Botterill reflects productively on the distinctions between oral and written approaches (esp. 20–5).
6. See Rino Caputo, 'Dante by Heart and Dante Declaimed: the "Realization" of the *Comedy* on Italian Radio and Television', in *Dante, Cinema, and Television*, ed. Amilcare A. Iannucci (Toronto: University of Toronto Press, 2004), 213–24.
7. Admittedly, this list of 16 includes some commentaries in multiple versions (the *Ottimo Commento* in two variants, Pietro Alighieri's in three), and some responses constituted by extensive sets of glosses rather than complete formal commentaries: https://dante.dartmouth.edu/commentaries.php.
8. The text appears in *Rime due e trecentesche tratte dall'Archivio di Stato di Bologna*, ed. Sandro Orlando (Bologna: Commissione per i testi di lingua, 2005), 205–6; Orlando's volume documents several other Dantean quotations from *Inferno* and *Purgatorio* that appear in other early fourteenth-century notarial registers from Bologna. See also Armando Antonelli and Riccardo

Pedrini, 'Appunti sulla più antica attestazione dell'*Inferno*', *Studi e problemi di critica testuale* 63 (2001): 29–41. Dante's early reception by notaries and administrators active in Bologna is discussed by Justin Steinberg, *Accounting for Dante: Urban Readers and Writers in Late Medieval Italy* (Notre Dame: University of Notre Dame Press, 2007), 17–60. See also the allusion to this type of quotation/copying, linking legal and poetic cultures, in Nicolò Crisafi and Elena Lombardi's essay in this volume.

9. See also John Ahern, 'Singing the Book: Orality in the Reception of Dante's *Comedy*', in *Dante: Contemporary Perspectives*, ed. Amilcare A. Iannucci (Toronto: University of Toronto Press, 1997), 214–39.

10. *Familiares* XXI. 15. 14–17: letter to Boccaccio, 1359.

11. Novella 114, in Franco Sacchetti, *Il Trecentonovelle*, ed. Davide Puccini (Turin: UTET, 2004): text dated *c.*1385–93.

12. Paola Nasti and Claudia Rossignoli, 'Introduction', in *Interpreting Dante*, 1–16 (1–2).

13. See the brief but incisive overview of Ernst Robert Curtius, 'Dante as a Classic', in *European Literature and the Latin Middle Ages*, trans. Willard R. Trask (Princeton: Princeton University Press, 1953), 348–50, with notes about historical resistance to Dante as well as about his acceptance as a 'classic' or 'canonical' author, or even a 'modern' *avant la lettre*. Harold Bloom's chapter on 'The Strangeness of Dante: Ulysses and Beatrice', in *The Western Canon. The Books and School of the Ages* (London: Macmillan, 1995), 76–104, has itself become a 'classic' piece of canon-proclamation; see also the fresh, lively discussion in Federica Pich, 'Dante's "Strangeness": the *Commedia* and the Late Twentieth-Century Debate on the Literary Canon', in *Metamorphosing Dante. Appropriations, Manipulations, and Rewritings in the Twentieth and Twenty-First Centuries*, ed. Manuele Gragnolati, Fabio Camilletti and Fabian Lampart (Berlin: Turia + Kant, 2010), 21–35.

14. Although the *Monarchia* was a focus of clerical condemnation from 1327/28, and remained on the *Index librorum prohibitorum* until 1881, the *Commedia* escaped with only recommendations for censorship (often little enforced) of more controversial passages: see Pier Giorgio Ricci, 'Monarchia', in *ED*, III (1971), 993–1004. On concerns about orthodoxy during and immediately after Dante's lifetime, see Maria Picchio Simonelli, 'L'Inquisizione e Dante: alcune osservazioni', *Dante Studies* 97 (1979): 129–49 (esp. 142–3). Davide Dalmas discusses Cinquecento debates over Dante in the context of Protestant and Counter-Reformation controversies in *Dante nella crisi religiosa del Cinquecento italiano: da Trifon Gabriele a Lodovico Castelvetro* (Rome: Vecchiarelli, 2005). Lino Pertile gives a shorter overview of how sixteenth- and seventeenth-century commentary came under Inquisitorial scrutiny, in 'A Text in Movement: Trifon Gabriele's *Annotationi nel Dante*, 1527–1565', in *Interpreting Dante*, 341–58. See also Dennis Looney's '*Dante politico*: an Introduction', in the special issue *Dante Politico: Ideological Reception Across Boundaries*, ed. Dennis Looney and Donatella Stocchi-Perucchio, *Mediaevalia* 38 (2017): 1–12. On other controversies, see for instance on responses from within Islam (and Judaism), Jan M. Ziolkowski's 'Introduction' to *Dante and Islam*, ed. Jan M. Ziolkowski (New York: Fordham University Press, 2015), 1–28 (esp. 1–5, 13–17). In 2012 the liberal human rights NGO, Gherush92, suggested that the poem be removed from Italian state school curricula for content potentially offensive to minority communities: 'Via la *Divina Commedia* dalle scuole', (http://www.gherush92.com/news.asp?tipo=A&id=2985) [accessed 6 December 2018].

15. See Formisano; Audeh and Haveley; Stefano Jossa, *L'Italia letteraria* (Bologna: il Mulino, 2006), 26–8, 61–3; Joseph Luzzi, *Romantic Europe and the Ghost of Italy* (New Haven: Yale University Press, 2008). The nineteenth-century canonisation of Dante as the 'father' of Italian literature is most strongly associated with Francesco De Sanctis, and his *Storia della letteratura italiana* of 1870–1; for discussion of De Sanctis's influence, see the essays collected as a themed segment, *Francesco De Sanctis (1817–1883). La storia della letteratura, ancora? La història de la literatura, encara?*, ed. Rossend Arquès, in *Quaderns d'Italià* 16 (2011): 3–100.

16. Mahnaz Yousefzadeh, *City and Nation in the Italian Unification: the National Festivals of Dante Alighieri* (New York: Palgrave Macmillan, 2011). See also Christian Satto, 'Simbolo cittadino, gloria nazionale. Dante nella Capitale', *Annali di Storia di Firenze* 10–11 (2015–16): 213–35; Rossella Bonfatti, 'Performing Dante or Building the Nation? The *Divina Commedia* between Dramaturgy of Exile and Public Festivities', in *Dante Politico*, 37–67.

17. Yousefzadeh, 1.

18. Henry Clark Barlow, *The Sixth Centenary Festivals of Dante Allighieri in Florence and at Ravenna by A Representative* (London: Williams and Norgate, 1866), 7, 24.

19. Yousefzadeh, 83–7. See also Anne O'Connor 'Dante Alighieri – from Absence to Stony Presence: Building Memories in Nineteenth-Century Florence', *Italian Studies*, 67.3 (2012): 307–35; and the opening remarks invoking the statue by Zygmunt G. Barański, 'On Dante's Trail', *Italian Studies* 72.1 (2017): 1–15 (1–3).

20. Roberto Benigni, 'Benigni legge Dante', article published in *La Repubblica* on 29 December 2008: http://ricerca.repubblica.it/repubblica/archivio/repubblica/2008/12/29/benigni-legge-dante.html [accessed 6 December 2018].

21. See for instance Stefano Albertini, 'Dante in camicia nera: uso e abuso del divino poeta nell'Italia fascista', *The Italianist*, 16.1 (1996): 117–42.

22. The Disney version *L'Inferno di Topolino* was published in 1950, with drawings by Angelo Bioletto and text by Guido Martina: see Ronald de Rooy, 'Divine Comics', *European Comic Art* 10.1 (2017): 94–109 (97).

23. D. Medina Lasansky, *The Renaissance Perfected: Architecture, Spectacle, and Tourism in Fascist Italy* (University Park, PA: Pennsylvania State University Press, 2004), 60–3, also discussing the programme of urban remodelling associated with the centenary; on parallel events and architectural programmes at Ravenna, Luigi Scorrano, 'Il Dante "Fascista"', *Deutsches Dante-Jahrbuch* 75.1 (2000): 85–123 (121–3).

24. *Le Opere di Dante. Testo critico della Società Dantesca Italiana*, ed. Michele Barbi, Ernesto Giacomo Parodi, Flaminio Pellegrini, Ermenegildo Pistelli, Pio Rajna, Enrico Rostagno and Giuseppe Vandelli (Florence: Bemporad, 1921), directed by Michele Barbi. The volume was reissued in 1960, ahead of the forthcoming centennial in 1965.

25. Dante Alighieri, *La Divina Commedia*, ed. Karl Witte (Berlin: Decker, 1862); Dante Alighieri, *De Monarchia Libri III*, ed. Karl Witte (Vienna: Braumüller, 1874); *La Vita nuova di Dante Alighieri*, ed. Karl Witte (Leipzig: Brockhaus, 1876); *Tutte le opere di Dante Alighieri*, ed. Edward Moore (Oxford: Oxford University Press, 1894). On these editions, and on the larger horizon of philological work on Dante prior to, and within, the nineteenth century, see John Lindon, 'Notes on Nineteenth-Century Dante Commentaries and Critical Editions', in *Interpreting Dante*, 434–49 (on Witte and Moore, 438–9).

26. See Francesco Mazzoni, 'Edizione Nazionale', in *ED*, II (1970), 630–2; and also the note on the SDI's website, https://dantesca.org/cms/edizione-nazionale/ [accessed 6 December 2018], combining information on the original series and on the new edition's published and forthcoming volumes.

27. Albertini, 117; Scorrano, 85–9, 103–23; De Rooy, 'Dante all'insegna dell'Unità', 67–8; Jossa, 29.

28. Domenico Venturini, *Dante Alighieri e Benito Mussolini* (Rome: Nuova Italia, 1932), 49–52; see Albertini, 126–8.

29. See Albertini, 136–7; Thomas L. Schumacher, *The Danteum: a Study of the Architecture of Literature* (Princeton: Princeton Architectural Press, 1985).

30. Scorrano, 86, 91–103, who does point out, however, that the variety of academic Dante studies in the period could accommodate reflections on their contemporary relevance, in a pro- or anti-regime spirit.

31. For an overview of the two philosophers' positions on Dante, see Enrico Ghidetti, 'Il Dante di Croce e Gentile', in *Croce e Gentile* (2016): http://www.treccani.it/enciclopedia/elenco-opere/Croce_e_Gentile/1 [accessed 6 December 2018]. Croce's evolving position with regard to fascism in government is usefully summarised in the 'Conclusion' to Fabio Fernando Rizi's *Benedetto Croce and Italian Fascism* (Toronto: University of Toronto Press, 2003), 261–7. On Gentile as *Dantista*, see also Donatella Stocchi-Perucchio, 'Giovanni Gentile's Reading of Dante as Prophet of the State *in interiore homine*', in *Dante Politico*, 169–207.

32. Erich Auerbach, *Mimesis: The Representation of Reality in Western Literature*, trans. Willard R. Trask (Princeton: Princeton University Press, 1953); first published as *Mimesis: Dargestellte Wirklichkeit in der abendländischen Literatur* (Bern: Francke, 1946). On Auerbach in Istanbul, see Kader Konuk, *East West Mimesis: Auerbach in Turkey* (Stanford: Stanford University Press, 2010).

33. Frank Rosengarten, 'Gramsci's "Little Discovery": Gramsci's Interpretation of Canto X of Dante's *Inferno*', *Boundary* 2, 14.3 (1986): 71–90. Gramsci's and Auerbach's readings are explored in Betsy Emerick, 'Auerbach and Gramsci on Dante: Criticism and Ideology', *Carte Italiane* 1.1 (1980): 9–22. Pich also notes the particular appeal of *Inferno* X for several ideological and theoretical 'positioning' essays in twentieth-century Dante criticism.

34. Attilio Momigliano wrote of the consolation found in Dante and Tasso while in hiding under the occupation: see Enrico Ghidetti, 'Attilio Momigliano', in *Dizionario biografico degli italiani*, 90 vols (Rome: Istituto dell'Enciclopedia Italiana, 1960–2017) 75 (2011), 481–6. I thank my UCL colleague Carlotta Ferrara degli Uberti, and Guri Schwartz, for referring me to Resistance examples, including Dante material in the diaries of Jewish partisan Emanuele Artom.

35. Primo Levi, *Se questo è un uomo* (Turin: De Silva, 1947; Einaudi, 1958). See also the focused survey of responses to, and memories and readings of, Dante in the concentration camps, in Thomas Taterka, *Dante Deutsch: Studien zur Lagerliteratur* (Berlin: Erich Schmidt Verlag, 1999).

36. Osip Mandelstam, 'Conversation about Dante', in Osip Mandelstam, *The Complete Critical Prose and Letters*, ed. and trans. Jane Gary Harris and Constance Link (Ann Arbor: Ardis, 1979), 397–442. The essay was composed *c*.1930–3, though not published until 1967.

37. Dennis Looney, *Freedom Readers: The African American Reception of Dante Alighieri and the 'Divine Comedy'* (Notre Dame: University of Notre Dame Press, 2011).

38. T. S. Eliot, *The Waste Land* (New York: Boni and Liveright, 1922); Dan Brown, *Inferno* (New York: Doubleday, 2013).

39. An enjoyable resource for Dante 'citings and sightings' in contemporary culture is the website 'Dante Today', maintained by Arielle Saiber and Elizabeth Coggeshall: https://research.bowdoin.edu/dante-today/ [accessed 6 December 2018].

40. Of numerous possible examples, two are offered from contemporary UK and Italian sources. Within this volume a photograph (Fig.9.2) in Claire Honess and Matthew Treherne's chapter shows how local British activism in support of refugees, in the 'City of Sanctuary' programme in Wakefield, was linked to Dante in the public-facing activities of a major research project on 'Dante and Late Medieval Florence'. From Italy, a project for resettlement of refugees developed in 2007 between the European Union, the UNHCR and Italy's Ministry of the Interior was christened the 'Piano Dante', in deliberate reference to Dante Alighieri's fourteenth-century exile, as well as to the notion of transformative movement from the 'infernal' situation of displacement to decent living and working conditions in resettlement: *Uno sguardo verso il futuro: Ipotesi per un "Piano Dante", Studio di Fattibilità per un Programma Italiano di Reinsediamento*, ed. Flavio Di Giacomo (https://www.resettlement.eu/sites/icmc/files/FA.RE_.%5B1%5D.pdf), alluding to Dante in detail on p.11 [accessed 6 December 2018].

41. There are for instance passages paying close attention to Dante in the following works, as well as elsewhere in their writings: Giorgio Agamben, *Homo Sacer: il potere sovrano e la nuda vita* (Turin: Einaudi, 1995); Alisdair MacIntyre, *Three Rival Versions of Moral Enquiry: Encyclopaedia, Genealogy, and Tradition* (London: Duckworth, 1990); Martha Nussbaum, *Upheavals of Thought: The Intelligence of Emotions* (Cambridge: Cambridge University Press, 2001).

9

Responses to Dante in the New Millennium

Claire E. Honess and Matthew Treherne

There have never been so many opportunities for the public to engage with Dante's works: translations, introductions and online resources are being produced all the time. Yet Dante can be intimidating. One of the consequences of the long tradition in Dante studies, and the vast amounts of scholarship on the poet, is that the sheer volume of writing on Dante, rather than making him more accessible, can seem to present a barrier to engaging with his work. Even full-time specialists are hardly able to keep up with the volume of new scholarship being published each year on Dante; this arguably prevents new, multidisciplinary voices from entering debates in Dante studies and it can be off-putting to non-academic readers.

In discussing responses to Dante in the new millennium, this essay directly addresses the question of how specialist and non-specialist Dante audiences were able to come together in creative ways under the auspices of a large-scale, international research collaboration, investigating 'Dante and Late Medieval Florence'. This project, funded by the Arts and Humanities Research Council (AHRC) in the UK, ran at the Universities of Leeds and Warwick from 2011 to 2017. The academics leading the research shared a strong conviction that their scholarly activities needed to be allied with a commitment to using that work to provide a platform for the public to engage with Dante. They were keen to avoid any sense that, as researchers' understanding of Dante and his contexts deepened, increased specialisation might somehow create yet further barriers to new readers of Dante. Indeed, they sensed that the project's approach to Dante's engagement with theology and religious culture offered new opportunities to capture the imagination of the public and to facilitate new and creative approaches to Dante's works.

The project itself emerged from a number of collaborative activities on Dante's theology. Such activities helped in various ways to identify the importance of understanding the local conditions in which Dante and his contemporaries would have experienced theology and religious culture.[1] The project aimed, therefore, to recover the multiple experiences of theology in late medieval Italy, focusing on Florence in the 1280s and 1290s, and to examine the way in which Dante engages with the forms of these experiences in his works. The project drew together a team of seven researchers, based in the Leeds Centre for Dante Studies at the University of Leeds and in the Department of Italian at the University of Warwick, in partnership with the Devers Program in Dante Studies at the University of Notre Dame in the USA. The team sought to cast light on the ways in which medieval theology was mediated and experienced within a specific historical and geographical context, while paying close attention to its varieties and their effects upon different publics.[2]

It did so through four strands of research. The first, 'Theological learning in Dante and Dante's Florence', examined the sites of theological learning in Florence. It asked what an educated layman such as Dante might have learned at the *Scuole* of Santa Croce and Santa Maria Novella in the 1280s and 1290s, and the forms that learning might have taken.[3] The second, 'Religious culture and the mediation of theological ideas in Dante and Dante's Florence', examined the ways in which theological ideas were mediated in late medieval Florence beyond the learned context, in particular in the form of preaching.[4] The project's third theme, 'Dante and the theological poetics of the social encounter', examined the theologians who appear as characters in the *Commedia*. In so doing this theme considered the templates that existed for mediating the theologian as a historical figure and explored the model of theological discourse presented in Dante's poem, as a personal, social interaction with individually named and characterised theological authorities.[5] Finally the fourth strand, 'Dante, theology, and socio-political thought', examined the close interaction between Dante's religious thought and his social and political ideas. In particular, it considered the ways in which the prophetic mode informed and helped to shape political discourse, connecting the social context of its audience with broader questions of theological significance.[6]

Drawing on these four strands of research, we were able to explore opportunities for bringing Dante to new audiences in fresh and engaging ways. The first of these was rooted in the desire to consider the full range of ways in which theology and religious culture were experienced in the context of Dante's Florence. The project's attention to the ways in which theology was mediated to non-learned and lay audiences, alongside its interest in the higher scholastic forms in which theology was practised and studied, was intended to highlight the vibrant and diverse ways in which theology entered the fabric of Florentine life – including through visual culture, architecture, ritual, vernacular song, preaching and storytelling. Through the activity of the mendicant orders and associated groups, one might see late thirteenth-century Florence as marked by experimentation in modes of engaging the public in theological ideas (albeit with varying senses of the hierarchies of authority). This diversity of experience – engaging the senses as well as the mind – seemed to us entirely in keeping with the way in which Dante's *Commedia* offered a rich, multilevelled approach to the spiritual, poetic, philosophical and political questions it wished to address. It also offered a diversity of models for engaging the public in our research.

Secondly, we saw Dante's work as aiming not merely to encapsulate a set of ideas for his readers to receive passively, but rather to provoke thought and responses. Indeed, as we explored the forms of popular engagement with theology in Florence – including through the activities of confraternities, pilgrimage and preaching – we gained an increasingly strong sense of the desire in Florentine society to be active participants in, rather than passive recipients of, religious culture. It was therefore entirely right, in our view, to help support well-informed but nonetheless creative responses to Dante and to his context.

Finally, it was clear to us that, while both Florence and Dante had strong visibility in twenty-first-century Western society and attracted a good deal of interest among the public, there were limited openings for thinking about the two together. The packaging and branding of the tourist experience of Florence strongly emphasised its Renaissance heritage, with the medieval city featuring far less prominently in tourist material and publicity. We felt that through the research project's emphasis on the rich context of late medieval Florence, it would be possible to make the most of the strong interest in Florence in order to offer a more coherent understanding of the ways in which the late medieval city would have been experienced.

Two sets of public engagement activities were developed to try to maximise the benefits of the project for the public. The first, focused on engagement with Florence itself, was carried out by Lois Haines, Leeds Undergraduate Leadership and Research Scholar, and Ruth Chester, AHRC Cultural Engagement Fellow. Together, they developed a set of materials to engage the public in the context of late medieval Florence.[7] In particular, Chester led on the development of new tourist material, now available in tourist offices in Florence, which offers a walking itinerary through Dante's Florence. Produced in collaboration with the Comune di Firenze and with UNESCO, this offers a new way for visitors to Florence to look beneath the Renaissance city and develop a sense of the diverse, vibrant forms in which Dante's Florence was renewing its economic, cultural, and religious life. It also offered a structure to well-attended public lectures, presented by a number of project team members and orchestrated by Chester and Haines. Audience members reported that the imaginary 'walking tour' format gave a memorable and inviting entry point to understanding the late medieval city.[8]

The second set of activities focused on bringing ideas and experiences from late medieval Florentine society into direct dialogue with contemporary experience in a more local context – not in Italy this time, but in contemporary northern England. This activity was particularly closely linked to the fourth strand of the AHRC project, which asked to what extent Dante's social and political thought was shaped by his theological understanding and religious practice, and was driven by the desire to understand the often conflicted relationship between an individual and her or his community.

The city of Wakefield is a city of around 300,000 inhabitants, situated in the south of the county of West Yorkshire.[9] Originally built on industry and coal mining, the city, like much of the surrounding area, has significant areas of social deprivation,[10] although there have been some attempts at cultural regeneration in recent years.[11] Through creative engagement with the ideas on community found in the *Commedia*, the Leeds Centre for Dante Studies attempted to encourage local residents with no previous knowledge of Dante to reflect on the meanings of community for them and for their city.

Starting from the point of view that all three realms of Dante's afterlife are communities of sorts, the project explored the ways in which twenty-first-century communities – taking Wakefield as a case study – might be construed as heavenly, purgatorial or hellish, characterised by community, learning or isolation. Hell, from this perspective, is a 'city' made up of many individuals, but which entirely lacks any sense of community. It is a 'città dolente' [grieving city] (*Inf.*, III. 1) – a city which is also a wilderness, in which citizens are punished together, but each is alone in isolation from God and from her or his fellow-citizens.[12] In contrast, Purgatory is a place of education, where the souls, as part of their process of cleansing and renewal, learn to live and work together towards a common goal. Paradise is a place of perfect community, where the desire for the common good overpowers all selfishness and cupidity and leads to an existence of perfect peace. This is perhaps best exemplified in the Heaven of Jupiter, where Dante sees a huge eagle made up of a great multitude of individual souls but which speaks with a single communal voice. The concept is visually depicted, in John Flaxman's memorable image, on the cover of the present volume:

> [...] io vidi e anche udi' parlar lo rostro,
> e sonar ne la voce e 'io' e 'mio',
> quand'era nel concetto e 'noi' e 'nostro'.

(*Par.*, XIX. 10–12)

[I saw and also heard the beak speaking, and the voice sounding both *I* and *mine*, though logically it was *we* and *ours*.]

Participants in the project were asked to consider how Wakefield's citizens might be working together today to create community so that they can live together in peace and harmony, and how it might feel to be deprived of a community, isolated in the midst of others, as is the case in Dante's Hell.[13] At the most basic level, they explored the ways in which a city such as Wakefield can be a heaven or a hell for its citizens, but they also probed the ways in which art and poetry might be one method by which community is communicated or even created.

Working with the Education Department at Wakefield Cathedral and with a local poetry group known as the Black Horse Poets, responses to these questions were invited in the form of photographs of Wakefield itself, seen in the guise of Heaven, Purgatory or Hell, and through the medium of poetry.[14] Around 30 images and 13 poems were submitted. The six photographs which were felt best to represent the potential relationships between Dante's *Commedia* and Wakefield were exhibited in Wakefield Cathedral throughout the month of May 2016. Alongside these were exhibited three poems (one for each *cantica* of the *Commedia*), accompanied by the three extracts from Dante's own text which had been used to stimulate the reflections of participating poets and photographers. All submissions were included in a project booklet that was freely available in the cathedral throughout the period of the exhibition.[15] Space, in the present context, does not permit a detailed discussion of the contributions to the project, but a few examples will allow the immediacy, reflectiveness and nuance of the responses received to emerge.

Fig. 9.1, then, presents an image of litter on Wakefield's Kirkgate Station on a rainy day, epitomising the bleakness and loneliness of Dante's Hell. There are no people in this city, although wet footprints suggest the

Figure 9.1 Charlotte Harvey, *Exit via Subway* (pedestrian subway at Wakefield Kirkgate Station). Used by permission of photographer.

presence of others who remain out of sight and out of contact with the viewer. But this image also hints ironically, with its sign proclaiming 'Way out via subway', at the overall trajectory of Dante-pilgrim's journey through Hell, descending ever further into the depths of the earth before emerging, via the narrow passage which leads from Hell to Purgatory, to see the stars.

In contrast, Fig. 9.2 shows a peaceful demonstration in support of refugees. This seemed to sum up the way in which, in Purgatory, the souls provide moral and physical support for one another; they suffer, but also work to make themselves, and by extension their community, better. In this image the individuals' anonymity gives them a universality, in the same way that Dante-pilgrim in the *Commedia* is often seen as an Everyman figure.[16] The *Purgatorio* is also evoked in the image of Wakefield Cathedral's stone floor labyrinth, installed in 2013 (Fig.9.3). At the beginning of this *cantica*, Virgil tells the souls who are newly arrived in Purgatory, '"noi siam peregrin come voi siete"' ['we are pilgrims here, as you are'] (*Purg.*, II. 63), and the journey through this second realm is, indeed, a pilgrimage of sorts. Like the journey of the labyrinth, however, there is only one way through Purgatory – and it is impossible, having undertaken it, to lose the 'diritta via' [straight way] (*Inf.*, I. 3), for this journey inevitably leads to God. In the same way, the worshipper walking the Wakefield labyrinth is led to the centre; here, facing east, s/he is naturally turned towards the altar and towards God.[17]

Figure 9.2 Harriet Evans, *Solidarity* (peaceful demonstration in support of refugees by Wakefield City of Sanctuary on the steps of Wakefield Cathedral). Used by permission of photographer.

Figure 9.3 Rich Wainwright, *Pilgrimage* (sandstone labyrinth, Wakefield Cathedral). Used by permission of photographer.

Figure 9.4 Rich Wainwright, *Community* (Wakefield city centre during the Tour de Yorkshire, May 2015). Used by permission of photographer.

Finally, Fig. 9.4, which shows the crowds and excitement in Wakefield's city centre when the Tour de Yorkshire passed through the city, is an image that seemed to reflect Dante's conception of Paradise – not in a religious sense, but precisely in the way in which the heavenly community is expressed through the image of the eagle in *Paradiso* XIX. Here a spontaneous coming-together, with a single purpose and speaking with a single voice, is shown to lead, above all, to joy: 'la bella image che nel dolce *frui* | liete facevan l'anime conserte' [that image made by the joyous souls woven together in their sweet *frui*] (*Par.*, XIX. 2–3).

Very similar ideas emerged from the poems submitted by members of the Black Horse Poets. In his poem *The Streets of Me*, Michael Yates conveyed the idea of both the pointlessness of Hell's punishments – the endless circling of the free city bus recalls all those punishments in the *Inferno* that involve circling, such as those of the avaricious, the fortune-tellers and the hypocrites – and also the isolation of the sinners, even in the midst of crowds of their fellows. Yates describes how:

> There is no transport but a circle;
> the Free City Bus running round forever,
> and the station with its machines clickety tickety,
> where the only change will be *small* change.
> Though I step outside my semi-detached,
> I am never detached from the Streets of Me.
>
> (*The Streets of Me*, lines 19–24)

In a different way Angie de Courcy Bower's poem *If Heaven's Too Bright*, constructed entirely around doubt and negativity, was reminiscent of the negativity of Dante's Wood of the Suicides. Compare the following extracts, for example:

> What if deeds are never good
> if water's thicker than blood
> if dreams should not be chased
> if there's an end to space [...]
> if cats don't have nine lives
> if two wrongs make a right
> if heaven's too bright?

(*If Heaven's Too Bright*, lines 1–4; 22–4)

> Non fronda verde, ma di color fosco;
> non rami schietti, ma nodosi e 'nvolti;
> non pomi v'eran, ma stecchi con tòsco.

(*Inf.*, XIII. 4–6)

[Not green leaves, but dark in colour, not smooth branches, but knotted and twisted, no fruit was there, but thorns with poison.]

In complete contrast, the opening line of Michael Yates's poem about Paradise, *In Cathedral Square*, captures entirely – even if in a tongue-in-cheek way – the focus on community that characterises the *Paradiso* in its assertion that 'Paradise is other people'. Peter Bedford's poem, *The City at a Distance*, while confronting Wakefield's real social and political issues directly, offers a conclusion of hope. His poem's nod to the city's more recent attempt to reinvent itself as an artistic hub combines with an understanding of the city's much earlier history,[18] and above all with a statement of faith in the resilience of its people.

> Somewhere in the eighties
> In a place where politicians play
> They stole its heart away [...]
> Depart King Cotton. Depart King Coal
> Four horsemen came-a-riding
> Rough shod, merciless, over the hill
> Closure, Demolition, Dispersal, Landfill
> Decline could not be declined.

[...]

On that cold and frosty morning
You may see through history's mist
Shrouding this nursery-rhyme town
A wealth that pays no heed to money
A running seam of richness
Footsteps on pathways, voices on the air
Sculpture living in hands of people
New music growing and dancing
A place for painters, poets, artists all
And rarely, in an occasional hush
The tallest spire, a dying prince
And a mulberry bush.

(*The City at a Distance*, lines 13–15; 20–24; 37–48)

This idea of resilience and of hope emerged even more strikingly in the poems that focused on the idea of Purgatory, which constituted perhaps the most interesting of the poems submitted. The idea of education, in particular, and of change, growth and development, seemed to resonate with those who took the idea of Purgatory as a learning community and applied it to their own time and place. Michael Yates again approaches the topic with wit in his reference to a 'Diploma in Guilt Management', an almost perfect condensation of the theology of Purgatory. But his poem concludes more seriously by exploring the hope of 'graduating' – aided by a combination of self-assessment (Dante's Purgatory depends on the souls recognising, repenting and then working to remove the stain of their own sins) and the help of a guide (some Virgil or Beatrice figure, perhaps):

Higher Diploma,
Guilt Management

[...]

With the help of self-assessment,
the mercy of a Personal Tutor,
I still dream I will graduate,
be a living soul again,
between Thornes Park and Lightwaves.

(*Purgatory: The Full-Time Course*, lines 8–9; 24–8).

Perhaps the most striking of all the poems submitted, however, was that entitled *Purgatorio* by Paul Crossley. In this work a latter-day Dante stumbles through twenty-first-century Wakefield in a haze of alcohol and drugs; he eventually gets into a fight in a club ironically named 'Paradiso', finds himself arrested and ultimately wakes up to the tentative hope of redemption. The author of this poem has not only grasped something of the tension that exists in Dante between human sinfulness, which translates into selfishness, aggression, greed and violence towards those around us, and the ever-present – however unlikely – possibility of redemption. He has also managed to reflect something of Dante's stylistic novelty: not only in choosing to write his poem in *terza rima,* but particularly by mixing stylistic registers in the work. *Purgatorio* thus engages inventively with the real, earthy, everyday language of the city, blending this with more erudite references (such as that to Newton's final Law of Motion):

> We kicked off at mid-day, me and my guide –
> I woke, stiff as a bread-stick, on the floor –
> With two Red-Bulls, leftover Southern-Fried
>
> And after that two Fosters. Then two more
> While taking turns to play Assassin's Creed
> On – was it the X-Box or the PS4?
>
> Well, that was when we started on the weed –
> My guide does, on the side, a little dealing –
> His dividend smelt very good indeed
>
> And I suspect we shared the same appealing
> Getting-It-On-While-Listening-to-Marvin-Gaye-
> Singing-'Let's Get It On' – type of feeling.
>
> […]
>
> Double Jack and Red-Bull in my hand
> Told me that all was well – but then this shit-head
>
> Grabbed my neck and, barking some command,
> Dragged me toward the doors. I should've said
> 'Excuse me Sir, you fail to understand … '
>
> But my glass was already swinging for his head.
> It didn't land, though Newton's Final Law
> Meant something final came at me instead,

Connecting very neatly with my jaw
As bodies clambered into the affray
And that was me. Out. Stars were all I saw.

(Paul Crossley, *Purgatorio*, lines 1–12; 44–54)

Taken as a whole, the poems and images generated by the Wakefield project stand as an eloquent testimony to the way in which Dante is still able to speak to audiences today. He does so particularly, perhaps, through his attention to human beings as 'political animals',[19] and to human lives as inextricably bound up with one another. Moreover, and even more significantly, the way in which this project engaged Dante with the gritty reality of life in a real twenty-first-century community reflected precisely those more scholarly ideas that lay behind the desire to explore Dante in his late medieval context and gave rise to the AHRC-funded project. That is, it illuminated even more clearly the need to read Dante in his own context; the conviction that questions of theology, community, art and poetry could not be easily separated; and, following from this, the belief that reading Dante in this highly contextualised way might open up new perspectives on his work for scholars and non-specialists alike.

Notes

1. Most notably, *Dante's 'Commedia': Theology as Poetry*, ed. Vittorio Montemaggi and Matthew Treherne (Notre Dame: University of Notre Dame Press, 2008); and *Reviewing Dante's Theology*, 2 vols, ed. Claire Honess and Matthew Treherne (Berlin: Peter Lang, 2013).
2. The project team comprised Matthew Treherne (Principal Investigator; University of Leeds), Simon Gilson (Co-Investigator; University of Warwick, now University of Oxford); Claire Honess (Co-Investigator; University of Leeds); Anna Pegoretti (postdoctoral research fellow, University of Warwick; now Università di Roma Tre); Nicolò Maldina (postdoctoral research fellow, University of Leeds; now University of Edinburgh); Kevin Marples and Abigail Rowson (both of whom successfully completed their PhDs at the University of Leeds under the auspices of the project).
3. See for instance Anna Pegoretti, 'Filosofanti', *Le Tre Corone* 2 (2015): 11–70; and the same author's essay in this volume.
4. For an example of the outputs of this strand, see Nicolò Maldina, *In pro del mondo. Dante, la predicazione e i generi della letteratura religiosa medievale* (Rome: Salerno, 2018); and the same author's essay in this volume.
5. See Abigail Rowson, 'Theologians as Persons in Dante's *Commedia*', unpublished PhD thesis, University of Leeds (2018).
6. The strand built on Honess's long-standing interest in Dante's political thought – as in, for example, her *From Florence to the Heavenly City: The Poetry of Citizenship in Dante* (Oxford: Legenda, 2006). See also Kevin Marples, 'Theology, Prophecy and Politics in Dante', unpublished PhD thesis, University of Leeds (2017).
7. Haines's Undergraduate Leadership and Research Scholarship was financed by a philanthropic gift to the University of Leeds, where she was then working for a BA in French and Italian. Chester had recently completed her PhD in the Leeds Centre for Dante Studies.
8. The lecture series, 'Three Evenings in Dante's Florence', was held in Leeds in November 2012.

9. The 2011 census gives Wakefield a population of 325,837; see http://localstats.co.uk/census-demographics/england/yorkshire-and-the-humber/wakefield [accessed 20 June 2018].

10. Wakefield is in the bottom quintile of local authorities in England according to the 2015 Index of Multiple Deprivation (coming in 65th place out of 326 authorities). This source also shows that 47,400 people in the district (14.4 per cent of the population) live in neighbourhoods that are in the top 10 per cent of the most deprived in England. In particular, the district shows high levels of education and skills deprivation, as well as worsening indicators of deprivation in income and health. See http://www.wakefieldjsna.co.uk/site/wp-content/uploads/Poverty-Profile.pdf and, for the full data set, https://www.gov.uk/government/statistics/english-indices-of-deprivation-2015 [accessed 20 June 2018].

11. The Hepworth Wakefield, which opened in 2011 and was awarded the title of Art Fund Museum of the Year in 2017, has been central to this cultural renewal. Simon Wallis, Director of the Hepworth, spoke of 'the value and power of culture in transforming the quality of people's lives in the Wakefield district' when collecting the award. See https://hepworth-wakefield.org/news/the-hepworth-wakefield-wins-art-fund-museum-of-the-year-2017/ [accessed 21 June 2018].

12. All references to the *Commedia* are taken from *La Commedia secondo l'antica vulgata*, ed. Giorgio Petrocchi, 2nd edn, 4 vols (Florence: Le Lettere, 1994). Translations are taken from *The Divine Comedy of Dante Alighieri*, ed. and trans. Robert M. Durling; introduction and notes Ronald L. Martinez and Robert M. Durling, 3 vols (Oxford: Oxford University Press, 1996–2011). For a fuller discussion of these issues, see Honess, *From Florence to the Heavenly City*, 51–63.

13. Participants in the Wakefield project were provided with a booklet with a brief explanatory introduction and three short extracts from Dante's text (one from each *cantica*), namely: *Inferno* III. 1–30; *Purgatorio* XIII. 82–111; *Paradiso* III. 67–90.

14. The authors are grateful to Tracey Noble and to the clergy and staff of Wakefield Cathedral, to members of the Black Horse Poets and to Simone Lomartire for their practical support and for their enthusiasm for the project.

15. Around 80 copies of the booklet were distributed during May 2016. The complete poems and the photographs can be viewed via the Leeds Centre for Dante Studies webpages at: https://ahc.leeds.ac.uk/leeds-centre-dante-studies/doc/community-projects [accessed 30 November 2018].

16. The opening line of the poem, 'Nel mezzo del cammin di *nostra* vita' [In the middle of the journey of *our* life] (*Inf.*, I. 1; our emphasis) is often seen as indicative of this universal perspective: the character's life is also our life, the life of his readers.

17. While Hell is a journey of dead ends whose end-point (Lucifer, frozen in the ice-lake of Cocytus) is ultimately static, the journey through Purgatory can have only one outcome – reunion with God in Heaven. See for example Virgil's words to the penitent souls in *Purg.*, III. 73–5.

18. A mulberry bush in the prison yard at Wakefield's notorious Category A prison is thought to be the origin of the nursery rhyme 'Here we go round the Mulberry Bush'; the dying prince is, of course, Richard, Duke of York, who was killed at the Battle of Wakefield in 1460, very close to where the Hepworth Gallery now stands.

19. 'Sì come Aristotile dice, l'uomo è animale civile' [As Aristotle says, man is a social animal] (*Cvo*, IV. xxvii. 3). See Dante, *Convivio*, ed. Cesare Vasoli and Domenico De Robertis, in *Dante Alighieri: Opere Minori*, 2 vols (Milan and Naples: Ricciardi, 1979–88), vol.I. 2; translation taken from *The Banquet*, trans. with intro. and notes Christopher Ryan (Saratoga, CA: Anma Libri, 1989).

Bibliography

Primary sources

Bible

Biblia Sacra iuxta Vulgatam versionem, edited by Robert Weber and Bonifatius Fischer, 2 vols. Stuttgart: Württembergische Bibelanstalt, 1969; 3rd edn Stuttgart: Deutsche Bibelgesellschaft, 1983.

Biblia Latina cum glossa ordinaria: Facsimile Reprint of the Editio Princeps Adolph Rusch of Strassburg 1480/81, edited by Karlfried Froehlich and Margaret T. Gibson. Brepols: Turnhout, 1992.

The Bible. Authorized King James Version, introduction and notes by Robert Carroll and Stephen Prickett. Oxford: Oxford University Press, 1996.

The Vulgate Bible: Douay-Rheims Translation, edited by Swift Edgar and Angela M. Kinney, 6 vols. Cambridge, MA: Harvard University Press, 2010–13.

Works by Dante

1. Editions of the 'Commedia'

Dante Alighieri. *La Divina Commedia*, edited by Karl Witte. Berlin: Decker, 1862.

Dante Alighieri. *La Commedia secondo l'antica vulgata*, edited by Giorgio Petrocchi, 4 vols. Milan: Mondadori. 1966–7; 2nd edn Florence: Le Lettere, 1994.

Dante Alighieri. *The Divine Comedy*, translated by Allen Mandelbaum, 3 vols. Berkeley: University of California Press, 1981.

Dante Alighieri. *The Divine Comedy*, translated and edited by Robin Kirkpatrick, 3 vols. London: Penguin, 2006–7.

Dante Alighieri. *The Divine Comedy of Dante Alighieri*, edited and translated by Robert M. Durling; introduction and notes by Ronald L. Martinez and Robert M. Durling, 3 vols. New York–Oxford: Oxford University Press, 1996–2011.

Dante Alighieri. *Inferno*, edited and with commentary by Saverio Bellomo. Turin: Einaudi, 2013.

Dante Alighieri. *Commedia*, revision of the text and commentary by Giorgio Inglese. Rome: Carocci, 2016.

2. Editions of Dante's Collected Works

Dante Alighieri. *Tutte le opere di Dante Alighieri*, edited by Edward Moore. Oxford: Oxford University Press, 1894.

Dante Alighieri. *Le Opere di Dante. Testo critico della Società Dantesca Italiana*, edited by Michele Barbi, Ernesto Giacomo Parodi, Flaminio Pellegrini, Ermenegildo Pistelli, Pio Rajna, Enrico Rostagno and Giuseppe Vandelli. Florence: Bemporad, 1921.

Dante Alighieri. *Le Opere*, edited by Marco Santagata, 2 vols. Milan: Mondadori, 2011–14. Vol.1: *Rime*, edited by Claudio Giunta; *Vita nova*, edited by Guglielmo Gorni; *De vulgari eloquentia*, edited by Mirko Tavoni. Vol.2: *Convivio*, edited by Claudio Giunta and Gianfranco Fioravanti;

Monarchia, edited by Diego Quaglioni; *Epistole*, edited by Claudia Villa; *Egloge*, edited by Gabriella Albanese.

3. Editions of Dante's Minor Works

Dante Alighieri. *De Monarchia Libri III*, edited by Karl Witte. Vienna: Braumüller, 1874.

Dante Alighieri. *La Vita nuova di Dante Allighieri*, edited by Karl Witte. Leipzig: Brockhaus, 1876.

Dante Alighieri. *La Vita Nuova*, translated by Mark Musa. Bloomington–London: Indiana University Press, 1962.

Dante Alighieri. *The Letters of Dante*, translated by Paget J. Toynbee, 2nd edn. Oxford: Clarendon Press, 1966.

Dante Alighieri. *Il convivio*, edited by Maria Simonelli. Bologna: Pàtron, 1966.

Dante Alighieri. *Dante's Lyric Poetry*, translated by Kenelm Foster and Patrick Boyde, 2 vols. Oxford: Oxford University Press, 1967.

Dante Alighieri. *Convivio*, edited by Cesare Vasoli and Domenico De Robertis, in *Dante Alighieri: Opere Minori*, 2 vols. Milan and Naples, Ricciardi, 1979–88.

Dante Alighieri. *The Banquet*, translated with introduction and notes by Christopher Ryan. Saratoga, CA: Anma Libri, 1989.

Dante Alighieri. *Dante's 'Il Convivio' (The Banquet)*, translated by Richard H. Lansing. New York: Garland, 1990.

Dante Alighieri. *Convivio*, edited by Giorgio Inglese. Milano: BUR, 1993.

Dante Alighieri. *Convivio*, edited by Franca Brambilla Ageno. Florence: Le Lettere, 1995.

Dante Alighieri. *Das Gastmahl*, translated by Thomas Ricklin, introduction and commentary by Francis Cheneval, Ruedi Imbach and Thomas Ricklin, 4 vols. Hamburg: Meiner, 1996.

Dante Alighieri. *Monarchy*, edited and translated by Prue Shaw. Cambridge: Cambridge University Press, 1996.

Dante Alighieri. *De vulgari eloquentia*, edited and translated by Steven Botterill. Cambridge: Cambridge University Press, 1996.

Dante Alighieri. *Four Political Epistles*, translated by Claire Honess. London: Modern Humanities Research Association, 2007.

Dante Alighieri. *Epistole, Ecloge, Questio de situ et forma aque et terre*, edited by Manlio Pastore Stocchi. Rome–Padua: Antenore, 2012.

Dante Alighieri. *Egloge*, edited by Marco Petoletti, in Dante Alighieri, *Le opere*. V. *Epistole, Egloge, Questio de aqua et terra*, edited by Marco Baglio, Luca Azzetta, Marco Petoletti and Michele Rinaldi. Rome: Salerno Editrice, 2016.

Philip H. Wicksteed and Edmund G. Gardner. *Dante and Giovanni del Virgilio: including a critical edition of the text of Dante's 'Eclogae Latinae' and of the poetic remains of Giovanni del Virgilio*. New York: Haskell House Publishers, 1970.

Commentaries on Dante's 'Commedia':

Except where other details are provided, the editions are the same as those used by the Darmouth Dante Project, indicated with the abbreviation 'DDP' and accessible at: https://dante.dartmouth.edu/.

Alighieri, Pietro. First, second and third redactions. DDP.

Benvenuto da Imola. DDP.

Berthier, P. Gioachino. DDP

Boccaccio, Giovanni. DDP.

Bosco, Umberto and Reggio, Giovanni. DDP.

Casini, Tommaso and Barbi, S. A. DDP.

Chiavacci Leonardi, Anna Maria. DDP.

Chimenz, Siro. DDP.

Daniello, Bernardino. DDP.

Del Lungo, Isidoro. DDP.

Fosca, Nicola. DDP.

Francesco da Buti. DDP.

Gabriele, Trifon. DDP.

Grabher, Carlo. DDP.
Gregorio di Siena. DDP.
Guido da Pisa. DDP.
Hollander, Robert. DDP.
Jacopo della Lana. DDP.
Johannis de Serravalle. DDP.
Landino, Cristoforo DDP.
Mattalia, Daniele. DDP.
Ottimo Commento. First and third redactions. DDP.
Pietrobono, Luigi. DDP.
Sapegno, Natalino. DDP.
Singleton, Charles S. DDP.
Steiner, Carlo. DDP.

Other primary sources

1. Manuscripts

Bartholomaeus Anglicus. *De proprietatibus rerum*. Copenhagen, Kongelige Bibliotek, MS 213.
Bartholomaeus Anglicus. *De proprietatibus rerum*. Troyes, Bibliothèque de Troyes, MS 979.
Florilegium of moral and historical texts, with *notabilia* from *Nic. Eth.*, Seneca (*Epist.* and other), Orosius, Valerius Maximus, Pompeius Trogus, Solinus, Macrobius, *Institutiones* of *Corpus Iuris Civilis*. Florence, Biblioteca Medicea Laurenziana, MS Plut. 6 sin. 10.

2. Print and online sources

Aelian. *De natura animalium libri XVII*, edited by Rudolf Hercher. Leipzig: Teubner, 1864–6.
Aelredus Rievallensis. *Sermones de tempore*, in *Patrologia Latina*, 195. All references from the *Patrologia Latina (PL)*, unless otherwise stated, were consulted via the 'Patrologia Latina Database', the complete electronic version of the first edition of Jacques-Paul Migne's *Patrologia Latina* (1844–55 and 1862–5) by ProQuest Information and Learning Company.
Alanus de Insulis. *Distinctiones dictionum theologicalium*. In *PL*, 210.
Albert the Great. *Ethica*. In *Opera Omnia*, edited by Auguste Borgnet, 38 vols, VII. Paris: Vives, 1891.
Albertus Magnus. *Super Ethica Commentum et Quaestiones*, edited by Wilhelm Kübel. In *Opera Omnia*, XIV.I. Münster: Aschendorff, 1968–72.
Anselm of Laon. *Enarrationes in Cantica canticorum*. In *PL*, 162.
Antoninus of Florence. *Confessionale di Santo Antonino arcivescovo fiorentino*. Venice: appresso Girolamo Scotto, 1566.
Antonius. *Vita S. Simeonis*. In *PL*, 73.
Aristotle. *Nicomachean Ethics*. In Aristoteles Latinus, *Ethica Nicomachea: Translatio Roberti Grosseteste Lincolniensis sive 'Liber Ethicorum' B. Recensio Recognita*, edited by René-Antoine Gauthier, XXVI, parts 1–3, fasc.4. Leiden: Brill; Brussels: Desclée de Brouwer, 1972–4.
Aristotle. *Historia animalium*. In Aristote, *Histoire des animaux*, edited by Pierre Louis. Paris: Les Belles Lettres, 1964–9.
Athanasius. *Vita B. Antonii Abbatis*. In *PL*, 73.
Augustine of Hippo. *City of God*, translated by Henry Bettenson, edited by Gillian R. Evans. London: Penguin, 2003.
Augustine of Hippo. *De trinitate libri XIV*, edited by William J. Mountain, 2 vols. Turnhout: Brepols, 1968.
Augustine of Hippo. *Liber de natura et gratia contra Pelagium*. In *Opera Omnia* (*PL* 44) at: http://www.augustinus.it/latino/natura_grazia/index.htm.
Augustine of Hippo. *Enarratio in Psalmum*, LXIX; XL. In *PL*, 36–37.
Augustine of Hippo. *Tractatus in Iohannis Evangelium*. In *PL* 35.
Barney, Stephen A., Lewis, W. J., Beach, J. A. and Berghof, Oliver, eds. *Etymologies of Isidore of Seville*. Cambridge: Cambridge University Press, 2006.
Bartholomaeus Anglicus. *De proprietatibus rerum*. In Bartholomaei Anglici, *De genuinis rerum coelestium, terrestrium et inferarum rerum Proprietatibus, Libri XVIII*. Frankfurt: apud Wolfangum Richterum, 1601; anast. reprint, Frankfurt a. M.: Minerva, 1964.

Bede, the Venerable. *The Commentary on the Seven Catholic Epistles of Bede the Venerable*, edited and translated by David Hurst, O.S.B. Kalamazoo: Cistercian Publications, 1985.

Bede, the Venerable. *Allegorica expositio in Cantica canticorum*. In *PL*, 91.

Bedford, Peter. *The City at a Distance*. In *Wakefield: Heaven, Purgatory or Hell?*, at: https://ahc.leeds.ac.uk/leeds-centre-dante-studies/doc/community-projects.

Bestiario moralizzato. In *Bestiari medievali*, edited by Luigina Morini, 487–547. Turin: Einaudi, 1996.

Bestiario toscano. In Garver, Milton Stahl and McKenzie, Kenneth, eds. 'Il bestiario toscano secondo la lezione dei codici di Parigi e di Roma.' *Studj romanzi* 8 (1912): 1–100.

Boethius. *De Consolatione Philosophiae*, edited by Karl Büchner. Heidelberg: Editiones Heidelbergenses, 1960.[2]

Brown, Dan. *Inferno*. New York: Doubleday, 2013.

Bruno of Asti. *Expositio in Apocalypsim*. In *PL*, 165.

Compagni, Dino. *Cronica*, edited by Davide Cappi. Rome: Istituto Storico Italiano per il Medioevo, 2000.

Crossley, Paul. Purgatorio. In *Wakefield: Heaven, Purgatory or Hell?*, at: https://ahc.leeds.ac.uk/leeds-centre-dante-studies/doc/community-projects.

Curtius Rufus. *Historiae Alexandri Magni*, edited by Carlo M. Lucarini. In 'Bibliotheca Teubneriana Latina (BTL) und Thesaurus linguae Latinae (TLL) Online', at: https://www.degruyter.com/view/db/btltll.

De Courcy Bower, Angie. *If Heaven's Too Bright*. In *Wakefield: Heaven, Purgatory or Hell?*, at: https://ahc.leeds.ac.uk/leeds-centre-dante-studies/doc/community-projects.

De Liguori, Alfonso Maria, St. *Opere ascetiche*, edited by Oreste Gregorio, Giuseppe Cacciatore and Domenico Capone. Rome: Edizioni di Storia e Letteratura, 1960.

Detto del gatto lupesco. In *Poeti del Duecento*, edited by Gianfranco Contini, 2 vols, II, 285–93. Milan: Ricciardi, 1960.

Eliot, Thomas S. *The Waste Land*. New York: Boni and Liveright, 1922.

Filippi, Rustico. *Sonetti satirici e giocosi*, edited by Silvia Buzzetti Gallarati. Rome: Carocci, 2005.

Flodoardus Remensis. *De triumphis Christi Antiochiae*. In *PL*, 135.

Foliot, Gilbert. *Expositio in Cantica canticorum*. In *PL*, 202.

Franceschi, Dora, ed. *Oculos pastoralis pascens officia et continens radium dulcibus pomis suis*. Turin: Accademia delle scienze, 1966.

Gervaise, *Bestiaire*. In *Bestiari medievali*, edited by Luigina Morini, 287–361. Turin: Einaudi, 1996.

Giamboni, Bono. *Libro de' vizi e delle virtudi*, edited by Cesare Segre. Turin: Einaudi, 1968.

Gillebertus de Hoilandia. *Sermones in Canticum Salomonis*. In *PL*, 184.

Glossa ordinaria: Postilla Hugonis de Sancto Charo, 7 vols. Venice: apud Nicolaum Pezzana, 1703.

Gregory the Great. *Expositio super Cantica canticorum*. In *PL*, 79.

Gregory the Great. *Moralia in Iob*, edited by Marcus Adriaen. Turnhout: Brepols, 1979–85. In *Corpus Christianorum Latinorum*, 143.

Guibert of Nogent. *Tropologiae in prophetas Asee et Amos ac Lamentationes Ieremiae*. In *PL*, 156.

Haymo Halberstatensis. *Expositio in Apocalypsin*. In *PL*, 117.

Henricus de Castro Marsiaco. *Epistolae*. In *PL*, 204.

Holder, Arthur, ed. *The Venerable Bede: On the Song of Songs and Selected Writings*. New York: Paulist Press, 2011.

Hugonis Cardinalis. *Opera Omnia in Universum Vetus, et Novum Testamentum*. 8 vols, IV. Venice: apud Nicolaum Pezzana, 1703.

Humberti de Romanis. *Opera de vita regulari*, edited by Joachim J. Berthier, 2 vols. Rome: Typis A. Befani, 1888–9.

Isidore of Seville. *De fide catholica*. In *PL*, 83.

Isidore of Seville. *Etymologiae*. In Isidoro di Siviglia, *Etimologie o Origini*, edited by Angelo Valastro Canale. Turin: UTET, 2004.

Jacobus de Benevento. *De adventu Antichristi*. In *S. Thomae de Aquino Opera omnia*, recognovit ac instruxit Enrique Alarcón automato electronico. Pompaelone ad Universitatis Studiorum Navarrensis aedes a MM A.D., at: http://www.corpusthomisticum.org.

L'Inferno di Topolino, originally published in *Topolino* 7–12 (October 1949–March 1950), drawings by Angelo Bioletto, text by Guido Martina; republished in *L'Inferno di Topolino e altre storie ispirate a Dante Alighieri*, edited by Susanna Carboni. Florence–Milan: Giunti, 2016.

Latini, Brunetto. *Tresor*, edited by Pietro G. Beltrami et al. Turin: Einaudi, 2007.

Latini, Brunetto. *Poesie*, edited by Stefano Carrai. Turin: Einaudi, 2016.

Latini, Brunetto. *The Book of the Treasure–Li livres dou tresor*, translated by Paul Barrette and Spurgeon Baldwin. New York: Garland, 1993.

Levi, Primo. *Se questo è un uomo*. Turin: De Silva, 1947; Einaudi, 1958.

Mandelstam, Osip. 'Conversation about Dante.' In Osip Mandelstam, *The Complete Critical Prose and Letters*, edited and translated by Jane Gary Harris and Constance Link, 397–442. Ann Arbor: Ardis, 1979.

Marti, Mario, ed. *Poeti giocosi del tempo di Dante*. Milan: Rizzoli, 1956.

Martinus Legionensis. *Sermones*. In *PL*, 208.

Meister Eckhart. *Sermones*, edited by Ernst Benz, Bruno Decker and Joseph Koch. Stuttgart: W. Kohlhammer Verlag, 1987.

Mussato, Albertino. *Ep.* I, *Ad collegium artistarum*. In Enzo Cecchini, 'Le epistole metriche del Mussato sulla poesia'. In *Tradizione classica e letteratura umanistica per Alessandro Perosa*, edited by Roberto Cardini et al., 2 vols. Rome: Bulzoni, 1985. I, 95–119.

Nathan, Sarina, ed. *Amicitia di maestro Boncompagno da Signa*. Rome: La Società, 1909.

Onorius of Autun. *Expositio in Cantica canticorum*. In *PL*, 172.

Orlando, Sandro, ed. *Rime due e trecentesche tratte dall'Archivio di Stato di Bologna*. Bologna: Commissione per i testi di lingua, 2005.

Orosius, Paulus, *Historiarum adversum paganos libri VII*, Turnhout: Brepols Publishers, 2010. In *The Library of Latin Texts. Series B*, at: http://clt.brepolis.net/LLTA/pages/TextSearch.aspx?key=POROS0571.

Ovid, *Tristia*, translated by Anthony S. Kline, at: https://www.poetryintranslation.com/PITBR/Latin/OvidTristiaBkTwo.php.

Ovid, *Metamorphoses*, with an English translation by Frank J. Miller, 2 vols. Cambridge, MA–London: Harvard University Press, 1958.

Peraldus. *Summa virtutum ac vitiorum*, 2 vols. Paris: apud Ludovicum Boullenger, 1648.

Peter Damian. *Collectanea in Vetus Testamentum*. In *PL*, 145.

Peter Damian. *Dialogus inter Iudaeum et Christianum, ad Honestum*. In *PL*, 145.

Peter Damian. *Sermones*. In *PL*, 144.

Petrarca, Francesco. *Le familiari*, translated by Ugo Dotti, 5 vols. Racconigi Cuneo: Nino Aragno, 2004–9.

Petrarca, Francesco. *Rerum memorandarum libri*, edited by Marco Petoletti. Florence: Le Lettere, 2014.

Philip of Harveng. *Commentaria in Cantica canticorum*. In *PL*, 203.

Philippe de Thaün, *Bestiaire*. In *Bestiari medievali*, edited by Luigina Morini, 103–285. Turin: Einaudi, 1996.

Phisiologus Latinus Versio B Is, XXIV. In *Bestiari medievali*, edited by Luigina Morini, 54–60. Turin: Einaudi, 1996.

Phisiologus. Versio Y, XXIX. In *Bestiari tardoantichi e medievali*, edited by Francesco Zambon, 162–4. Milan: Bompiani, 2018.

Pliny. *Naturalis Historia*. In Gaio Plinio Secondo, *Storia naturale*, edited by Alessandro Barchiesi, Chiara Frugoni and Giuliano Ranucci. Turin: Einaudi, 1982.

Proverbia quae dicuntur supra natura feminarum. In *Poeti del Duecento*, edited by Gianfranco Contini, 2 vols, I, 521–55. Milan: Ricciardi, 1960.

Ps.-Hugh of Saint Victor, *De bestiis*. In *PL*, 177.

Quintus Curtius. *History of Alexander*, translated by John C. Rolfe. Cambridge, MA: Harvard University Press, 1971.

Rabanus Maurus. *Allegoriae in universam sacram scripturam*. In *PL*, 112.

Rabanus Maurus. *Commentaria in Ecclesiasticum*. In *PL*, 109.

Rabanus Maurus. *De universo*. In *PL*, 111.

Richard of Saint Victor. *De eruditione*. In *PL*, 196.

Richard of Saint Victor. *In Cantica canticorum explicatio*. In *PL*, 196.

Richart de Fornival, *Bestiaire d'amours*. In *Bestiari medievali*, edited by Luigina Morini, 362–424. Turin: Einaudi, 1996.

Rupertus Tuitiensis. *Commentarius in librum Ecclesiastes*. In *PL*, 168.

Rupertus Tuitiensis. *De victoria Verbi Dei*. In *PL*, 169.

Sacchetti, Franco. *Il Trecentonovelle*, edited by Davide Puccini. Turin: UTET, 2004.

Servius, *Commentarius in Vergilii Aeneidos libros*, Turnhout: Brepols, 2010. In *The Library of Latin Texts. Series A*, at: http://clt.brepolis.net/LLTB/pages/TextSearch.aspx?key=PSERACOAE.

Schneyer, Johannes B. *Repertorium der lateinischen Sermones des Mittelalters für die Zeit 1150–1350*, 11 vols. Münster: Aschendorff, 1969–90.

Schönberger, Rolf, Quero Sánchez, Andrés, Berges, Brigitte and Jiang, Lu, eds. *Repertorium edierter Texte des Mittelalters aus dem Bereich der Philosophie und angrenzender Gebiete*. Berlin–Boston: Akademie Verlag, 2011.

Seneca. *Epistulae morales ad Lucilium*, edited by Otto Hense. In 'Bibliotheca Teubneriana Latina (BTL) und Thesaurus linguae Latinae (TLL) Online', at: https://www.degruyter.com/view/db/btltll.

Seneca. *Epistulae morales ad Lucilium*, translated by Richard M. Gummere. Cambridge, MA: Harvard University Press, 1917–25.

Servasanto da Faenza. *Sermones de proprio sanctorum*. In *Bonaventurae opera omnia*, edited by Adolf C. Peltier, 15 vols, XIII (1868), 493–636. Paris: Ludovicus Vives, 1864–71.

Statuta Populi et Communis Florentiae, publica auctoritate collecta, castigata et praeposita, anno Salutis MCCCCXV, 3 vols. Florence [Freiburg]: Michaelem Kluch, 1778.

Statuto del Podestà [1325]. In *Statuti della Repubblica Fiorentina*, edited by Romolo Caggese, revised by G. Pinto, F. Salvestrini, A. Zorzi, 2 vols. Florence: Olschki, 1999.

Stegmüller, Friedrich. *Repertorium Biblicum Medii Aevii*. Madrid: Consejo Superior de Investigaciónes Cientificas, 1949–61.

Tassi, Francesco, ed. *Della miseria dell'uomo, Giardino di consolazione, Introduzione alle virtù di Bono Giamboni*. Florence: Guglielmo Piatti, 1836.

Tesoro della lingua italiana delle origini–Opera del vocabolario italiano (TLIO–OVI), database at: http://tlio.ovi.cnr.it/TLIO/.

Thomas à Becket. *Epistolae*. In *PL*, 190.

Thomas Aquinas. *Sententia libri Ethicorum*. In *Opera Omnia*, XLVII. Rome: Editio Leonina, 1882.

Thomas Aquinas, *In Jeremiam*. In *S. Thomae de Aquino Opera omnia*, recognovit ac instruxit Enrique Alarcón automato electronico. Pompaelone ad Universitatis Studiorum Navarrensis aedes a MM A.D., at: http://www.corpusthomisticum.org.

Thomas Aquinas. *Summa Contra Gentiles*. Rome: Editio Leonina Manualis, 1934.

Thomas Aquinas. *Super Isaiam*. In *S. Thomae de Aquino Opera omnia*, at: http://www.corpusthomisticum.org.

Thomas Aquinas. *The Summa Theologiae of Saint Thomas Aquinas: Latin-English*, translated by the Fathers of the English Dominican Province. Scotts Valley: NovAntiqua, 2008.

Thomas Cisterciensis. *Commentaria in Cantica canticorum*. In *PL*, 206.

Uncertain Author. *Expositio in Apocalypsin*. In *PL*, 17.

Uncertain Author. *Expositio in Cantica Canticorum* (attributed to Cassiodorus). In *PL*, 70.

Valerius Maximus. *Facta et dicta memorabilia*, edited by John Briscoe. In 'Bibliotheca Teubneriana Latina (BTL) und Thesaurus linguae Latinae (TLL) Online', at: https://www.degruyter.com/view/db/btltll.

Villani, Giovanni. *Nuova cronica*, edited by Giuseppe Porta. Parma: Guanda, 1990–1.

Virgil, *Eclogues. Georgics. Aeneid, Books 1–6*, translated by H. Rushton Fairclough. Cambridge, MA–London: Harvard University Press, 1999.

Walther, Hans and Schmidt, Paul Gerhard. *Proverbia Sententiaeque Latinitatis Medii Ac Recentioris Aevi: Nova Series/Lateinische Sprichwörter und Sentenzen des Mittelalters und der frühen Neuzeit in alphabetischer Anordnung*, 3 vols. Göttingen: Vandenhoek & Ruprecht, 1982–6.

Wakefield: Heaven, Purgatory or Hell? From Isolation, via Education, to Harmony: at: https://ahc.leeds.ac.uk/leeds-centre-dante-studies/doc/community-projects.

Wolbero Sancti Pantaleoni. *Commentaria in Cantica canticorum*. In *PL*, 195.

Yates, Michael. *Purgatory: The Full-Time Course*. In *Wakefield: Heaven, Purgatory or Hell?*, at: https://ahc.leeds.ac.uk/leeds-centre-dante-studies/doc/community-projects.

Yates, Michael. *The Streets of Me*. In *Wakefield: Heaven, Purgatory or Hell?*, at: https://ahc.leeds.ac.uk/leeds-centre-dante-studies/doc/community-projects.

Yates, Michael. *In Cathedral Square*. In *Wakefield: Heaven, Purgatory or Hell?*, at: https://ahc.leeds.ac.uk/leeds-centre-dante-studies/doc/community-projects.

Secondary sources

Abrams, Richard. 'Against the *Contrapasso*: Dante's Heretics, Schismatics and Others.' *Italian Quarterly* 27 (1986): 5–19.

Agamben, Giorgio. *Homo Sacer: il potere sovrano e la nuda vita*. Turin: Einaudi, 1995.

Ahern, John. 'Singing the Book: Orality in the Reception of Dante's *Comedy*.' In *Dante: Contemporary Perspectives*, edited by Amilcare A. Iannucci, 214–39. Toronto: University of Toronto Press, 1997.

Albanese, Gabriella. 'Tradizione e ricezione del Dante bucolico nell'Umanesimo. Nuove acquisizioni sui manoscritti della corrispondenza poetica con Giovanni del Virgilio.' *Nuova Rivista di Letteratura Italiana* 14 (2011): 9–80.

Albanese, Gabriella. '*De gestis Henrici VII cesaris*: Mussato, Dante e il mito dell'incoronazione poetica.' In *Enrico VII, Dante e Pisa*, edited by Petralia, G. and Santagata, M., 161–202. Ravenna: Longo, 2016.

Albanese, Gabriella and Pontari, Paolo. 'Il notariato bolognese, le *Ecloghe* e il Polifemo dantesco. Nuove testimonianze manoscritte e una nuova lettura dell'ultima *Egloga*.' *Studi danteschi* 81 (2016): 13–130.

Albertini, Stefano. 'Dante in camicia nera: uso e abuso del divino poeta nell'Italia fascista.' *The Italianist* 16.1 (1996): 117–42.

Antonelli, Armando and Pedrini, Riccardo. 'Appunti sulla più antica attestazione dell'*Inferno*.' *Studi e problemi di critica testuale* 63 (2001): 29–41.

Armour, Peter. 'Dante's *Contrapasso*: Contexts and Texts.' *Italian Studies* 55.1 (2000): 1–20.

Armstrong, Guyda. 'Boccaccio and Dante.' In *The Cambridge Companion to Boccaccio*, edited by Guyda Armstrong, Rhiannon Daniels, Stephen J. Milner, 121–38. Cambridge: Cambridge University Press, 2015.

Arquès, Rossend, ed. 'Dossier: Francesco De Sanctis (1817–83). La storia della letteratura, ancora? La història de la literatura, encara?' *Quaderns d'Italià* 16 (2011): 3–100.

Ascoli, Albert R. '"Ponete mente almeno come io son bella": Prose and Poetry, "pane" and "vivanda", Goodness and Beauty, in *Convivio* I.' In *Dante's 'Convivio' or How to Restart a Career in Exile*, edited by Meier, F., 115–43. Bern: Peter Lang, 2018.

Audeh, Aida and Havely, Nick, eds. *Dante in the Long Nineteenth Century: Nationality, Identity, and Appropriation*. Oxford: Oxford University Press, 2012.

Auerbach, Erich. *Mimesis: The Representation of Reality in Western Literature*, translated by Willard R. Trask. Princeton: Princeton University Press, 1953; first published as *Mimesis: Dargestellte Wirklichkeit in der abendländischen Literatur*. Bern: Francke, 1946.

Baika, Gabriella I. 'Tongues of Fire and Fraud in Bolgia Eight.' *Quaderni d'italianistica* 32.2 (2011): 5–26.

Baldan, Paolo. 'Dante, Mussato e il Colle di Romano.' In *Nuovi studi ezzeliniani*, edited by Giorgio Cracco, 575–88. Rome: Istituto Storico Italiano per il Medioevo, 1992.

Baldelli, Ignazio. *Dante e Francesca*. Florence: Olschki, 1999.

Barański, Zygmunt G., ed. *'Libri poetarum in quattuor species dividuntur': Essays on Dante and 'Genre'*. Supplement to *The Italianist* 15 (1995).

Barański, Zygmunt G. 'Dante Alighieri: Experimentation and (Self-)Exegesis.' In *The Cambridge History of Literary Criticism*, edited by Alastair J. Minnis and Ian Johnson, 559–82. Cambridge: Cambridge University Press, 2005.

Barański, Zygmunt G. 'Sulla formazione intellettuale di Dante: alcuni problemi di definizione.' *Studi e problemi di critica testuale* 90.1 (2015): 31–54.

Barański, Zygmunt G. 'On Dante's Trail.' *Italian Studies* 72.1 (2017): 1–15.

Barański, Zygmunt G. '"Oh come è grande la mia impresa": Notes towards Defining Dante's *Convivio*.' In *Dante's 'Convivio' or How to Restart a Career in Exile*, edited by Meier, F., 9–26. Bern: Peter Lang, 2018.

Barlow, Henry Clark, *The Sixth Centenary Festivals of Dante Allighieri in Florence and at Ravenna by A Representative*. London: Williams and Norgate, 1866.

Barolini, Teodolinda. *The Undivine Comedy: Detheologizing Dante*. Princeton: Princeton University Press, 1992.

Barolini, Teodolinda. 'Dante and Cavalcanti (On Making Distinctions in Matters of Love): *Inferno* V in its Lyric Context.' *Dante Studies* 116 (1998): 31–63.

Barolini, Teodolinda. 'Minos's Tail: The Labor of Devising Hell (*Aeneid* 6.431 and *Inferno* 5.1–24).' In Teodolinda Barolini, *Dante and the Origins of Italian Literary Culture*, 132–50. New York: Fordham University Press, 2006.

Barolini, Teodolinda. 'Dante and Francesca da Rimini: Realpolitik, Romance, Gender.' In Teodolinda Barolini, *Dante and the Origins of Italian Literary Culture*, 304–32. New York: Fordham University Press, 2006.

Barolini, Teodolinda. 'Dante's Sympathy for the Other.' *Critica del Testo* 14.1 (2011): 177–204.

Bartuschat, Johannes. 'La littérature vernaculaire et la philosophie en Toscane dans la deuxième moitié du 13ème siècle.' *Tijdschrift voor Filosofie* 75 (2013): 311–33.

Bartuschat, Johannes. 'La littérature vernaculaire et la philosophie en Toscane dans la deuxième moitié du 13ème siècle.' *Tijdschrift voor Filosofie* 75 (2013): 311–33.

Bartuschat, Johannes and Robiglio, Andrea Aldo. *Il 'Convivio' di Dante*. Ravenna: Longo, 2015.

Bates, Richard and Rendall, Thomas. 'Dante's Ulysses and the *Epistle* of James.' *Dante Studies* 107 (1989–1990): 33–44.

Bellomo, Saverio. *Filologia e critica dantesca*. Brescia: La Scuola, 2008.

Beltrami, Pietro G., ed. 'Introduzione.' In Brunetto Latini, *Tresor*, edited by Beltrami, P. G., et al., vii–xxvi. Turin: Einaudi, 2007.

Benigni, Roberto. 'Benigni legge Dante.' In *La Repubblica*, 29 December 2008, at: http://ricerca.repubblica.it/repubblica/archivio/repubblica/2008/12/29/benigni-legge-dante.html.

Benson, Joshua C. 'Matthew of Acquasparta's Sermons on Theology.' In *Franciscans and Preaching. Every Miracle from the Beginning of the World Came about through Words*, edited by Timothy J. Johnson, 145–74. Leiden–Boston: Brill, 2012.

Berg, Klaus and Kasper, Monica, eds. *'Das büch der tugenden'. Ein Compendium des 14.Jahrhunderts über Moral und Recht nach der 'Summa theologiae' II–II des Thomas Aquin und anderen Werken der Scholastik und Kanonistik*. Tübingen: Max Miemeyer Verlag, 1984.

Beringer, Alyson. *The Sight of Semiramis: Medieval and Early Modern Narratives of the Babylonian Queen*. Tempe: Arizona Center for Medieval and Renaissance Studies, 2016.

Bianchi, Luca. '"Noli comedere panem philosophorum inutiliter". Dante Alighieri and John of Jandun on Philosophical "Bread".' *Tijdschrift voor Filosofie* 75 (2013): 335–55.

Billanovich, Giuseppe. 'Giovanni Del Virgilio, Pietro da Moglio, Francesco da Fiano.' *Italia Medioevale e Umanistica* 6 (1963): 203–94.

Billanovich, Giuseppe. 'Tra Dante e Petrarca.' *Italia Medioevale e Umanistica* 8 (1965): 1–44.

Billanovich, Giuseppe. *La tradizione del testo di Livio e le origini dell'Umanesimo. I: Tradizione e fortuna di Livio tra Medioevo e Umanesimo*. Padua: Antenore, 1981.

Billanovich, Guido. 'Il preumanesimo padovano.' In *Storia della cultura veneta*, II. *Il Trecento*, edited by Girolamo Arnaldi, 19–110. Vicenza: Neri Pozza, 1976.

Black, Robert. *Humanism and Education in Medieval and Renaissance Italy: Tradition and Innovation in Latin Schools from the Twelfth to the Fifteenth Century*. Cambridge: Cambridge University Press, 2001.

Black, Robert. 'The Origins of Humanism, its Educational Context and its Early Development: a Review Article of Ronald Witt *In the Footsteps of the Ancients*.' *Vivarium* 40.2 (2002): 272–97.

Black, Robert. *Education and Society in Florentine Tuscany: Teachers, Pupils and Schools, c.1250–1500*. Leiden: Brill, 2007.

Black, Robert. 'Education.' In *Dante in Context*, edited by Lino Pertile and Zygmunt G. Barański, 260–76. Cambridge: Cambridge University Press, 2015.

Black, Robert and Pomaro, Gabriella. *La 'Consolazione della Filosofia' nel Medioevo e nel Rinascimento Italiano/Boethius's 'Consolation of Philosophy' in Italian Medieval and Renaissance Education: Schoolbooks and Their Glosses in Florentine Manuscripts*. Florence: SISMEL–Edizioni del Galluzzo, 2000.

Blackburn, Simon. *Lust*. Oxford: Oxford University Press, 2004.

Bloom, Harold. 'The Strangeness of Dante: Ulysses and Beatrice.' In Harold Bloom, *The Western Canon. The Books and School of the Ages*, 76–104. London: Macmillan, 1995.

Bloomfield, Morton W. *The Seven Deadly Sins*. East Lansing, MI: Michigan State College Press, 1952.

Blumenfeld-Kosinski, Renate. 'The Scandal of Pasiphae: Narration and Interpretation in the *Ovide moralisé*.' *Modern Philology* 93 (1996): 307–26.

Bologna, Corrado. 'Dante e il latte delle Muse.' In *Atlante della letteratura italiana*, edited by Luzzato, S. and Pedullà, G., I, 145–55. Turin: Einaudi, 2010.

Bolognesi, Davide. 'Il contrapasso come chiasma. Appunti su *Inferno* XXVIII.' *L'Alighieri* 36 (2010): 5–20.

Bonfatti, Rossella. 'Performing Dante or Building the Nation? The *Divina Commedia* between Dramaturgy of Exile and Public Festivities.' *Medievalia* 38 (2017): 37–67.

Bosco, Umberto, ed. *Enciclopedia Dantesca (ED)*, 6 vols. Rome: Istituto dell'Enciclopedia Italiana, 1984; 1st edn, 1970–8.

Botterill, Stephen. 'Reading, Writing and Speech in the Fourteenth- and Fifteenth-Century Commentaries on Dante's *Comedy*.' In *Interpreting Dante: Essays on the Traditions of Dante Commentary*, edited by Nasti, P. and Rossignoli, C., 17–29. Notre Dame: University of Notre Dame Press, 2013.

Boyde, Patrick. *Perception and Passion in Dante's 'Comedy'*. Cambridge: Cambridge University Press, 1993.

Branca, Vittore, ed. *Dante nel mondo*. Florence: Olschki, 1965.

Brilli, Elisa. 'Reminiscenze scritturali (e non) nelle epistole politiche dantesche.' *La Cultura* 3 (2007): 439–55.

Brugnoli, Giorgio. 'Epistula Catholica Beati Jacobi Apostoli.' In Giorgio Brugnoli, *Studi danteschi*, 3 vols, III, 19–24. Pisa: ETS, 1998.

Brundage, James A. *Law, Sex and Christian Society in the Middle Ages*. Aldershot: Variorum, 1993.

Brunetti, Giuseppina. 'Guinizzelli, il non più oscuro Maestro Giandino e il Boezio di Dante.' In *Intorno a Guido Guinizzelli, Atti della Giornata di studi (Università di Zurigo, 16 giugno 2000)*, edited by Luciano Rossi and Sara Alloatti Boller, 155–91. Alessandria: Edizioni dell'Orso, 2002.

Brunetti, Giuseppina. 'Nicolas Trevet, Niccolò da Prato: per le tragedie di Seneca e i libri dei classici.' *Memorie domenicane* 44 (2013): 345–71.

Brunetti, Giuseppina and Gentili, Sonia. 'Una biblioteca nella Firenze di Dante: i manoscritti di Santa Croce.' In *Testimoni del vero: su alcuni libri in biblioteche d'autore*, edited by Emilio Russo, 21–55. Rome: Bulzoni, 2000.

Bullough, Vern L. 'Medieval Concepts of Adultery.' *Arthuriana* 7.4 (1997): 5–15.

Busnelli, Giovanni. *Il simbolo delle tre fiere dantesche: ricerche e studi intorno al prologo della Commedia*. Rome: Civiltà Cattolica, 1909.

Cannata, Nadia and Signorini, Maddalena. 'Per trionfare o Cesare o poeta. La corona d'alloro e le insegne del poeta moderno.' In *Dai pochi ai molti. Studi in onore di Roberto Antonelli*, edited by Paolo Cannettieri and Arianna Punzi, 3–37. Rome: Viella, 2014.

Caputo, Rino. 'Dante by Heart and Dante Declaimed: the "Realization" of the *Comedy* on Italian Radio and Television.' In *Dante, Cinema, and Television*, edited by Amilcare A. Iannucci, 213–24. Toronto: University of Toronto Press, 2004.

Carapezza, Sandra. '"Grazia divina e precedente merto". L'Epistola di Giacomo come fonte della speranza.' *L'Alighieri* 58 (2017): 93–105.

Caretti, Lanfranco. 'Eros e castigo (*Inferno* V).' In *Antichi e moderni: Studi di letteratura italiana*, 7–30. Turin: Einaudi, 1976.

Carrara, Enrico. *La poesia pastorale*. Milan: Vallardi, 1906.

Carron, Delphine. 'Remigio de' Girolami dans la Florence de Dante (1293–1302).' *Reti Medievali Rivista* 18.1 (2017): 1–29. In themed segment, *Dante attraverso i documenti. II. Presupposti e contesti dell'impegno politico a Firenze (1295–1302)*, edited by Giuliano Milani and Antonio Montefusco.

Casagrande, Carla and Fioravanti, Gianfranco, eds. *La filosofia in Italia al tempo di Dante*. Bologna: il Mulino, 2016.

Casagrande, Carla and Vecchio, Silvana. *I peccati della lingua: disciplina ed etica della parola nella cultura medievale*. Rome: Istituto della Enciclopedia Italiana, 1987.

Casagrande, Carla and Vecchio, Silvana. *I sette vizi capitali. Storia dei peccati nel medioevo*. Turin: Einaudi, 2000.

Casella, Mario. 'L'amico mio e non de la ventura.' *Studi danteschi* 27 (1943): 117–34.

Cassell, Anthony Kimber. *Dante's Fearful Art of Justice*. Toronto: University of Toronto Press, 1984.

Castelli, Daniela. 'L'errore rigorista e la "fisica dell'anima" in una *Commedia* senza *lex talionis*.' *Studi danteschi* 78 (2013): 154–95.

Chiarini, Eugenio and Mengaldo, Pier Vincenzo. 'Ravenna.' In *ED*, IV, 857–66. 1973.

Chiffoleau, Jacques. 'Le crime de majesté, la politique et l'extraordinaire. Note sur les collections érudites de procès de lèse majesté du XVIIè siècle et leurs exemples médiévaux.' In *Le procès politique(XIVè-XVIIè siècles): Actes du colloque de Rome (20-22 janvier 2003)*, edited by Yves-Marie Bercé, 577–662. Rome: Collection de l' École française de Rome, 2007.

Chiffoleau, Jacques. *La Chiesa, il segreto e l'obbedienza*. Bologna: il Mulino, 2010.

Ciavolella, Massimo. *La malattia d'amore dall'antichità al Medioevo*. Rome: Bulzoni, 1976.

Ciavolella, Massimo. 'L'amore e la medicina medievale.' In *Guido Cavalcanti tra i suoi lettori*, edited by Maria Luisa Ardizzone, 93–102. Florence: Cadmo, 2003.

Ciccarese, Maria Pia. *Animali simbolici. Alle origini del bestiario cristiano*, 2 vols. Bologna: Edizioni Dehoniane, 2007.

Comba, Riccardo. '"Apetitus libidinis coherceatur". Strutture demografiche, reati sessuali e disciplina dei comportamenti nel Piemonte tardomedievale.' *Studi storici* 27 (1986): 529–76.

Comparetti, Domenico. *Virgilio nel Medio Evo*, edited by Giorgio Pasquali. Florence: La Nuova Italia, 1981; 1st edn, 1872.

Cornish, Alison. 'The *Epistle* of James in *Inferno* 26.' *Traditio* 45 (1989): 367–79.

Cox, Virginia and Ward, John O., eds. *The Rhetoric of Cicero in its Medieval and Early Renaissance Commentary Tradition*. Leiden: Brill, 2006.

Crisafi, Nicolò. 'Dante's Masterplot and the Alternative Narrative Models in the *Commedia*.' Unpublished DPhil thesis, University of Oxford, 2018.

Cristaldi, Sergio. *La profezia imperfetta. Il veltro e l'escatologia medievale*. Caltanissetta: Sciascia, 2011.

Curtius, Ernst Robert. 'Dante as a classic.' In *European Literature and the Latin Middle Ages*, translated by Willard R. Trask, 348–50. Princeton: Princeton University Press, 1953.

Dahan, Gilbert. 'La classificazione delle scienze e l'insegnamento universitario nel XIII secolo.' In *Le Università dell'Europa: le scuole e i maestri. Il Medioevo*, edited by Jacques Verger and Gian Paolo Brizzi, 19–43. Milan: Silvana Editoriale, 1994.

Dalmas, Davide. *Dante nella crisi religiosa del Cinquecento italiano: da Trifon Gabriele a Lodovico Castelvetro*. Rome: Vecchiarelli, 2005.

De Rooy, Ronald. 'Dante all'insegna dell'Unità.' *Incontri* 26.2 (2011): 64–72.

De Rooy, Ronald. 'Divine Comics.' *European Comic Art* 10.1 (2017): 94–109.

De Sanctis, Francesco. *Storia della letteratura italiana*, edited by Niccolò Gallo. Turin: Einaudi; Paris: Gallimard, 1996; 1st edn, 1870–71.

Dean, Trevor. *Crime and Justice in Late Medieval Italy*. Cambridge: Cambridge University Press, 2007.

Del Castello, Antonio. 'La tradizione del "Liber de virtutibus et vitiis" di Servasanto da Faenza. Edizione critica delle "distinctiones" I–IV.' Unpublished PhD thesis, University of Naples Federico II–École nationale des Chartes, 2011–13.

Dell'Oso, Lorenzo. 'Per la formazione intellettuale di Dante: i cataloghi librari, le tracce testuali, il *Trattatello* di Boccaccio.' *Le tre corone* 4 (2017): 129–61.

Di Giacomo, Flavio. *Uno sguardo verso il futuro: Ipotesi per un "Piano Dante", Studio di Fattibilità per un Programma Italiano di Reinsediamento* (https://www.resettlement.eu/sites/icmc/files/FA.RE_.%5B1%5D.pdf)

Diacciati, Silvia. *Popolani e magnati*. Spoleto: Fondazione Centro Italiano di Studi sull'Alto Medioevo, 2011.

Dizionario Biografico degli Italiani, 90 vols. Rome: Istituto dell'Enciclopedia Italiana, 1960–2017.

Emerick, Betsy. 'Auerbach and Gramsci on Dante: Criticism and Ideology.' *Carte Italiane* 1.1 (1980): 9–22.

English indices of deprivation 2015, at: https://www.gov.uk/government/statistics/english-indices-of-deprivation-2015.

Esposito, Anna. 'Adulterio, concubinato, bigamia: testimonianze dalla normativa statutaria dello Stato pontificio (secoli XIII–XVI).' In *Trasgressioni: Seduzione, concubinato, adulterio, bigamia (XIV–XVIII secolo)*, edited by Silvana Seidel Menchi and Diego Quaglioni, 21–42. Bologna: il Mulino, 2004.

Esposito, Enzo, ed. *L'opera di Dante nel mondo: edizioni e traduzioni nel Novecento*. Ravenna: Longo, 1992.

Falzone, Paolo. 'Il *Convivio* di Dante.' In *La filosofia in Italia al tempo di Dante*, edited by Casagrande, C. and Fioravanti, G., 225–64. Bologna: il Mulino, 2016.

Fenzi, Enrico. 'Dante ghibellino. Note per una discussione.' *Per leggere* 24 (2013): 171–98.

Ferrara, Sabrina. 'Il senso del tempo nelle *Egloghe* di Dante.' *Italianistica* 44. 2 (2015): 199–218.

Ferrara, Sabrina. *La parola dell'esilio. Autore e lettori nell'opera di Dante dopo l'esilio*. Florence: Cesati, 2016.

Fioravanti, Gianfranco. 'Introduzione.' In Dante Alighieri, *Convivio*, edited by C. Giunta and G. Fioravanti. In *Opere*, edited by M. Santagata, 5–79. Milan: Mondadori, 2014.

Fioravanti, Gianfranco. 'La nobiltà spiegata ai nobili. Una nuova funzione della filosofia.' In *Il Convivio di Dante*, edited by Bartuschat, J. and Robiglio, A.A., 57–63. Ravenna: Longo, 2015.

Fioravanti, Gianfranco. 'Il pane degli angeli nel *Convivio* di Dante.' In *Nutrire il corpo, nutrire l'anima nel Medioevo*, edited by Chiara Crisciani and Onorato Grassi, 191–200. Pisa: ETS, 2017.

Formisano, Luciano, ed. *Storia della letteratura italiana. 12: La letteratura italiana fuori d'Italia*. Rome: Salerno, 2005.

Gambale, Giacomo. 'Dante, l'*Epistula Iacobi* e il *De Peccato Linguae*. Per una lettura filosofica di *Inferno* XXVI.' *Studi danteschi* 74 (2009): 179–98.

Gambale, Giacomo. *La lingua di fuoco: Dante e la filosofia del linguaggio*. Rome: Città nuova, 2012.

Gargan, Luciano. 'Dante e Giovanni del Virgilio: le Egloghe.' In Luciano Gargan, *Dante, la sua biblioteca e lo studio di Bologna*, 112–41. Rome–Padua: Antenore, 2014.

Gasparini, Patrizia. 'L'amitié comme fondement de la "concordia civium". Le *Favolello* de Brunet Latin (et une nouvelle source du *Tresor*).' *Arzanà* 13 (2010): 55–108.

Gehl, Paul F. *A Moral Art: Grammar, Society, and Culture in Trecento Florence*. Ithaca–London: Cornell University Press, 1993.

Gentili, Sonia. *L'uomo aristotelico alle origini della letteratura italiana*. Rome: Carocci–Università degli studi di Roma La Sapienza, 2005.

Gentili, Sonia. 'La filosofia dal latino al volgare.' In *La filosofia in Italia al tempo di Dante*, edited by Casagrande, C. and Fioravanti, G., 191–224. Bologna: il Mulino, 2016.

Gherush92, 'Via la *Divina Commedia* dalle scuole', at: http://www.gherush92.com/news.asp?tipo=A&id=2985.

Ghidetti, Enrico. 'Attilio Momigliano.' In *Dizionario Biografico degli Italiani* 75 (2011): 481–6.

Ghidetti, Enrico. 'Il Dante di Croce e Gentile.' In *Croce e Gentile* (2016): http://www.treccani.it/enciclopedia/elenco-opere/Croce_e_Gentile/1.

Gianferrari, Filippo. '"Poca favilla gran fiamma seconda" (*Par.*, I. 34). Riscrivere un proverbio tra Cino, San Giacomo, e San Girolamo.' *Le tre corone* 7 (2020; forthcoming).

Gilson, Simon. 'Modes of Reading in Boccaccio's *Esposizioni sopra la Comedia*.' In *Interpreting Dante: Essays on the Tradition of Dante Commentary*, edited by Nasti, P. and Rossignoli, C., 250–82. Notre Dame: University of Notre Dame Press, 2013.

Giordano, Lisania. 'Iuramentum sive sacramentum: prassi giuridico-sacrale in Gregorio Magno.' *Annali della Facoltà di Scienze della Formazione* 2 (2003): 99–108.

Giunta, Claudio. 'Dante: l'amore come destino.' In *Dante the Lyric and Ethical Poet. Dante lirico e etico*, edited by Zygmunt G. Barański and Martin McLaughlin, 119–36. London: Legenda, 2010.

Giustiniani, Vito R. 'Gli umanisti e la *querelle des anciens et des modernes*.' In *L'educazione e la formazione intellettuale nell'età dell'Umanesimo. Atti del II convegno internazionale, 1990*, edited by Luisa Rotondi Secchi Tarugi, 63–71. Milan: Guerini, 1992.

Gorni, Guglielmo. *Dante nella selva. Il primo canto della 'Commedia'*. Florence: Cesati, 1995.

Gorni, Guglielmo. 'Francesca e Paolo. La voce di lui.' *Intersezioni* 16 (1996): 383–9.

Gowler, David B. *James Through the Centuries*. Hoboken: Wiley, 2014.

Gragnolati, Manuele, '*Inferno* V.' In *Lectura Dantis Bononiensis*, edited by Emilio Pasquini and Carlo Galli, 7 vols, II, 7–22. Bologna: Bononia University Press, 2012.

Gray, Jonathan Michael. *Oaths in the English Reformation*. Cambridge: Cambridge University Press, 2012.

Gross, Kenneth. 'Infernal Metamorphoses: An Interpretation of Dante's "Counterpass".' *Modern Language Notes* 100 (1985): 42–69.

Havely, Nick R. *Dante and the Franciscans. Poverty and the Papacy in the 'Commedia'*. Cambridge: Cambridge University Press, 2004.

Hennessey, Brendan, Hooper, Laurence E. and Leavitt IV, Charles L. 'Realisms and Idealisms in Italian Culture, 1300–2017.' *The Italianist* 37.3 (2017): 281–8.

Honess, Claire E. *From Florence to the Heavenly City: The Poetry of Citizenship in Dante*. Oxford: Legenda, 2006.

Honess, Claire E. '"Ecce nunc tempus acceptabile": Henry VII and Dante's Ideal of Peace.' *The Italianist* 33.3 (2013): 484–504.

Honess, Claire E. '"Ritornerò Poeta ... ": Florence, Exile, and Hope.' In '*Se Mai Continga ...*,' edited by Claire E. Honess and Matthew Treherne, 84–103. Ravenna: Longo, 2013.

Honess, Claire E. and Treherne, Matthew, eds. '*Se Mai Continga ... ' Exile, Politics and Theology in Dante*. Ravenna: Longo, 2013.

Honess, Claire E. and Treherne, Matthew, eds. *Reviewing Dante's Theology*, 2 vols. Bern: Peter Lang, 2013.

Hooper, Laurence. 'Dante's *Convivio*, Book 1: Metaphor, Exile, Epochē.' *Modern Language Notes* 127.5, Supplement (2012): 86–104.

Iannucci, Amilcare A., ed. *Dante: Contemporary Perspectives*. Toronto: University of Toronto Press, 1997.

Iannucci, Amilcare A. 'Forbidden Love: Metaphor and History (*Inferno* V).' In *Dante: Contemporary Perspectives*, edited by Iannucci, A. A. 94–112.

Imbach, Ruedi. *Laien in der Philosophie des Mittelalters: Hinweise und Anregungen zu einem vernachlässigten Thema*. Amsterdam: Grüner, 1989.

Imbach, Ruedi. *Dante, la philosophie et les laïcs*. Fribourg, Suisse: Éditions universitaires, 1996.

Imbach, Ruedi and König-Pralong, Catherine. *La sfida laica. Per una nuova storia della filosofia medievale*. Rome: Carocci, 2016; 1st edn, *Le défi laïque: existe-t-il une philosophie de laïcs au Moyen Age?* Paris: Vrin, 2013.

Indizio, Giuseppe. *Problemi di biografia dantesca*. Ravenna: Longo, 2013.

Indizio, Giuseppe. 'Le tappe venete dell'esilio di Dante.' In Indizio, G., *Problemi*, 93–114.

Indizio, Giuseppe. 'Giovanni del Virgilio maestro e dantista minore.' In Indizio, G., *Problemi*, 449–69.

Inglese, Giorgio. *Vita di Dante. Una biografia possibile*. Rome: Carocci, 2015.

Jacquard, Danielle and Thomasset, Claude Alexandre. *Sexuality and Medicine in the Middle Ages*. Princeton: Princeton University Press, 1988.

Jossa, Stefano. *L'Italia letteraria*. Bologna: il Mulino, 2006.

Kent, Bonnie. 'On the Track of Lust: *Luxuria*, Ockham, and the Scientists.' In *In the Garden of Evil: The Vices and Culture in the Middle Ages*, edited by Richard Newhauser, 349–70. Toronto: Pontifical Institute of Medieval Studies, 2005.

Kirkham, Victoria. '*Contrapasso*: The Long Wait to *Inferno* 28.' *Modern Languages Notes* 127.1 (2012): S1–S12.

Konuk, Kader, *East West Mimesis: Auerbach in Turkey*. Stanford: Stanford University Press, 2010.

Lanza, Antonio. *Primi secoli. Saggi di letteratura italiana antica*. Rome: Archivio Guido Izzi, 1991.

Lasansky, D. Medina. *The Renaissance Perfected: Architecture, Spectacle, and Tourism in Fascist Italy*. University Park, PA: Pennsylvania State University Press, 2004.

Ledda, Giuseppe. *La guerra della lingua: ineffabilità, retorica e narrativa nella 'Commedia' di Dante*. Ravenna: Longo, 2002.

Ledda, Giuseppe. 'Dante e la tradizione delle visioni medievali.' *Letture Classensi* 37 (2008): 119–42.

Ledda, Giuseppe. 'Modelli biblici e identità profetica nelle *Epistole* di Dante.' *Lettere Italiane* 60.1 (2008): 18–42.

Ledda, Giuseppe, ed. *Le teologie di Dante*. Ravenna: Centro Dantesco dei Frati Minori Conventuali, 2015.

Lévy, Jean-Philippe. 'Le Problème de la preuve dans les droits savants du Moyen Age.' In *Recueils de la Société Jean Bodin pour l'histoire comparative des institutions. La Preuve* 2, 38 vols. XVII, 137–67. Brussels: Éditions de la Librairie encyclopédique, 1964.

Lindon, John. 'Notes on Nineteenth-Century Dante Commentaries and Critical Editions.' In *Interpreting Dante: Essays on the Traditions of Dante Commentary*, edited by Nasti, P. and Rossignoli, C., 434–49. Notre Dame: University of Notre Dame Press, 2013.

Livi, Giovanni. *Dante: suoi primi cultori, sua gente in Bologna*. Bologna: Licinio Cappelli, 1918.

Lombardi, Elena. *The Wings of the Doves: Love and Desire in Dante and Medieval Culture*. Montreal: McGill–Queen's University Press, 2012.

Lombardi, Elena. '"Che libito fe' licito in sua legge". Lust and Law, Reason and Passion in Dante.' In *Dantean Dialogues. Engaging with the Legacy of Amilcare Iannucci*, edited by Maggie Kilgour and Elena Lombardi, 125–54. Toronto: University of Toronto Press, 2013.

Lombardi, Elena. '"Per aver pace coi seguaci sui": Civil, Religious and Erotic Peace in *Inferno* V.' In *War and Peace in Dante*, edited by John C. Barnes and Daragh O'Connell, 173–93. Dublin: Four Courts Press, 2015.

Lombardo, Luca. '"Quasi come sognando". Dante e la presunta rarità del "libro di Boezio" (*Convivio* II xii 2–7).' *Mediaeval Sophia* 12 (2012): 141–52.

Lombardo, Luca. *Boezio in Dante: la 'Consolatio Philosophiae' nello scrittoio del poeta*. Venice: Edizioni Ca' Foscari, 2013.

Lombardo, Luca. '"In sembianza di donna". Reperti boeziani nei testi toscani delle origini: dal rifacimento al *Convivio* di Dante.' *Le tre corone* 4 (2017): 11–46.

Lombardo, Luca. '"Ed imaginava lei fatta come una donna gentile". Boezio, Brunetto Latini e la prima formazione intellettuale di Dante.' *Le tre corone* 5 (2018): 39–71.

'Lonza.' In *ED*, III, 691. 1971.

Looney, Dennis. *Freedom Readers: The African American Reception of Dante Alighieri and the 'Divine Comedy'*. Notre Dame: University of Notre Dame Press, 2011.

Looney, Dennis. '*Dante politico*: an Introduction.' *Mediaevalia* 38 (2017): 1–12.

Looney, Dennis and Stocchi-Perucchio, Donatella, eds. *Dante Politico: Ideological Reception Across Boundaries*, Special Issue *Mediaevalia* 38 (2017).

Lucchesi, Valerio. 'Giustizia divina e linguaggio umano. Metafore e polisemie del contrapasso dantesco.' *Studi danteschi* 63 (1991): 53–126.

Luzzato, Sergio and Pedullà, Gabriele, eds. *Atlante della letteratura italiana*, 2 vols. Turin: Einaudi, 2010.

Luzzi, Joseph. *Romantic Europe and the Ghost of Italy*. New Haven: Yale University Press, 2008.

MacIntyre, Alisdair. *Three Rival Versions of Moral Enquiry: Encyclopaedia, Genealogy, and Tradition*. London: Duckworth, 1990.

Macrì-Leone, Francesco. *La bucolica latina nella letteratura italiana del XIV secolo, con una introduzione sulla bucolica latina nel Medioevo.* Turin: Loescher, 1889.

Maldina, Nicolò. 'Raccogliendo briciole. Una metafora della formazione dantesca tra *Convivio* e *Commedia.*' *Studi danteschi* 81 (2016): 131–64.

Maldina, Nicolò. *In pro del mondo. Dante, la predicazione e i generi della letteratura religiosa medievale.* Rome: Salerno, 2018.

Manescalchi, Romano. 'Osservazioni sulla "lonza" in Rustico Filippi e in Dante.' *Studi danteschi* 74 (2009): 127–47.

Margiotta, Giacinto. *Le Origini italiane de la Querelle des Anciens et des Modernes.* Rome: Editrice Studium, 1953.

Marples, Kevin. 'Theology, prophecy and politics in Dante.' Unpublished PhD thesis, University of Leeds (2017).

Martellotti, Guido. 'Dalla tenzone al carme bucolico.' *Italia medioevale e umanistica* 7 (1964): 325–36.

Martellotti, Guido. 'La riscoperta dello stile bucolico (da Dante a Boccaccio).' In *Dante e la cultura veneta. Atti del Convegno di studi organizzato dalla Fondazione 'Giorgio Cini', Venezia, Padova, Verona, 30 marzo–5 aprile 1966,* edited by Vittore Branca and Giorgio Padoan, 335–46. Florence: Olschki, 1966.

Martellotti, Guido. 'Egloghe.' In *ED*, II, 644–6. 1970.

Martellotti, Guido. 'Giovanni del Virgilio.' In *ED* III, 193–4. 1971.

Martellotti, Guido. 'Mussato, Albertino.' In *ED* III, 1066–8. 1971.

Maurer, Maria. 'The Trouble with Pasiphaë: Engendering a Myth at the Gonzaga Court.' In *Receptions of Antiquity: Constructions of Gender in European Art, 1300–1600,* edited by Alison Poe and Marice Rose, 199–229. Leiden: Brill, 2015.

Mazzi, Maria Serena. 'Cronache di periferia dello Stato fiorentino: Reati contro la morale nel primo Quattrocento.' *Studi storici* 27 (1986): 609–35.

Mazzoni, Francesco. *Saggio di un nuovo commento alla 'Divina Commedia': Inferno canti I–III.* Florence: Sansoni, 1967.

Mazzoni, Francesco. 'Edizione Nazionale.' In *ED*, II, 630–2. 1970.

Mazzoni, Guido. 'Dante e il Polifemo bolognese (*Eclogae*, II, 73 segg.).' In Mazzoni, Guido, *Almae luces malae cruces. Studi danteschi,* 349–72. Bologna: Zanichelli, 1941.

Mazzotta, Giuseppe. *Dante's Vision and the Circle of Knowledge.* Princeton: Princeton University Press, 1993.

Mazzotta, Giuseppe. 'Metaphor and Justice (*Inferno* XXVIII).' In Mazzotta, Giuseppe. *Dante's Vision and the Circle of Knowledge,* 75–95. Princeton: Princeton University Press, 1993.

Meier, Franziska. 'Educating the Reader: Dante's *Convivio.*' *L'Alighieri* 45 (2015): 21–33.

Meier, Franziska, ed. *Dante's 'Convivio' or How to Restart a Career in Exile.* Bern: Peter Lang, 2018.

Mengaldo, Pier Vincenzo. 'Gramatica.' In *ED*, III, 259–64. 1971.

Minnis, Alastair J. *Medieval Theory of Authorship: Scholastic Literary Attitudes in the Later Middle Ages.* London: Scolar, 1984.

Modesto, Filippa. *Dante's Idea of Friendship: the Transformation of a Classical Concept.* Toronto: University of Toronto Press, 2015.

Montemaggi, Vittorio and Treherne, Matthew, eds. *Dante's 'Commedia': Theology as Poetry.* Notre Dame: University of Notre Dame Press, 2008.

Nasti, Paola. '"Vocabuli d'autore e di scienze e di libri" (*Conv.* II xii 5): percorsi sapienziali di Dante.' In *La Bibbia di Dante: esperienza mistica, profezia e teologia biblica in Dante. Atti del convegno internazionale di studi (Ravenna, 7 novembre 2009),* edited by Giuseppe Ledda, 121–78. Ravenna: Centro dantesco dei Frati minori conventuali, 2011.

Nasti, Paola. 'Storia materiale di un classico dantesco: la *Consolatio Philosophiae* fra XII e XIV secolo tradizione manoscritta e rielaborazioni esegetiche.' *Dante Studies* 134 (2016): 142–68.

Nasti, Paola and Rossignoli, Claudia, eds. *Interpreting Dante: Essays on the Traditions of Dante Commentary.* Notre Dame: University of Notre Dame Press, 2013.

Nasti, Paola and Rossignoli, Claudia. 'Introduction.' In *Interpreting Dante: Essays on the Traditions of Dante Commentary,* edited by Nasti, P. and Rossignoli, C., 1–16. Notre Dame: University of Notre Dame Press, 2013.

Nussbaum, Martha. *Upheavals of Thought: The Intelligence of Emotions.* Cambridge: Cambridge University Press, 2001.

O'Connor, Anne. 'Dante Alighieri – from Absence to Stony Presence: Building Memories in Nineteenth-Century Florence.' *Italian Studies* 67.3 (2012): 307–35.

Oliger, Livarius. 'Servasanto da Faenza O.F.M. e il suo *Liber de virtutibus et vitiis.*' In *Miscellanea Francesco Ehrle. I: Per la storia della filosofia e della teologia*, 148–89. Rome: Biblioteca Apostolica Vaticana, 1924.

Padoan, Giorgio. *Inferno (canti I–VIII)*, edited by Giorgio Padoan, in *Opere di Dante: IX*, edited by Vittore Branca, Francesco Maggini and Bruno Nardi (Florence: Le Monnier, 1967), at: Dartmouth Dante Project, https://dante.dartmouth.edu/

Padoan, Giorgio. 'Tra Dante e Mussato.' *Quaderni veneti* 24 (1996): 27–45.

Pasquini, Emilio. 'Giovanni del Virgilio.' In *Dizionario Biografico degli Italiani* 38 (1990): 404–9.

Payer, Pierre J. *The Bridling of Desire: Views of Sex in the Late Middle Ages*. Toronto: University of Toronto Press, 1993.

Pegorari, Daniele Maria. 'La lonza svelata. Fonti classiche, cristiane e "interne" dell'allegoria della frode.' *Giornale storico della Letteratura italiana* 192 (2015): 523–41.

Pegoretti, Anna. 'Filosofanti.' *Le tre corone* 2 (2015): 11–70.

Pegoretti, Anna. '"Nelle scuole delli religiosi": materiali per Santa Croce nell'età di Dante.' *L'Alighieri* 50 (2017): 5–55.

Pegoretti, Anna. '"Da questa nobilissima perfezione molti sono privati": Impediments to Knowledge and the Tradition of Commentaries on Boethius' *Consolatio Philosophiae.*' In *Dante's 'Convivio': Or How to Restart a Career in Exile*, edited by Meier, F., 77–97. Bern: Peter Lang, 2018.

Perotti, Pier Angelo. 'Caina attende.' *L'Alighieri* n.s. 1–2 (1993): 129–34.

Pertile, Lino. 'Canto XXIX: Such Outlandish Wounds.' In *Lectura Dantis: 'Inferno'*, edited by Allen Mandelbaum et al., 387–91. Berkeley: University of California Press, 1998.

Pertile, Lino. 'Mal d'amore.' In Pertile, Lino, *La punta del disio. Semantica del desiderio nella Commedia*, 39–58. Florence: Cadmo, 2005.

Pertile, Lino. 'Le *Egloghe* di Dante e l'antro di Polifemo.' In *Dante the Lyric and Ethical Poet,. Dante lirico e etico,* edited by Zygmunt G. Barański and Martin McLaughlin, 153–67. London: Legenda, 2010.

Pertile, Lino. 'A Text in Movement: Trifon Gabriele's *Annotationi nel Dante*, 1527–1565.' In *Interpreting Dante: Essays on the Traditions of Dante Commentary*, edited by Nasti, P. and Rossignoli, C., 341–58. Notre Dame: University of Notre Dame Press, 2013.

Peters, Edward. '*Crimen exceptum*: The History of an Idea.' In *Proceedings of the Tenth International Congress of Medieval Canon Law: Syracuse, New York, 13–18 August 1996*, edited by Kenneth Pennington, Stanley Chodorow, Keith H. Kendal, 137–94. Vatican City: Biblioteca Apostolica Vaticana, 2001.

Petralia, Giuseppe and Santagata, Marco, eds. *Enrico VII, Dante e Pisa*. Ravenna: Longo, 2016.

Picchio Simonelli, Maria. 'L'Inquisizione e Dante: alcune osservazioni.' *Dante Studies* 97 (1979): 129–49.

Pich, Federica. 'Dante's "Strangeness": the *Commedia* and the Late Twentieth-Century Debate on the Literary Canon.' In *Metamorphosing Dante. Appropriations, Manipulations, and Rewritings in the Twentieth and Twenty-First Centuries*, edited by Manuele Gragnolati, Fabio Camilletti and Fabian Lampart, 21–35. Berlin: Turia + Kant, 2010.

Picone, Michelangelo. 'Il tema dell'incoronazione poetica in Dante, Petrarca e Boccaccio.' *L'Alighieri* 25 (2005): 5–26.

Picone, Michelangelo. '*L'amato alloro*: Dante fra Petrarca e Boccaccio.' In Picone, Michelangelo. *Scritti danteschi*, edited by Antonio Lanza, 649–69. Ravenna: Longo, 2017.

Pierotti, Gian Luca. 'La "legenda sancti Jacobi" nei canti del cielo stellato.' *Rivista di Letteratura Italiana* 28.3 (2010): 9–20.

Poleg, Eyal. *Approaching the Bible in Medieval England*. Manchester: Manchester University Press, 2013.

Prandi, Stefano. 'Canto XXV. "Ritornerò Poeta".' In *Lectura Dantis Romana. Cento Canti per Cento Anni. Paradiso. Vol. III.2. Canti XVIII–XXXIII*, edited by Enrico Malato and Andrea Mazzucchi, 723–46. Rome: Salerno, 2015.

Raimondi, Ezio. 'Dante e il modello ezzelianiano.' In *Dante e la cultura veneta. Atti del Convegno di studi organizzato dalla Fondazione Giorgio Cini, in collaborazione con l'Istituto universitario di Venezia, l'Università di Padova, il Centro scaligero di studi danteschi e i Comuni di Venezia, Padova, Verona (30 marzo–5 aprile 1966)*, edited by Vittore Branca and Giorgio Padoan, 51–69. Florence: Olschki, 1966.

Ricci, Corrado. *L'ultimo rifugio di Dante*. Milan: Hoepli, 1921; 1st edn, 1891.

Ricci, Pier Giorgio. 'Monarchia.' In *ED*, III, 993–1004. 1971.

Ricklin, Thomas. '" … quello non conosciuto da molti libro di Boezio". Hinweise zur *Consolatio Philosophiae* in Norditalien.' In *Boethius in the Middle Ages: Latin and Vernacular Traditions of the Consolatio Philosophiae*, edited by Maarten J. F. M. Hoenen and Lodi Nauta, 267–86. Leiden: Brill, 1997.

Rigo, Paola. 'Tempo liturgico nell'epistola ai Principi e ai popoli d'Italia.' *Lettere Italiane* 32 (1980): 222–31.

Rigo, Paola. *Memoria classica e memoria biblica in Dante*. Florence: Olschki,1994.

Rizi, Fabio Fernando. *Benedetto Croce and Italian Fascism*. Toronto: University of Toronto Press, 2003.

Rosengarten, Frank. 'Gramsci's "Little Discovery": Gramsci's Interpretation of Canto X of Dante's *Inferno*.' *Boundary* 2, 14.3 (1986): 71–90.

Rossi, Aldo. 'Dante, Boccaccio e la laurea poetica.' *Paragone*, n.s. 12 (1962): 3–41.

Rowson, Abigail. 'Theologians as Persons in Dante's *Commedia*.' Unpublished PhD thesis, University of Leeds (2018).

Ruggiero, Guido. '"Più che la vita caro": Onore, matrimonio, e reputazione femminile nel tardo Rinascimento.' *Quaderni storici* 66 (1987): 753–75.

Saiber, Arielle and Coggeshall, Elizabeth. 'Dante Today'. At: https://research.bowdoin.edu/dante-today/.

Salsano, Fernando. 'Arte.' In *ED*, I, 397–9. 1970.

Salsano, Fernando and Ragonese, Gaetano. 'Fiera.' In *ED*, II, 857–61. 1970.

Samuel, Irene. 'Semiramis in the Middle Age: The History of a Legend.' *Medievalia et Humanistica* 2 (1944): 32–44.

Santagata, Marco. *Dante. Il romanzo della sua vita*. Milan: Mondadori, 2012.

Sarolli, Gian Roberto. 'Giacomo (Iacopo) Maggiore.' In *ED*, III, 147–8. 1971.

Satto, Christian. 'Simbolo cittadino, gloria nazionale. Dante nella Capitale.' *Annali di Storia di Firenze* 10–11 (2015–16): 213–35.

Scheil, Andrew. *Babylon Under Western Eyes. A Study of Allusion and Myth*. Toronto: University of Toronto Press, 2016.

Schumacher, Thomas L. *The Danteum: a Study of the Architecture of Literature*. Princeton: Princeton Architectural Press, 1985.

Scorrano, Luigi. 'Il Dante "Fascista".' *Deutsches Dante-Jahrbuch* 75.1 (2000): 85–123.

Shapiro, Marianne. 'Semiramis in *Inferno* V.' *Romance Notes* 16 (1975): 455–6.

Skinner, Quentin. *Visions of Politics*, 3 vols. Cambridge: Cambridge University Press, 2002.

Slotemaker, John T. and Witt, Jeffrey C. *Robert Holcot*. Oxford: Oxford University Press, 2016.

Smalley, Beryl. *English Friars and Antiquity in the Early Fourteenth Century*. New York: Barnes & Noble, 1961.

Smalley, Beryl. 'Glossa Ordinaria.' In *Theologische Realenzyklopädie*, 36 vols. III, 452–7. Berlin: De Gruyter, 1984.

Società Dantesca Italiana. 'Edizione Nazionale' at: https://dantesca.org/cms/edizione-nazionale/

Spagnolo, Luigi. 'La lingua delle *muliercule*: ideologia preumanistica e questioni di autenticità nel Dante latino.' *La lingua italiana* 11 (2015): 37–65.

Steinberg, Justin. *Accounting for Dante: Urban Readers and Writers in Late Medieval Italy*. Notre Dame: University of Notre Dame Press, 2007.

Steinberg, Justin. *Dante and the Limits of the Law*. Chicago: Chicago University Press, 2013.

Steinberg, Justin. 'Dante's Justice? A reappraisal of the *contrapasso*.' *L'Alighieri* 44 (2014): 59–74.

Stocchi-Perrucchio, Donatella. '*Dante Politico*: Toward a Mapping of Dante's Political Thought.' *Medievalia* 38 (2017): 13–36.

Stocchi-Perucchio, Donatella. 'Giovanni Gentile's Reading of Dante as Prophet of the State *in interiore homine*.' *Medievalia* 38 (2017): 169–207.

Suitner, Franco. 'Le tre fiere di Dante, la *Queste* e il *Gatto lupesco*.' In *Dante e il mondo animale*, edited by Giuseppe Crimi and Luca Marcozzi, 34–48. Rome: Carocci, 2013.

Suitner, Franco. 'Sul condizionamento della rima in Dante: primi appunti.' *Letteratura Italiana Antica* 20 (2019), forthcoming.

Tanturli, Giuliano. 'La corrispondenza poetica di Giovanni del Virgilio e Dante fra storia della tradizione e critica del testo.' *Studi Medievali* 52 (2010): 809–45.

Taterka, Thomas. *Dante Deutsch: Studien zur Lagerliteratur*. Berlin: Erich Schmidt Verlag, 1999.

Tavoni, Mirko. 'La cosiddetta battaglia della Lastra e la biografia politica di Dante.' *Nuova Rivista di Letteratura Italiana* 17. 2 (2014): 51–87.

Tavoni, Mirko. *Qualche idea su Dante*. Bologna: il Mulino, 2015.

Terlizzi, Francesco Paolo. 'Le incoronazioni poetiche.' In *Atlante della letteratura italiana*, edited by Luzzatto, S. and Pedullà, G. I, 141–4. Turin: Einaudi, 2010.

The Hepworth, Wakefield at: https://hepworthwakefield.org/news/the-hepworth-wakefield-wins-art-fund-museum-of-the-year-2017/.

Théry, Julien. '"Atrocitas/enormitas." Per una storia della categoria di "crimen enorme" nel basso Medioevo (XII–XV secolo),' translated by Benedetto Borello. *Quaderni storici* 44, 131.2 (2009): 329–75.

Tonelli, Natascia. *Fisiologia della passione. Poesia d'amore e medicina da Cavalcanti a Boccaccio*. Florence: Galluzzo, 2015.

Uitti, Karl D. 'The Codex Calixtinus and the European St. James the Major: Some Contextual Issues.' In *'De Sens Rassis': Essays in Honor of Rupert T. Pickens*, edited by Keith Busby et al., 645–66. Amsterdam: Rodopi, 2005.

Vallone, Aldo. 'Lectura Dantis.' In *ED*, III, 606–9. 1971.

Venturini, Domenico. *Dante Alighieri e Benito Mussolini*. Rome: Nuova Italia, 1932.

Villa, Claudia. 'Il problema dello stile umile e il sorriso di Dante.' In Claudia Villa, *La protervia di Beatrice. Studi per la biblioteca di Dante*, 215–32. Florence: SISMEL–Galluzzo, 2009.

Vincent-Cassy, Mireille. 'Les animaux et les péchés capitaux: de la symbolique a l'emblématique.' In *Le monde animal et ses représentations au Moyen Âge*, edited by Francis Cervan, 121–32. Toulouse: Université de Toulouse–Le Mirail, 1985.

Wakefield Census Demographics United Kingdom at: http://localstats.co.uk/census-demographics/england/yorkshire-and-the-humber/wakefield.

Wakefield State of the District: Poverty at: http://www.wakefieldjsna.co.uk/site/wp-content/uploads/Poverty-Profile.pdf.

Weijers, Olga. *Le maniement du savoir: pratiques intellectuels à l'époque des premières universités (XIIIe-XIVe siècles)*. Turnhout: Brepols, 1996.

Weisheipl, James A., O. P. 'The Nature, Scope, and Classification of the Sciences.' In *Science in the Middle Ages*, edited by David C. Lindberg, 461–82. Chicago: University of Chicago Press, 1978.

Witt, Ronald G. *In the Footsteps of the Ancients: The Origins of Humanism from Lovato to Bruni*. Leiden: Brill, 2000.

Witt, Ronald G. 'Un poeta laureato: Albertino Mussato.' In *Atlante della letteratura italiana*, edited by Luzzato, S. and Pedullà, G. I, 134–9. Turin: Einaudi, 2010

Witt, Ronald G. *The Two Latin Cultures and the Foundation of Renaissance Humanism in Medieval Italy*. Cambridge: Cambridge University Press, 2012.

Worsham Musgrove, Margaret. 'Cyclopean Latin: intertextual readings in Dante's *Eclogues* and Góngora's *Polifemo y Galatea*.' *Classical and Modern Literature* 18.2 (1998): 125–36.

Yousefzadeh, Mahnaz. *City and Nation in the Italian Unification: the National Festivals of Dante Alighieri*. New York: Palgrave Macmillan, 2011.

Zabbia, Marino. 'Albertino Mussato.' In *Dizionario Biografico degli Italiani*, 67(2012): 520–4.

Zanin, Enrica. '"Miseri, 'mpediti, affamati": Dante's Implied Reader in the "Convivio".' In *Dante's 'Convivio': Or How to Restart a Career in Exile*, edited by Meier, F., 207–21. Bern: Peter Lang, 2018.

Ziolkowski, Jan M. 'Introduction.' In *Dante and Islam*, edited by Jan M. Ziolkowski, 1–28. New York: Fordham University Press, 2015.

Index

public lectures 129–31, 147
public officials 85
public reception of Dante's work 8
punishment
  as distinct from rectification 85
  outside the norm 83, 90
  of souls and of sin 80–3
Purgatorio (Dante's) 1, 7, 55, 64–5, 68–70,
  80–1, 113, 119, 149, 154–5
Purgatorio (poem by Crossley) 153–5
Purgatory 147, 149
Pythagoreans 81, 84

Ravenna 111, 114, 117–18, 120
reactions to Dante 8–9
reciprocal justice 81, 85, 87
religious culture, participation in 146
Remigio de'Girolami 3–4
Revelation, Book of 51
rhetorical deftness of Dante 2
rhythm and rhyme 24
Ricci, Pier Giorgio 136
Richard of Saint Victor 50–1
Rime, Dante's 1, 14–15, 18, 99
Risorgimento patriotism 133, 136
Roman Empire and Roman military power
  102–6, 136
Roman law 72, 86
Rome, city of 133, 137

Sacchetti, Franco 132–3
sacrilege 81, 88
Sallust 3
Scarpetta degli Ordelaffi 118–19
scholarship on Dante 137–9, 144–5
Second Coming of Christ 56
self-perception and self-depiction, Dante's 2,
  11–12
self-proclaimed masters 96
Semiramis 64, 66–71, 74, 76
Seneca 3, 6, 31–2, 35–6
sententiae 72, 97
Servasanto da Faenza 6, 10, 30, 33–41
sexcentenary of Dante's death 133–5
sexual relationships and sexual offences 65, 93
Shaw, Prue 136
she-wolves 55–6
Sicily 120
sin and punishment 82–3
Skinner, Quentin 3
Smalley, Beryl 30
social ideas in Dante 145
social ties 85
Società Dantesca Italiana 135, 139
sodomy 68, 73
Song of Solomon 51, 65

Steinberg, Justin 7, 11, 72–3; *author of*
  Chapter 5
striking the sovereign 86, 88
swearing to truthfulness 64
symbolism 56–7
  medieval 52–4
  see also animal symbolism

Terragni, Giuseppe 137
Tesoretto 22–3
testimony 7, 64, 71, 73–6
  female 76
  medieval 75
theology, theologians and theological ideas
  9, 145–6
tongue, the, Saint James's imagery of 96–8,
  102, 104
tourist experience 146–7
Treherne, Matthew 9, 130–1; *author of*
  Chapter 9
Trevet, Nicholas 31
truthfulness 64, 76
'TuttoDante' events *see* Benigni, Roberto
Turin 133

Ugolino 75
Ulysses 97, 137
Unification of Italy 133–34
United Nations Educational, Scientific and
  Cultural Organization (UNESCO) 147

Valerius Maximus 6, 31–4, 37
Venturini, Domenico 136
Veltro 56–7
Venus 53
vernacular culture and poetry 21–5, 37, 39,
  49, 64, 65, 67, 68–9, 72, 76, 112–13, 117,
  129, 132–3
Victor Emmanuel II, King 133–4
violence, *legitimate* and *illegitimate* 52, 86
Virgil 10, 52–3, 55–6, 75, 82–3, 113–16,
  119–20, 135, 149, 153; *see also* Aeneid, the
visions, interpretation of 54
Vita nova 6, 17, 19, 22, 38, 135
voluntary and *involuntary* actions 84–5

Wakefield 147–55
  Cathedral 148–50
walking itineraries 146–7
Warwick University 144–5
White Party of Florence 19, 118–19
Wisdom, Book of 2
Witte, Karl 135
wolf-imagery 6, 54–6

Yates, Michael 151–3
Yousefzadeh, Mahnaz 133

Lightning Source UK Ltd.
Milton Keynes UK
UKHW051428040822
406850UK00017BA/273